NKf
Jan 2001

THE ROAD TO HARMONY

An Appalachian Childhood

After leaving Harmony, J. D. Ballam studied English at the University of York, where he graduated with First Class Honours. He was later awarded a PhD by the University of Bristol for his research in Modernist Poetry. He now lives with his wife and daughter near Bath.

To Nan and to Wren —
one who told, and one who asked.

THE ROAD TO HARMONY

An Appalachian Childhood

J.D. BALLAM

PAN BOOKS

First published 1999 by Long Barn Books

This edition published 2000 by Pan Books
an imprint of Macmillan Publishers Ltd
25 Eccleston Place, London SW1W 9NF
Basingstoke and Oxford
Associated companies throughout the world
www.macmillan.co.uk

ISBN 0 330 48183 5

Printed and bound in Great Britain by
Mackays of Chatham plc, Chatham, Kent

Preface

From the broken mountain, with its green rocks and running springs, to Hawbottom, with Catoctin on the right and South Mountain across the valley to the left, The Hollow Road turns past the silent stones of the old distillery before dropping away to the stream and past Mosker's Farm. After The Corner it twines up the little hill between the houses, and around Orpha's barn, before resting at the first farm on the right. This is the road home – the road to Harmony – where a hog can root the mortgage off a farm faster than Hell can send a feather and four saddlebags of gold lie buried at Bootjack Spring. From here there's a way to Wistman Lane Falls, following the path through the pink and white dogwoods, or to stop and ask old Hank for some groundhog pie. (There are mushrooms to hunt for in the mayapples up by Fisher's Lodge, and wild spring daisies as big as a child's hand and in time for Easter.) A little farther on is where my people are – the ghosts in the underbrush along Ford Fields, where the Tuscarora braves used to wait for the deer to come down in the winter. But remember, if you decide to stay, don't build your house with white stones in the wall, for the Fords believe that these attract lightning.

Harmony, Maryland, USA. Climb ten feet up in the poplars in Shultz's meadow, and there in the bark is my heritage:

C.E. Ford
1926 A.D.

Smiling old faces above long beards crowd together in the albums. Young ones, too, remembering the day when the schoolhouse burnt down, or Charlie Ford swore for the first and last time. They ate fresh scrapple and chewed tobacco, and the noise of the threshers with their long belts surrounded them. Now in their places there is nothing but the silvering remains of their Festival boards, and the crashing echo of baseballs high in the walnut trees. But while there's still time, it's good to ask Dutch about Sadie (because Sadie was good to her, if not to many else), and she'll point out the place where lightning struck twice.

Somewhere in these things there is the history of a people – small and poor, democratic and proud. It is a history that is part fiction, and part the determination of a community to believe in itself. It is the story of this community, in a recollection larger than my own, that this book seeks to tell.

CHAPTER ONE

Ain't Got Time To Die

Emma Blanche Ford was the youngest of ten children. About a year after her mother's death, she was riding home in the darkness of a winter's evening with her father, when he attacked her. Blind drunk, Will Ropp leaned across from the driver's seat and made a lunge for her – which she resisted by leaping from the speeding car. She then ran through the dense forest for nearly three miles, crossing the lower end of Catoctin Mountain, and presented herself at her cousins' house. She was nine years old.

It had been Will's habit to beat his wife into a stupor, and this, combined with a relentless program of child-bearing, led to her death at the age of thirty-eight. Tall, slim, fair-complexioned, with powerful hands and eyes like an April sky, everyone spoke of his remarkable Bavarian good looks. For this too, his youngest daughter hated him. Exactly resembling the mother she had loved intensely, she would grow to become a short, stocky heavy-armed woman, whose straight coal-black hair, olive-complexion, flattened bulbous nose and narrow eyes made her seem Mongolian.

Almost her first decision after leaving home was to change her name. Although her parents called her Emma Blanche, she hated the name Emma, and silently reversed the order. There was no birth certificate to contradict her. It was, in its way, an important decision that made not the least difference to anyone, because for the rest of her life she was known as Dutch.

Until the age of twelve, Dutch attended a one-room school on a hillside near her cousin's home. She then left school in order to look after her foster family's younger children, and to help with the household chores. Counting her entire extended family, Dutch reckoned that in her long life she personally oversaw the rearing of twenty children.

Dutch had one child herself, and the experience of childbirth was nearly fatal. It was in July 1934, and Dutch was nineteen years old. Although the temperature was over ninety degrees Fahrenheit, her in-laws had selected an attic room immediately beneath a simmering red tin roof as the birthing chamber. After labour was positively established mid-morning, a doctor was sent for. Despite half a day's work in the boiling heat, no child appeared. In despair, Dutch's husband brought in an aged midwife. This midwife's first action was to tear a bed sheet into long strips, plait them together to form a rope, and then tie both ends to the foot board of the bed. The purpose of this rope was to give Dutch something to pull against during her contractions. When this was done, the midwife placed an axe under the bed. This was intended to 'cut' the bleeding. Within two hours, Dutch was delivered of a healthy baby girl. She named her daughter Jane Lois. Thirty years later, this child became my mother.

Dutch was married at the age of eighteen to Clarence Elmer Ford – C.E – the only son of a prosperous family established on Catoctin Mountain for more than 200 years. Two of his distant forebears had been in George Washington's army, and his grandfather, William Henry Ford, had built the family homestead at Ford Fields. As the only son of the only child of the only son of his eldest son, I have inherited his cherished hand-carved gunpowder flask. But it was William Henry's son Charles Clinton who was the true patriarch of the Ford family.

A portrait made of Charlie Ford around his twentieth birthday, in 1986, shows a handsome, intelligent, rugged man with auburn hair and a golden flame in his eyes. As a teenager he taught himself carpentry, and by early manhood he had become a master barn-builder. The role of the barn-builder was to imagine the entire structure of a building, including every one of its constituent parts, with a view to their final assembly. With this in mind, the builder would select from the timber felled by the farmer himself, choosing the wood best-suited to each purpose. Each log would then be hewn or sawn by hand, trial-fitted, then marked with Roman numerals. On the day of the barn-raising, the farmer's friends and family would arrive at sunrise to be welcomed with a hearty breakfast. When this was completed, supervised by the builder, the raising could begin, lasting without interruption until nightfall. Using horses, ropes and muscle, the enormous timbers were raised into position and hammered down with wooden pegs. The flooring and outside of the building were then covered with poplar sheathing, and the roof finished with split cedar shingles. If the master carpenter's imagination had proven to be fully comprehensive, the entire building – upon which a family's whole subsistence might depend – could be finished in a single day.

For his part, Charlie seldom failed, and the building trade proved to be very profitable. Driving around the Valley now, it is possible to see his handiwork still in daily use on many farms. Then one day in 1899, Charlie decided to get a wife. According to Sadie Mae Kinna, the decision to marry was certainly his. She described herself as having been 'caught in a cornfield'.

The match with Sadie was a fortunate one. She brought to it a dowry of $200 and a ferocious temper. The $200 was used to buy a small farm, and the temper was never truly spent, but lasted her throughout sixty years of married life. The farm the couple purchased consisted of five parcels of land, each individually named. There was a stream, a spring and a powerful well. There were arable fields, pasture land and hardwood timber. The farm buildings included a barn, a small waggon-shed, a pig pen (with corn-crib), a chicken coop, a smokehouse, a washhouse and a springhouse. The living accommodation was at least sixty years old when the couple purchased it. Like many Maryland farmhouses it was built of logs with pine cladding painted white. There were four bedrooms, an enormous kitchen, a sitting room and a parlour. The kitchen and the parlour had separate doors, about six feet apart – the former for daily use, and the latter to be used by visitors only. The cellars were reachable from the outside, as was the toilet (movable, but usually on the hill behind the barn). It was in this house that the couple raised their five children, including my grandfather C.E.

Now C.E. was a precocious child. His first memory was the sound of the church bells ringing at the end of the Great War. His second memory was climbing into his father's Model T Ford and driving it into the fence opposite the barn. As a teenager he hated farmwork and was quick to learn that if he threw two shocks of wheat into the thresher backwards, then two more the right way around, then two more backwards, the machine would jam for at least half-an-hour, allowing time for a rest and some lemonade. He was not sorry when his parents decided to sell the farm and move to a more profitable business at the opposite end of the village.

This business was twofold. On one side of the road was the building known as The Corner. Diagonally across the junction was the Cider Press. Between the two, clockwise from the corner was The Mary House and opposite it The Patch. The Corner itself was one of the oldest buildings in the county. Constructed originally as a grist mill, it was a meeting place during the Revolutionary War for British sympathisers and local Indians. The original 'purchase' of its adjacent land, including space for a three-quarter-mile mill race, was negotiated with the Tuscarora tribe based on measurements achieved by bowshot. That is, Tuscarora braves shot arrows in the air in a given direction an agreed-upon number of times in succession from the point where each arrow fell, until a large, lop-sided rectangle was marked out. Some time in the eighteenth century the mill's purpose was changed from grinding wheat to weaving wool, and then in the 1870's it was converted to a large house and shop. There was also a spring house and an outdoor toilet (under the walnut trees). The geographical area served by the Ford's new shop formed a trapezoid with sides of two, three, seven and eleven miles. All sorts of goods were available, including horseshoes and petrol, hominy and asparagus, salt fish and shoes. The business flourished.

The Cider Press was Charlie Ford's brainchild. While barn-building occupied him throughout spring and summer, and the shop could be managed by his wife and daughters, he saw an opportunity to profit by the late autumn harvest. The result was a large shed with a steam-powered press and a queue of laden waggons stretching throughout the village. Trade was brisk. The Ford family enterprise expanded to include the manufacture of apple butter – a thick, brown, spreadable concoction of apples, brown sugar and nutmeg.

In the idle winter months, Charlie converted The Mary House into a workshop. This building was made of logs with a brick veneer and one room on each of two floors. It also had a fireplace and a vegetable garden bordering two streams. Its name, like the names of many of the village houses, was derived from that of its most notable occupant. In this case, the surname of the woman responsible for its appellation was lost altogether. Many houses continued to be known by the names of people who had left them generations before. My own family's house was called after someone else for more than thirty years after we moved in, our own stake in the matter taking that long to be recognised.

Anyway, from his new workshop Charlie produced some fine furniture, including glazed cupboards, benches, cabinets and other household and agricultural items. He also took to caning chairs with fine-patterned wickerwork. In the fourth parcel of land, known as The Patch, the Fords grew their own vegetables.

It was in an attic room of The Corner that Dutch gave birth to my mother. It was a very full household, but one that apparently got on well together. This must have been due in part to the family's unusual receptiveness to innovation. For instance, the Fords were reputedly the first family in the area to own a car. They were certainly the first to have electric lights, the electricity being supplied by a private generator and run through wiring installed by C.E. Later, shortly after the Second World War, C.E. built a television and put it prominently in the front of the shop with a few benches for onlookers. For years, Saturday nights were standing room only.

But even before this time C.E. was achieving a growing notoriety in other areas. Like his father, he was skilled in head and hands. Although he left school at sixteen, he taught himself algebra, calculus and trigonometry. While still a teenager, he also taught himself to play the guitar. With this and a few friends, he formed a small band, and throughout the remainder of the Depression-era they made a night-time summer circuit of local festivals, carnivals and beer-joints, earning money re-playing popular jazz and bluegrass tunes. On one particular occasion, while Dutch waited in the car, too scandalised by the surroundings to watch any closer, some of the music-lovers got a bit rowdy. The band wisely decided that this was a good time to take a short break. As he left the bandstand, C.E. propped his guitar on his chair, and was walking towards his car when a fight broke out. Within minutes there was gunfire. No one was hurt, and when the smoke and tempers cleared somewhat, the band ran back to their former places to pick up their instruments. As he leaned down to pick up his guitar, C.E. noticed that a bullet had gone through the back of his chair. His career as a professional musician ended that night.

This loss in income was more than made up for by the winter trade in furs. The rich deep forests of Catoctin Mountain are the home of racoons, minks, foxes, muskrats and skunks, all of which contributed to the thriving fur-garment industry. C.E. saw a way into this, and bought himself nearly a hundred steel traps. These were carefully installed into

11

cunningly concealed places on the mountain, over an area of two miles wide and nearly ten miles long. Now fur-trapping is an extremely painstaking, dirty and laborious business. The traps themselves are prepared with intense care, the parts being cleaned and boiled to remove every trace of human scent along with that pervasive note of death to which all animals are alert. The bait usually consisted of fetid meat – attractive to scavengers and detectable at great distances. Once prepared, it takes a deft hand and a level insight to place the traps in such a way that makes them invisible to their prey. For instance, to catch that most clever of animals, the fox, you must first find proof of his habits. Where does he sleep? Where has he fed? Where does he empty his bowel? Then getting as close to the ground as possible (without actually touching it with your own skin) you must look for the likely paths that connect these places. If you are very lucky, one of these paths will be partially blocked by a fallen tree limb. The trap can then be concealed in the moss and leaves close to one side of this limb, in the hope that the fox will land on it in jumping over the obstruction. To avoid distressing the animals unnecessarily (as well as ruining the furs) the traps must be checked as frequently as possible. This normally meant inspecting every trap on alternate days. Doing this meant walking through the entire circuit, in any weather, carrying a gun to dispatch those animals not already dead, and returning with a bagful of small carcasses. These carcasses must be dressed immediately, and the work requires both a strong stomach and a skilful touch. C.E. was matchless as a skin-dresser, once winning first prize in a nation-wide competition sponsored by Sears, Roebuck & Company, the purchaser of his furs.

The mountain wildlife also provided sustenance of another kind. Despite the bad eyes inherited from his mother, C.E. was a crack shot with a rifle. Throughout the season, family fare included rabbits and squirrels. C.E. was also a talented fly-fisherman, bringing home great numbers of trout from the high mountain streams that fed into Middle Creek.

But like many men, C.E. had a passion for a pursuit outside his abilities. Of medium height, with a broad powerful frame, long nose and weak green-grey eyes, he was the mirror-image of his mother, and like her he found running impossible. Although he could walk twenty miles laden with game, he lost every foot-race he ever entered. For this reason, when the Second World War came, he considered himself immensely lucky to be drafted into the navy – a further irony of war for a man who had never even seen salt water. But he felt his handicap most when he watched his favourite sport: baseball.

When Springtime laid her green hand on the meadows and the sweet trill of the mockingbird glistened on the air, C.E.'s thoughts turned to the pennant race. He knew everything about baseball, from the odds facing the Red Sox to The Babe's favourite brand of tobacco. But he also knew better than to try and play ball himself. Instead, he helped others to play. He was the Manager for the Harmony Little League team and a keen supporter of the Men's league.

This Men's League was founded in order to give the villagers a chance to join in the national sport in an organised, even dignified, way. Uniforms and equipment were paid for by subscription, and the team was allotted a makeshift diamond in an improved piece of pasture land. Throughout the summer months the team played 'away' games at other villages, and hosted visitors at the local ground. Always on the lookout for new talent, the local fellows were overjoyed when a lanky young man crossed South Mountain to join them. He was tall, skinny and clean-shaven and known only by a few of the locals. He was a poor runner, but a steel-nerved infielder, being unbreakable as a first baseman. But his talent, his real talent, was with a Louisville Slugger. Batting left-handed, his copper-brown eyes could read the path of a speeding baseball even as it left the pitcher's hand. He quickly became batter number four – the clean-up man, the power-hitter for the team.

One hot afternoon in August 1952 the Harmony Men's League faced defeat. It was the bottom of the ninth, they were trailing by three runs, and there were two men out. The local assembly (it could never be called a crowd) was silent. The bases were loaded and the young man stepped to the plate. Everyone knew it was a horrible position to be in, and embarrassment looked certain. The pitcher leant forward and took his signal for the first pitch. Before anyone could move, a shout went up behind the home-team bench:

'C'mon Moosey, knock one inda the walnut trees!'

The pitcher rocked on to his heels and let go a fast ball that was right down the pike. There was a split second when no one breathed, then a sound like the crack of a rifle-shot. Then, as surely as God made little green apples, the old horsehide was on its way through the walnut trees. As the locals cheered themselves hoarse, Harmony won 4-3.

Standing with a clipboard near the homeplate umpire was the official score-keeper Jane Lois Ford. She had earned this position through teaching herself shorthand, and through showing a flair for accountancy in the Ford family shop. Moose, the young slugger from South Mountain, had made her task as a book-keeper more than usually lively of late. She certainly knew the score when C.E. gave the young man a new fielder's mitt. It was a top-quality one and cost $22.00. C.E. extracted a promise that the young man would repay the cost of the mitt at the rate of $1.00 for each fielding error he committed with it. That season he paid back $2.00. He also became a frequent guest to supper. In the autumn of that year, the following conversation took place:

Moose (shyly) I wuz wondrin if ya wannet a ring?

Jane (coyly) What kindova ring?

Moose (peevishly) A rowund one.

They were married in November 1952, and the bridal bed was put in the same attic room where Jane had been born eighteen years earlier. Eleven years later, Jane and Moose had a son named John David, and thirty-five years on, he began to write this book.

I was awakened to my own life in the summer of 1970. It was in that year that the past was given to my five senses when I learned that we were to move to the farm once owned by Charlie Ford and Sadie. The farm had been out of our family for nearly a generation when my father spent almost every penny we had (and a great many more we didn't have) to get it back. I was neither frightened nor excited, but simply uncomprehending. I was told that it was a very old house and that practically all of our family had lived there at one time or another.

So I looked around me for what that might mean. I thought of C.E.'s sister Carrie. She had lived in this farmhouse and now had one of her own. She was beautiful – hair like a white tulip and cheeks like a red one – and like C.E., she was seldom without a smile. Her own farmhouse was magical – long corridors to run in, great green shutters to open and close, a high balcony and a tall sunny kitchen. I was encouraged too when I thought of C.E.'s sister Viola. Though she no longer lived in a farmhouse, the old one had plainly left its stamp on her spirit. Smaller and frailer than Carrie, she had once waded into Little Catoctin Creek to retrieve a lost rubber ball for me.

There was C.E. himself – my beloved grandfather and the craftiest adult I had ever met. He said the letters F A R M spelt 'work'. I must

14

have looked confused, because when he turned to smile at his friend Guy, Guy said no, it didn't. F A R M spells '*shit*'. Both men giggled until Dutch gave them a look that turned them both into sheep.

I was more troubled when I thought of my great-grandmother Sadie Mae. In late middle age she had joined a dark old-fashioned religious sect that had done nothing to improve her sunny disposition. Gone were the peacock-feathered hats as big as bushel baskets, replaced by black-buttoned frocks and netted caps. When my mother asked Sadie what she thought of her prospective grandson-in-law, she replied, 'Uf he ever fulls out he'll beuh man.' Two years later Sadie was told she was to be a great-grandmother. Her reply, 'at's nuthin tuh be prowd uv', came to represent her whole world outlook.

I cannot recall her ever speaking to me. Bedridden for the last years of her life, I visited her daily, accompanying Dutch as she tended her. I knew that Sadie had crippling arthritis, but I was never allowed to get too close to her for fear that her behaviour or appearance might become too shocking. My memories are of red, gnarled hands and a crooked, scaly voice. We sat together in the same room, often for hours, nearly every day for years – the two of us spanning four generations – and yet I truly believe we never even said hello. Perhaps, I wondered, this was the result of the work spelt F A R M.

Yet there was Charlie Ford to reflect upon. At ninety-four, he was the oldest human I had ever seen. When he was born, Ulysses S. Grant was president and it was the year of the Centennial. Now his auburn hair had turned to dove-white and his great left arm – once as strong as an ash tree – rested easily upon his wheelchair. He was graceful and kind. He hid Christmas gifts of whiskey in the bureau, taking a medicinal drop before bedtime. Every morning he drank a cup of hot water and ate fresh fruit and oats, convinced that this was the key to longevity. He was calm and sensible and, most importantly, he still had dreams. In the earth-brown silence of his parlour, broken only by the whiz-ping of the clock and the square of fern-coloured light by his chair, he sat daily, poring over atlases and books of foreign travel, imagining the mountains of Tibet and the rivers of Brazil. This man, who had once voted for Teddy Roosevelt and who had had maggots injected into his heel to cure gangrene, shook my hand, laughed at my jokes, and glowed with pride at my achievements. Surely here was a goodness unmarred by work.

But the truth about my parents' plans became plain to me whenever I tried to discuss them with my grandmother. In Dutch's eyes we were not moving three quarters of a mile down the road, we were moving to another world. For me that world would be one of enigmas and secrets, mysteries and promises. For her, it had been a world of boiled white laundry and huckleberry jelly, hurricane lamps and shadowless August days. Her eyes filled with tears when she recalled the back-breaking harvests and the stillborn calves, the flight of young rabbits and the smell of new hay.

On a fine autumn morning, as we walked home from church hand in hand, Dutch paused by the drooping iron chain that marked the churchyard boundary. As I watched she laid a small bunch of flowers at the base of a worn grey stone that read 'William Henry Ford'. I asked her why she did this and she told me that he was Charlie Ford's father. I didn't feel that this had answered my question at all, but I was quiet for a minute. Finally, I asked whether he had died a long time ago. Without looking me in the eye, she let go of my hand and said no, no not really. The people who had died a long time ago were buried up on the mountain, above Ellerton, at the old Meeting House near Ford Fields. I tried to recall this place and what I saw was a green sloping hillside with small, silvery stones, none of which I could read. But one windy day around Easter I had run up and down this hillside like a bird learning to fly, and now, today, that mattered. They were mine and I was joined to them as I was joined to no one else. Without knowing how it had happened, I had come into a memory larger than my own.

CHAPTER TWO

Foggy Mountain

A fur-trapper walking north-northeast of Harmony for ten miles could cross the summit of the mountain and find himself at Catoctin Furnace. This abandoned ironworks by the side of Little Hunting Creek was one of my favourite places to visit as a child. It had been built in the early eighteenth century by Thomas Johnson, first Governor of Maryland, and continued in use until the early years of the twentieth century. At its peak, there had been over 20,000 acres of woodland used to produce charcoal to smelt the low-grade ore dug from the mountainside pits. This iron eventually became frying pans, Dutch ovens and cannon balls for the Maryland 'Old Line' regiment of George Washington's army. I knew it as a high, L-shaped pair of crumbling green-stone walls and a squat bulging stone tower with arches on four sides, at the base of which in the sand and leaves were fantastic bubbly pieces of jade-coloured slag. The works themselves were overgrown with trees and temptingly dangerous to walk on, as were the paths through the water-filled pits. Across the road from the furnace were the collapsing mist-grey remains of the Ironmaster's home, lost in a century of neglect. The village, pouring out along both sides of the road, was made up largely of the crouching heavy-walled cottages of the ironworkers. Rising menacingly near the cross-roads was the evil spectre of the Company Store. It was here that the workmen exchanged the chits they were given as wages for all the goods needed to support their families. The Store was, of course, owned by the furnace's proprietors, which meant that the men's wages simply cycled through their pockets and back into the business. Heaven help you if you traded for a commodity elsewhere. The men themselves were capable of almost anything. In the early nineteenth century, for some reason that is still unclear, the Furnace men saw the sale of newfangled matches in a nearby town as evidence of a threat to their personal safety.

In retaliation they armed themselves with clubs, hammers, axes and bats and attacked the town. In the ensuing melee several people were killed and the ironworkers were beaten back to their lair. Still, they were not totally without a sense of humour. In a nearby churchyard one man is now buried under a headstone that reads,

Here lies the body of an atheist – all dressed up and no place to go.

Follow the blue gravel road beside the Creek as it whirls upward on to the mountain, water-green with oak, elm and pine. Don't leave the road unless you know the way, for the sumac bushes fool all but the best. If it is summer, keep your eyes to the ground lest you stumble on a rattlesnake asleep in the sun. Give a wide berth to the huge blackish leaf-bags that hang in the trees, because hornets are easily provoked and slow to forgive. When you reach the Ridge Road, turn left towards Mink Farm. In the small meadow here on a glorious morning in June, I saw what I believe I shall never see again. A light shower of rain had sprung from some high hollow clouds and now dripped gently from the branches. As I came forward from the woods I saw, or thought I saw, the wide parti-coloured stump of a rainbow rooted near the opposite side of the field. With my chin on my chest and my eyes like pennies, I watched as the flatish panel of metallic light swung backwards, away from me, as if turning on an axis overhead, disappearing at last in the trees beyond.

The Ridge Road itself was a gravel track running just below the spine of the mountain. There are no roads to the left except for dirt trails leading to little clusters of 'fire-ponds'. These fire-ponds were dug in order to provide water for the great pumping engines in the event of a forest fire. Thankfully, they have only been used once, and now rest tranquilly, a home for cat-tails, migrating ducks and the floating peach-white blossom of the dogwood trees. After Mink Farm, there is a small washed-out road that loops pointlessly into the forest, rejoining the main road slightly farther on. This is Ford Fields, home now to no one but the pheasants and the deer. Yet lying in neat rows among the green briar canes are the stone foundations of a small farmhouse, not quite forgotten.

In about a mile the Ridge Road divides at a place called Five Forks. Don't turn right. This is the Delaney Road and midway down the slope the road runs between a house and barn. Mr Delaney lives here in constant fear of the road's being improved and made more accessible to wheeled traffic. He is prepared to defend the status quo with arms and is best avoided. Instead, go straight on past the Meeting House Road to Wistman Lane. Follow the quartz-bright trail past the fallen-in shed into the laurel trees until you reach the Falls. Here, in a clearing made by fallen boulders, Little Catoctin Creek leaps from her mountain and plunges through the branches to rest in a twenty-foot pool. The air is creamy with a fragrant mist, and even the birds are silent with awe. I used to come here whenever I was in love, or wished I was, to let my thoughts turn around me like the eddies at my feet.

Taking the Ridge Road south, carry on past Fisher's Hollow, Coxey Brown and Hawbottom, and look up the hill towards Bootjack Spring. After an 1844 bank robbery in Baltimore, two men on horseback paused to rest here. The law was hot on their trail and their way had been slowed by four heavy saddlebags full of gold. In the gritty soil under the shade of the pines beside the spring, the two men decided to hide their treasure and return for it later, after they had made good their escape. The two men then split up, hoping to confuse their pursuers. Within days one of them was killed near Harper's Ferry. The other one got as far as Ohio, but died there under mysterious circumstances. To this day, the gold has never been found. You really ought to look for it. Everyone else has.

A little farther down the hill, where a small stream leads to Carroll Creek, there is gold for the taking. A solitary prospector earned a very difficult living here until the early years of this century. His work consisted of diverting a channel of water through a system of wooden troughs filled with sand from the stream. Peering deeply into the water, he removed the soft, gold-bearing stones with his fingers and sold them by the bagful to a local jeweller. Through some geological quirk, the tiny vein of gold upon which he had established his living, surfaces at some point on the mountain crossed by this stream, and the crumbly, reddish-golden rocks washed downwards until extracted by his crude sluices. The gold – never plentiful – surfaced nowhere else in the vicinity. But once, after a heavy flood, a sandbank formed in a meadow further downstream. C.E. was the first to realise the potential of this accident, and brought home a gold nugget the size of a dried pea. For my part, I once dropped down the steep muddy banks near the old working site to have a look. There among the thick black rotting planks, nose to the water, I carefully plucked out a palmful of slivery dusk-red pebbles that twinkled like the eyes of a god – useless and impure, but the stuff of boyhood pride.

About a mile west, near the old Shookstown Road, on a patch of hillside too rocky to support a tree, there stands a fireplace and chimney. This ruin marks the sight of the original home of the Ropp family. The house had disappeared even before Will Ropp was born, but until recently the view remained. On a clear day, it was possible to see the dim blue outline of the great chasm where the Shenandoah River spills into the Potomac twenty miles away. In between, the farms lay warmly dressed in lime-green hay and pale silver grain. Carrie's house is just out of sight beyond a low fall of land, and to walk there you must cross the Stotter Farm.

This farm has a melancholy history. Mr Stotter was born around the same year as Charlie Ford. He had two children and his wife died when they were still young. Shortly after his children came of age, Mr Stotter was overcome by depression. He contacted his lawyer and drew up his will. This will specified that in the event of Mr Stotter's death, the farm would pass to whomever of his children had not married. His assumption was that if his daughter married first, her husband would have a farm of his own, and if his son married first, his own farm would become a dowry for his daughter. Shortly after making this will, Mr Stotter's body was found face down in the stream that curves through the meadow behind his house. He had committed suicide by lying down in a pool of water that barely covered his head. For more than fifty years after the reading of his will, Mr Stotter's children lived on in their parents' home, neither one the sole legal possessor. Motivated by greed, or thwarted by ill-fortune, neither child ever married. A broken and frustrated man, Mr Stotter the Younger was found one autumn morning face down in the same shallow pool where his father had ended his own life. His sister, now the legal heir to the family home, never took possession of the property in her own right. Instead, within two years she died insane, the captive of a cruel Fate.

Down the hill from the Stotter Farm, sharing a stream with my great-aunt Carrie, there was a small property with a small house and a small barn, all as brightly polished as a fresh red apple. Scrupulously kept, with impeccable white fences, there were ten acres of steeply slanted land that had been in the same family for generations. The last heir to this tiny kingdom was named Launcelot Somers. He was an only child and his parents died when he was still a young man. What was remarkable about his life was not that his farm was so tidy – all good farms are that – or that he earned a living on so small a ground. What made Launcelot special among farmers was that he could barely walk. With knees pointed inwards like a newly-born foal, he struggled single-handedly six days a week to plough his fields, milk his cows, and bale his hay. If his poor legs did little to ease his daily toil, his spirits found no repose in his voice. Launcelot was practically mute. It was only with fierce gesticulations and rumbling, tensely-muscled moans that he could make his words understood. Naturally shy, he never married and had few contacts with the outside world. At last, after a lifetime of dedicated and sometimes brutal labour, his pristine family farm fell under the auctioneer's hammer. Stricken in years, Launcelot bid farewell to the bottomless blue skies and the yellow-green shade of the pear trees, to end his days inside four white walls, under a nurse's care, in a town he barely knew. But his legacy, as a proud, efficient and independent member of an honourable profession still lives.

Leaving Launcelot's farm, turn right for the Harmony Road. In five hundred yards you'll see the first of the four great iron bridges across Little Catoctin Creek. Resembling a pair of huge green longbows resting on their strings, these bridges were built in the 1890's from contributions by the locals. Each one carried a small plaque commemorating this achievement in generosity, placed midway along their centre posts and invisible unless you climbed up on to the ribbed iron supports. Fifty yards to the right, and about a mile downstream from The Corner, was Shultz's Mill. Like Charlie Ford's cider press, the Shultz family built the mill as a subsidiary interest to their surrounding farm. With two hundred acres themselves, and grain-growing farms in every direction, it seemed like a sure thing.

The business failed in less than a generation. To remove this blot from their family's honour, the next scion of the Shultz family decided to have the building demolished. A special steam-powered derrick with a huge wrecking ball was brought in to speed up the process of destruction. On the appointed day, young Mr Shultz was surprised to find that none of the villagers came to watch the proceedings. As the great machine wheeled into place, roaring and gasping, a creeping doubt took possession of Mr Shultz. With its boom in place, the engineer released the chains and the mighty wrecking ball descended.

There followed the sound of a splitting crack as a hole opened up in the first floor brickwork. This was followed by a grating rush as the shattered masonry collapsed on to the flooring inside, leaving a circular hollow in the wall nearly eight feet across. As the wrecking ball was drawn back, Shultz's heart sank. He ran to the engineer and called off the whole operation. In a flood of sentiment, Shultz lost the will to demolish completely something for which his whole family had made sacrifices. The steam engine was dragged away and for eighty years the building gradually imploded. The roof caved in, the floors sagged and gave way, and two of the walls folded inwards. But stiff and upright, a half-stone-half-brick wall, with a gaping wound long softened by the winter frosts, still remained, a monument of loss and recovery.

On the high ground above the silver roof of the Shultz farmhouse, beyond the second iron bridge, there is a tiny triangular vale. Nestled deep in the honeysuckle, under the whir of intoxicated bees and the drip-click song of bluejays, there lie the unmarked graves of the Shultz family's slaves. Callously referred to as The Boneyard, the exact whereabouts of the place is known only to a few. But here in the shade of the locust trees, untended and unmourned, time and circumstance only have given solace to the remains of an unnamed family who worked side-by-side with the Shultzs for nearly a century.

Many of the nearby farms had kept slaves, the descendants of whom have long since moved away. Dutch recalled that as a young girl she had known only one survivor. This person was an old woman even in Dutch's youth. As a child she had been a slave on the farm neighbouring the Shultz's – one later bought by Dutch's uncle George Ropp. Dutch never knew the woman's name, but could recall only that she lived in a single room above the washhouse, near the rear corner of the family's own home. She had lived there as a slave and remained there as a freewoman until her death in the 1920's. Her identity, like the exact whereabouts of her remains, will probably never be known.

The farm that George Ropp bought was the largest ever in his family's possession. Never affluent, he was able to buy the property with funds gathered from a tragic windfall. In the summer of 1917, General 'Black Jack' Pershing's call for volunteers to fight the war in France was heard on Catoctin Mountain. George Ropp answered the call, and months later he arrived on the Western Front. It was there on a vile autumn day, 3000 miles from Harmony and in a war against his own ancestral homeland, that George 'Sock' Ropp gave his right arm for the Argonne Forest. When he returned home he was given the customary pension awarded to soldiers thought to be too maimed for further work. Nothing daunted, Uncle Sock spent the money on a two-hundred-acre property, meaning to farm it with the aid of the new machinery then becoming available. This entailed learning to drive in such a way that he had to pass his left arm through the steering wheel to change gears – a feat that would later terrify his great-niece Jane. (By comparison, Charlie Ford, although complete in his limbs, never used first gear, believing that any gear so quickly changed out of was obviously worthless). In any case, the scheme prospered, and Uncle Sock's great-grandchildren now manage the business he founded.

The far corner of the Ropp Farm borders a place owned by Russell Waterman. Now Russ's profession was ostensibly that of farmer. But he did little farming. Instead, he devoted his time to his hobby – junk. If it was capable of rust and corrosion, Russ owned at least three examples. I suspect that in the four acres or so surrounding his house and farmyard there is enough ferrous oxide to dye the county orange. He owned more than a century's worth of decay. It pervaded his whole attitude. Among the spiffy working farms that surrounded him, Russ's place shone like an unpainted beacon. The whitewash used by his forebears had so far gone that it left no trace in living memory. I myself am certain that at one time or another as a child I played on the floor of every house in the village except his. There were two reasons for this. First, he is said to have had little available floor space and, secondly, my parents regarded his house as in imminent danger of collapse. This was not an unjustified fear. The annexe on the right-rear of the house had already broken off, leaving its jagged edge exposed, unpainted and unaltered for years. Still, Russ realised an unexpected boon from this unconventionality. Besides an obvious pride of ownership, on rare occasions he could be persuaded reluctantly to part with an isolated item from his collection. C.E. recalled that in his boyhood, his father Charlie's hay rake struck a stone with its iron wheel and popped two of its spoke-rods. As hay-making is a very time-sensitive business, Charlie was anxious to repair this as quickly as possible. His thoughts turned hopefully to Russ's inestimable store of spares. C.E. said it took his father three-quarters of an hour to so far insinuate himself into Russ's confidence that Russ would initiate a search for the necessary wheel.

The two men, with C.E. in tow, then walked behind the dingy corner of the barn where, invisible to the public eye, C.E. said there was a pile of iron wheels that reached well above his father's head. All bore that distinctive amber-rich hue that characterised Russ's possessions. According to C.E., the three of them worked like termites on a heap of sawdust for close to an hour until a wheel of the correct sort was found. When at last the other unwanted consumer-durables had been replaced, Charlie dropped two silver dollars in to Russ's hand and the transaction was complete. Both men, no doubt, felt they had become a little richer and a little poorer.

Turn left from Russ's place on to the Brethren Church Road. Walk by Mary-Bill Gadshill's on the right and round the corner past Edda-Mae Hunter's, but stop for a bit to visit Russ's sister-in-law Florry Waterman. Florry and her husband Henry were ideally partnered. She was five foot tall, he, six-and-a-half. She was frail, arthritic and sadly humpbacked. He was robust, youthful and as strong as a stallion. But both shared a talent for rural crafts that took patience, a light touch, and the low voice of persuasion.

Like many of the villagers, Henry had a small farm. Although like his brother Russ, his attitude to painting farm buildings was incompletely formed, Henry raised the usual crops of hay and corn, while Florry minded the cows and chickens. What made Henry's farm unusual was his small harvest of broom corn. For Henry was a broom-maker. Now as a boy I had a great love of any and all mechanical things, and I thought that the broom-shop was pure magic. It was an upstairs room above the stables, with a wooden floor, cut and scrapped by hard use. It smelt deliciously of grease and wood and straw. In one corner, there was a prickly pile of bundled broom corn. Beside it stood a sinister chopping machine, with a hinged knife and a yellow litter of decapitations. To the left were the great crimping irons where the broom would be held while Henry, astraddle the wooden bench, carefully stitched up the corn with emerald green twine. But most marvellous of all, looming majestically in front of the window, was the broom-machine itself. To a curious boy, it was fascinating in its combination of technology and agriculture. Silvery new wire spooled in from overhead, a hand-powered rivet-puncher swivelled in from one side, wooden handles turned slowly as the foot-treadle was played, and fingered a few at a time, the warm stalks of corn were spun into a whole. Out of this wonderwork there came many masterpieces of the sweeper's repertoire: little whisk brooms for those almost unreachable nooks, great flat models for that broad expanse of floor. All needs were catered for with a great show of reluctance. You see Henry's expertise, however well-founded, was employed only for the persistent. No brooms could be had for the asking. Only cajoling, teasing, tempting with home-made pies, or bartering with fresh strawberries might avail against his stubborn Waterman refusal to employ himself for his own profit.

Motivated more by modesty, Florry had a similar way with her wares. If you were lucky, spoke softly and flattered her weedless columns of pole beans, she might consent to sell you a pound of her freshly-churned butter. With the colour of a marigold and the minty softness of an August breeze, it came in firm irregular rectangles with her initials pressed crookedly on the surface. Spread thinly over a steaming corncake with the bee-bright honeyed breath of molasses, it taught me the lesson of delectation. Florry's other gift was to be mistress of the village quilters. Her cedar chests were piled to bursting with some of the finest needlework in the county. Year in and year out, this tiny woman with her crippled spine and her jaded red-blue hands won top prizes at the largest exhibition of needlework in the state. If asked, she would hobble to an immense cupboard, seize one corner of a log-cabin, a wedding-ring, or nine-ladies-dancing and, rocking back and forth, pluck it on to the floor. Unable to lift it easily, she would nonchalantly, even haphazardly, throw this work of 1000 hours patience into the air like a fisherman casting his nets, revealing a beauty achieved through bold scraps of cloth and the tense pacing of her needle. My last glimpse of her was on a gold-washed morning in July. She was standing among the straight rows of her vegetables, the long handle of her hoe protruding several feet behind her, her figure lost in ankle-length calico, her face hidden in the shadow of her bonnet. Around her there was no sound except the clank of cowbells and the low red hum of locusts; nothing in fact to disturb her work but the dream of the patterns she held in her hands.

Across the road from Henry and Florry, lived Henry and Russ's sister Annie and her husband Arthur. Go down the hill past their flower-fringed vegetable garden to the Brethren Meeting House. Here in the cemetery was the only tombstone I ever saw for a man who hadn't died.

After 'Cost' Foster retired from shopkeeping up on the Old National Pike, he had time to consider his own mortality. At sixty-eight, he knew he wouldn't last forever and he was concerned that after his demise his final resting-place might go unremembered. In view of this, he bought himself a large red granite memorial – simple, unostentatious, unadorned – and had his name and birth-date inscribed on it. It was then carefully placed near the roadside, where it could be seen by passers by. Although neatly kept, the stone remained otherwise unaltered for another twenty years. Yet today, long after the second date has been entered, some kind hand never lets an Easter go by without placing a few white daffodils above his head, out of regard for the old man's worst fear.

Below the Meeting House, the road curves sharply to the right, through two steep banks, and past the Lutheran Church. Opposite the church is a square empty patch of gravel that marks the site of C.E.'s third memory. Here in the autumn of 1922, the schoolhouse burnt down. C.E. said it was the greatest day of his life. From that day onwards, lessons were held in a large borrowed parlour until pedagoguery was given up in Harmony altogether, and the local children walked the three miles to the next village.

We'll go on then further downhill, waving to Hen Hubble on the right and Guy Taylor on the left, until we come to The Corner. Here I'll leave the decision to you. Shall we go straight on, round The Mary House, past Mame Hunter's and over the third iron bridge? It's a steep walk up the Hollow Road, so we could jump down to the creek and count the sunfish, or walk along gathering chestnuts for Mrs Clover. Or maybe you'd like to turn right, to the fourth and biggest of the iron bridges? We could lower ourselves down by the side, and inch our way along the outer support rods, hovering over the water and hanging by our knees. At the other side, if Dutch isn't looking, we'll throw a stone at the old tin sign on the Cider Press. We could play horseshoes alongside the stream (they're hidden in the toolbox inside the lean-to). We could even ask Dick Taylor – who has lived in great-uncle Dick Kinna's House for thirty years – to show us the stairs that connect his cellar to a kitchen cupboard, or go on down to say how-do at great-aunt Viola's. But as it's a warm day, why don't we join The Loafers.

The Loafers is not an official convocation. It has no constitution, no membership fee is charged, and dress is casual. It helps to be invited by someone who has himself been a member for at least twenty years, but this is not essential. Meetings are generally convened on The Bench. The Bench has two principal parts, and one small outrider. In the wide square of road in front of The Corner, opposite The Mary House, the bench is tucked alongside the bridge, underneath the walnut trees, with its back to the stream. Its larger section consists of a painted grey pew, donated by the Lutherans. At its far end, there is a plank recovered from the bridge-floor, raised on two short logs. If you sit here, don't wriggle or you'll roll down the steep drop behind you. When it rains, the assembly-point is across the road on a bench built by Charlie Ford, along the back wall of the Store-Porch, sheltered by the High-Porch above. The Loafers is led by Black Label, a man known by the brand of beer he invariably holds in his left hand. With a merry smile, and a face like a red egg, Black Label has spent his entire leisure life within a stone's throw of The Bench. As a lithe youth, he was notorious for riding his bicycle, unhanded, over the high iron braces of the bridge – ten inches wide and thirty feet above the rocky creek bed. But as a man, within his limited sphere, his role in the community is immense in its diversity. If you need to drive out from a blind corner, he is a traffic warden. If you are lifting your potatoes, he is an agricultural worker with a bucket and a strong back. If you are curious about any piece of village news, he is a journalist with many secret sources. In short, he is the merchant of village social commerce.

Some of the other loafers you have met before: C.E., Guy, Henry, Cost, Hen, Dick Taylor. If the sun's too hot to drink beer, or its Sunday, or like the other loafers, you're teetotal, you can buy a bottle of pop on the Store Porch. This was C.E.'s idea and it ought not to have worked. Everybody said so. After all, even the most distantly aboded of the loafers lived only a ten minutes walk away, so why would anyone pay fifteen cents for a cold drink when he could just walk home and have one for free? C.E. proved the doubting ones wrong on a blistering Sunday afternoon in July. The sky was as empty as a hot dry skillet, not a leaf trembled in the parched immovable air, and the ground lay buried in almond-coloured dust. As the loafers sat about fanning their sweaty foreheads in the dim shade of the trees, C.E. made his move. Striding moodily across the boiling tarmac, he dropped his money into his own machine and bought a bottle of purple fizzy grape juice. He quietly rejoined his comrades, pressing the cool dewy surface of the bottle

27

against his forehead. There was a clink-ping, as he popped off the lid with an opener kept in his pocket, and in the silence the crisp knocking of the idle bubbles sent out their call. There was a gentle thunking noise as his Adam's apple rocked in its sleeve, transporting the drink downwards. Taking it away, smiling abstractedly, he lay back on the bench like Nero after a long debauch. No one had spoken throughout this performance, and the slow voices gradually rose up again, dusty and hoarse. At last, one by one, each man slipped away towards the Store Porch. In less than ten minutes conviviality prevailed. Without ever referring to their behaviour, or the changes wrought to their habits or revenues, a handful of lives had been altered. Cold drinks at The Bench had become a naturalised part of summer afternoons.

With Black Label's pudgy arm as a pointer, we'll turn left up the low hill towards the Band Hall.

The Band Hall was actually a church built in the 1890's, but used as such for less than ten years. The builders, a mysterious sect of outsiders, quietly and completely disappeared after failing to attract local converts. The building itself is apparently unique in its design. Built of heavy unshaped stones in the form of a rectangle it has a tangentially attached bell-tower. The top half of the tower, building and roof are covered with whitening brown, unpainted, hand-cut shingles in the shape of little rounded feathers. The entrance follows a switchback path up the hill, then a long flight of stairs through the tower and into the hall. Inside, remnants of the stained glass remain, but as an otherwise 'plain' sect, the previous occupiers left no other traces of their beliefs. Even the tower is empty except for a choir of pigeons and one clerical owl. Fortunately, when the faithful interlopers who built this edifice found themselves too financially straitened to remain, they found a buyer for the property in the assembly known as the Harmony Band.

These noble children of Pan had been organised first in the mid-nineteenth century. Their numbers ranged from ten to twenty active members, their crimson and gold ranks at one time or another including my great-uncle 'Meardy' Ropp, and my mother Jane. The Band's activities were various, but their music maintained a singularly consistent style, more noted for gusto than finesse. Still, they were financially self-supporting and available for all manner of functions from village festivals to Independence Day parades.

Onwards now past great-aunt Grace's house on the left, and her chicken coop on the right, and round the sharp bend past Gaetha Fox's to the jelly-bean red home of Floyd Pine. Here, in his shingled workshop, the third pillar of village society rests. Once a month, a space is cleared for the benches, rocking chairs, gliders, stools and cane-bottom comforts of the Harmony Community Club. The Club is open to men and women, provided you pay your fifty-cent dues. As you're a newcomer and I'm too young to vote, we'll just sit on the rug by the window while folks discuss the four main issues of Club business. These four issues are always the same: the principal source of revenue, the principal source of expenditure, the principal public relations exercise, and the principal plan of public development. Or, to put it another way: bingo, street lamps, the festival and a new baseball diamond.

Club finances came almost exclusively from Saturday night bingo at the Band Hall. With C.E. to call the numbers, and Dutch to cook the eats, the trade in low-grade gambling flourished. From the proceeds of this came the funds to maintain the street lamps. Oh, yes, Harmony had them – around a dozen to illumine the cold mountain darkness and to single us out from our neighbouring villages as people who embraced the future. The third piece of business was organising the festival. For two, or sometimes three weekends in the summer, our Friday and Saturday nights sparkled with merriment. But all of these things rocked easily on, like the legs of Floyd's chair, one meeting just like another. The real debate, against which committees and sub-committees formed from the crème of The Loafers broke their wits was the dream of a new baseball diamond. We certainly needed one. Although the Band Hall was rented at a nominal fee, for everything else – that is baseball and the festival – we depended on Floyd's generosity. After 'Old Man' Somers died, and his widow let out the farm to tenants, she felt that it wasn't fair to them to clutter up a meadow with festival stalls. So Floyd stepped in and allowed the Club to put up its stalls in one of his two pastures. A few years later, the same thing happened at the other end of the village, when the old diamond was converted to grazing for young heifers. Once again, Floyd chipped in and let the Club rake the grass off part of the second of his two fields, so that village athletics might have a new home. All this from a shy unassuming little man with thick white hair and a face lined like damp earth on a dry day, who stood beside me singing tenor in the church quartet. But what the Club really wanted was independence. What they hoped for was a family park: baseball diamond, bandstand, picnic tables, swings, slides and sandpits, permanent stalls for the festival. The dilemma was in finding a suitable place. It had to be near to the village centre, and accessible from a public road. It also had to be flat, and worst of all, it had to be cheap. Cunningly developed dialogues were opened with all the local sultans, but despite sifting every argument and refuting every argument, no deal was ever struck. Instead, for twenty-five years monthly meetings of the Harmony Community Club dragged on into the night, prolonged by head scratchings and chin rubbings, as the worthy villagers formulated fresh strategies to win some new ground for their dream.

Well, it's nearly supper time now, but I'll walk with you as far as Orpha's barn, for that's my turning. You can go straight on if you want to, and maybe sit for a while with Junior and Ebbie, the tenants on the Somers' Farm. They'll play you a game of Michigan Rummy if you have time. Or you can walk with me up the Coxey Brown Road and we'll throw a stone at the water skippers under the bridge. We'll have the whole dark mountain in front of us, and a burnt little sun at our backs. We could have a rich black yeasty glass of root beer at my house and sit on the bench under the maple trees. I don't know what's for supper, but I expect we'll find something.

CHAPTER THREE

Salty Dog Rag

My first real memory of my family's new home is as a nightmare. From my earliest infancy we had gone up the Coxey Brown Road to cut Christmas trees at the farm owned by Viola's son Willie. In summer, along this way, just after a low rattling plank bridge, there was a dense jungle of trees, dotted with the star-light burst of multaflora briars and a buttery sprinkle of honeysuckle. But in winter, when the blossoms were lost in a dry heap of leaves milled to dust by the wind, it was just possible to make out the smoke-grey home of the Dog-Woman. Once, on a hard cold morning in December, as we came home past the sagging pink shed by the path to her lair, I convinced myself that I had seen her. Small and arched, with her nickel-coloured hair blowing about her ears and her ancient hands cupped to her mouth, I imagined her walking towards me through the ruinous clutter of her farmyard. Now nothing, absolutely nothing, could have persuaded me to go nearer than the gravel path bordering the road.

The Dog-Woman's story began in New York. Sally Caxton was a vaudevillian and Gay Nineties belle. She had prestige, she had glamour, and she had money – lots of money. But she also had a husband, and that husband was a rich captain in the merchant marine. One fine spring day, while her husband was at sea, Sally's loneliness overtook her. Her career was over and her name obscure. She had no family and no connections and she decided to run away. Taking trunkful after trunkful of sequinned ball gowns and strong-boxes full of greenbacks, she absconded to a tiny village in the Appalachian Mountains. Once there she bought a small neat farm from a man whose daughter had just married and who had moved out of her parents' old home. That man's name was Charlie Ford.

For a few years things went along smoothly enough. Though reclusive, Sally bothered no one, and even let out her fields for use by her neighbours. She employed local men to do her outdoor chores. She tended her grapes and trained her rose bushes in solitude. Then one day in midsummer, a storm came down from the north that broke Sally's mind. Eyewitnesses recalled the event exactly. It was early afternoon and Sally was at work in the vegetable garden behind her house. Like the local women, she was dressed in a long calico-print dress and broad-brimmed bonnet. As she knelt in the sun weeding her onions, her neighbour Clarence Farley was working ten feet in front of her, pulling up the dead pea-vines, and preparing to dig over the soil. As Clarence straightened out his back and lifted his straw hat to wipe away the sweat, he saw a man turn the corner by Orpha's barn. Clarence didn't know the man, and he watched him as he walked nearer up the Coxey Brown Road. When he reached the hollow apple tree that overhangs the road just below the farmhouse, Clarence saw that the man was in his shirtsleeves but, despite the heat, he had a dark blue cap on his head. His hands were empty. Curious, Clarence walked past Sally, who anyway was working with her back towards the house and road, and strolled around the front of the house, waiting by the picket fence to get a better look. To his surprise, the man turned in at the gravel entrance to the farm and walked straight towards him. Clarence said hello, but the short square man with thick black hair and eyebrows walked right past him, through the gate, and round the front of the house. When he got to a spot just below the black maple tree he stopped. In front of him, just beyond the grape arbour, Sally was still on her hands and knees, hard at work. As Clarence drew up close to him, the man put his hands to his mouth and shouted at the crouching woman, 'Glynna Willerup!'

According to Clarence, a deep shudder ran over Sally's whole frame and then she went rigid. Without turning, without even moving, she groaned, 'I haven't got it. I haven't got it.' The stranger's shoulders dropped and he stood motionless in the shade for a moment. Then, without uttering another word, the man turned on his heel and walked slowly away, the same way he had come. He was never seen in the village again.

From that day onwards things changed at Sally Caxton's. When the leases on her fields ran out, she refused to renew them. She no longer had anyone in to help with the heavy chores. Strangest of all, she brought in a firm of builders all the way from Frederick to build her an enormous kennel. Dug into the hillside behind the farmhouse, it was a state-of-the-art construction. Built of cement blocks with neatly painted green woodwork and silver-green shingles, there was a vast and luxurious accommodation for at least a dozen dogs. There was a chimney and wood stove to provide heating, and a large room with water and electricity for the preparation of meals and clean-up. Each dog had a large wooden-floored galley with a sturdy oak kennel. From these, full sized doors provided separate indoor and outdoor access to the galleys, each of which had an immaculate sixty-foot run. Not long after the builders' work was done, Sally found occupiers for her kennel, and from some still unknown source, dogs of every breed and dimension were accommodated. Then tragedy struck. With her human contacts practically at an end and her once beautiful farm in tatters, Sally abandoned her beloved dogs to their fate. When rumours began to circulate among the villagers, the County Sheriff was called in to investigate. What he found was a complete horror. Dead and dying dogs, some half-buried in filth, others starving in their once fine home, littered the ground. Sally herself was arrested and carried off raving. She died in a sanatorium soon after.

Full proof of her madness lay inside the house itself. To the Sheriff's astonishment, the house – though vile-smelling and unbelievably dirty – was crammed with money. It was hidden, or half-hidden in every orifice. One sofa had $15,000 stuffed into a cushion. The pockets of every garment contained coins, newspapers were interfolded with bank notes, and in the ashes of the stove were the scorched remains of $20 bills.

The Sheriff's search was, of course, motivated by more than mere idle curiosity. All the money seized in the property would revert to the State treasury. With this as an inspiration, his men pursued their work relentlessly. Floorboards were pulled up, century-old plaster was hacked off, ceilings were dragged down and every crevice probed. One by one, every article of furniture was ripped to shreds, cushions were disgorged, and all of the household belongings rifled. When the last of the rubble had been hauled outside and smashed to pieces, anything salvageable was removed for sale. The remainder was heaped in the front garden where it was set alight. Then, as the remains of Glynna Willerup's ill-fated adventure were consumed in the flames, one of the deputies opened up a window in a second floor bedroom. From here the contents of the two huge walk-in wardrobes – hundreds of sequinned dresses, ball-gowns and silken day-coats – were hurled into the fire

33

below. Though the blaze was tremendous and lasted well into the night, it failed to obliterate the memory of 'Sally Caxton' from the villagers' minds. For more than half a century her former home was known as The Dog Woman's House.

On a rainy morning in February The Dog Woman's House was offered for sale at public auction on the steps of the County Court House in Frederick, Maryland. My father, then thirty-four, was present in the small crowd. Standing about twenty feet away, with his eyes steadily fixed on him, was a man who shared my father's interest in the property. This man was Athanasius Barnstaple, President of The Myersville Savings Bank, and owner of fifty-one percent of the shares thereof. Earlier in the week, Moose had paid him a little visit in order to discuss some plans. Athanasius listened intently, nodded sympathetically, and agreed that he would back Moose on the day for a sum not exceeding $11,000. Friendly, but wary, Athanasius had come along to watch the proceedings.

With a humming rat-a-tat drone, the auctioneer got down to business. Several bidders fell off early, but two persisted. The bid landed at $10,000 and Moose's opponent hesitated. Then, with the barely perceptible nod that signifies financial commitment on these occasions, the man assented. The heavy-browed, Stetson-hatted little auctioneer wheeled his pendulous open mouth around the onlookers before hovering expectantly before my father.

Here-and-there-right-sir-hear-the-bid-what-are-you-gonna-give-for-it? Ten-thousand-ten-thousand-ten-thousand-is-the-bid-what-are-you-gonna-give-for-it? Here-and-there-right-sir-do-I-hear-eleven-thousand? Eleven-eleven-eleven-thousand-is-the-bid-sir-what-you-gonna-give-for-it?

His damp eye ceased its roving. Though it was a cold day, Moose was sweating. He looked dry-mouthed towards Athanasius. Athanasius ran his tongue over his lips, closed his eyes, and let his head drop down on to his chest. It was the signal Moose was waiting for. He swallowed hard and his lips formed the words 'Eleven thousand.' The auctioneer's eyes opened a little wider.

Here-and-there-right-sir-hear-the-man-bids-eleven-thousand. Eleven-eleven-eleven-thousand-is-the-bid-sir-do-I-hear-more?

Sensing the kill was near, the auctioneer waved his arm expansively around the assembly. The previous bidder was rock hard and silent.

Eleven-eleven-eleven-thousand-is-the-bid-sirs-goin-once!

   (Silence)

Goin-twice!

   (Silence)

Sold-to-the-gentleman-in-the-red-wool-coat!

With his morning's work completed, Moose returned to his family. I cannot now recall my mother's response to the news that she had just become the co-owner of a small farm. What I am certain of is that either as a matter of delicacy or of policy, she was not allowed to see the property for six months after we purchased it.

When at last the day came and we were allowed to see our new home, I am sure that my bewilderment could not have been greater. Although my father had worked diligently, steadily and almost relentlessly for the whole of this time, the place was still incredible. Nothing was good. If it possessed roots, it was wild, unguarded and overgrown. If it was made of wood, some part of it was rotten. If it was built of stone, some part of it had collapsed. My most potent memory of the day was my first tentative entry into the small downstairs sitting room where, in years gone by, the walls had echoed with the music of C.E. and his friends. All around me lay crumpled paper, broken glass, twisted metal and splintered wood. None of this had any meaning for me at all. But there, beginning just above the pantry door, a great triangle of ceiling had been pulled downwards, making a peach-coloured waterfall of tiles that spilled forwards to my feet. With every step I took I could hear the crisp grating sound of the broken shards. I realised then that the letters FARM spelt time.

What I didn't know then was how much time a labour of even the greatest love can take. My father had toiled slavishly for half a year just to make our new property safe and accessible to his family. Yet what we saw on our first visit was almost unbelievable. It was impossible to touch anything for fear that it might fall, crumble, or spread contagion. But my mother, always the heart-wood of patience, smiled faintly when she saw the crestfallen look that crossed her husband's face as he beheld our all-too-obvious disappointment. She knitted her brows and extracted a promise that we must all be allowed to help him, materially, starting immediately. The next day was a Saturday, and like every Saturday, Sunday and Monday-till-Friday-night, we worked – all of us, side by side.

The first thing to be done was to clear a little space to move about in. Moose had cut back the thicket of miscellaneous brambles, seedlings and weeds that had virtually choked the entrance to the property, leaving a space just wide enough to park our elderly pickup truck. From here, he had widened a little unpaved trail to the steps that led to the ground floor entrance. Although these stairs were ten feet wide, a passageway of two feet only was clear to the right-front doorway. On either side were heaps of broken kitchen utensils, flowerpots and other domestic rubbish. This path crossed the porch diagonally, and I was not allowed to diverge from the course marked out for me. I was also forbidden to touch anything, throw anything, jump off anything, or to speculate for too long on how any of this sometimes fascinating junk could be put to good use as a plaything. Instead, I was apprenticed to the Honourable Company of Hauliers, and given the task of transporting bags, boxes and bucketfuls of rubbish from the front door, down the steps, along the path to the truck, and then given leave to whirl the contents on board. After only one repetition I grew bored, so I invented ways to pass the time. Sometimes I ran all the way, sometimes I walked backwards. I tried hopping on one foot, but I was forbidden to pick up anything I dropped, and my losses from this method were a little too high. I loaded the truck from every available angle. I threw bucketsful side-arm, overhead, behind the back and like a fastball, slider, and curve (I never mastered the knuckle-ball). After two days of this tedium, I was allowed over the threshold for the second time, and what I saw cheered me up tremendously. Practically all of the junk and rubbish was cleared away and my mother even swept the floor. I was still not allowed upstairs, but what I could see so far made me hopeful. I was even proud that I had helped.

Alongside the ongoing remedial work, we were at last in a position to make some positive changes. Summer was wearing away and my parents did not want to see the house sit throughout the long bitter winter without some type of heating to dry out the old timbers. The first thing we needed was a new chimney. The original chimney snaked its way along like an elongated zed from the kitchen to the attic, dropping bricks and creek-bed sand on every floor. It was completely unlined and, if pushed, actually wobbled in places. The problem was how to remove it.

This problem, like all of our problems, was made up of four related elements: little money, little experience, little help and large pride. The first and last of these obstacles were naturally insurmountable, the second was gradually wearing away, but the third posed a special challenge. In a small village, everyone is proud, and my father was no exception. But to live together in pride of this kind, it is necessary to have absolute confidence in one another, and confidence in oneself. As a relative newcomer, securely in debt, physically exhausted and surrounded by a host of difficulties, he had neither. What he needed was a good strong fellow like himself, with a bit of experience, who would keep his opinions of our little bombsite to himself. What he found was Vernon Postmayer.

Vernon's people lived on a small place further up the mountain near Spruce Run – a place still notorious for moonshine and witchcraft 'cures'. He was about my father's age and build and when I was a boy he was one of the most frightening men I knew. Lacking in both the dignity of the older generation and modernity of the new, he was rough, unshaven, unwashed and willing to do work for money – something a good neighbour almost never is. What bothered me most was the unwholesome look in his filthy eye, his more than usually inarticulate voice, and the cracked red sores on his hands. Still, Vernon had unshakeable nerves, and he was the best we could get. We were all glad to have him.

He climbed on to our corrugated tin roof like a monkey, and as I watched from the shade of the black maple tree, bricks began to fall like rain. In no time he slid down the roof feet first and swung dextrously into an upstairs window. There followed a strange series of, to me, inexplicable noises. There was no crunching of hammer on to masonry, no scrape of mortar falling on to floorboards. Instead, there was the high whinny of nails being drawn and the biting whip of splitting wood. Shortly afterwards there was the pounding of feet on the stairs to the ground floor. Jane, as much afraid of Vernon as I was, came down the front steps and stood beside me. Minutes later, Moose emerged from the front door, his face deeply creased with apprehension. He was gasping slightly and unable to speak for bad nerves. Inside the house there was a slow steady smashing of sledgehammer against dull brickwork. All at once there was a pause as the hammer was thrown into a corner. This was followed by a low creaking noise, and then an explosion like thunder on an August night, as the entire chimney passed downwards through a series of holes in the floorboards, resolving itself into a great belch of green-black dust from the open windows and a mountain of debris on the kitchen floor. Seconds later, black as soot, Diabolo himself appeared from inside, grinning triumphantly.

Countless hours of working like an ant were required to deposit the residue of the old chimney into the sagging bed of our old trunk. When at last the space was clear, the new chimney went up apace through the gaping hole. However, we were not yet through with Vernon. Though a skilled builder himself, Moose faced a major difficulty with this particular project. That difficulty centred on the uppermost six feet of the chimney. You see, Moose was afraid of heights. Work went on smoothly until the top of the chimney brushed the underside of the attic ceiling, and there it halted. For a small fee, Vernon had secured us the use of a rickety wooden double-extension ladder. With this, and a pulley to raise the materials, he climbed to his perch once again. Shortly after, when the last trowelful of cement was in place, Vernon called out to ask if there was anything further to be done on the roof. No, my father shouted excitedly, but there was some beer to be drunk at ground-level. Giggling oafishly, Vernon swung himself on to the ladder. Then, in a feat of bravado I wouldn't have thought mechanically possible, he tipped the toes of his workboots on to the outside of the ladder and rocketed bumpily thirty feet to the ground. Being the only one who knew he had no soul, I was also the only one not surprised he wasn't dead.

The next major enhancement the farmhouse needed was running water. Although there was a good spring fifteen feet from the front door, my parents reckoned that it might prove insufficient for the needs of a modern family. A better alternative was a powerful well that had been dug in the field immediately behind the barn. This well's sole purpose had been to supply water for The Dog Woman's kennels and no pipe connected it to the farmhouse. Fortunately, the pump was in good working order, but we still needed a 300 metre trench dug between the well-head and the nearest wall of the house. This trench had to be more than a metre deep in order to avoid the danger of the penetrating frosts. Once again specialist help was needed.

This time Moose called on a boyhood friend. This friend was employed as a sub-contractor for a large firm whose line of work was road-building for the State Highway Department. His particular specialism was in the use of a massive JCB to excavate sites for bridges, build embankments and so on, and a perk of the job was to be allowed to quarter his own twenty-ton digger at home, and use it at will for pleasure or gain.

I was stunned when this colossal piece of technology arrived. It was the largest moving yellow object I had ever seen and its destructive power was horrible. The small gap we had hacked into the brushwood blocking the farm entrance was widened almost instantaneously. The ground shuddered with its passing and the twisted brambles and sooty remains of our front garden were pulverised under its great tracks. The tumbling and rotten picket fence, where once as a tiny girl Jane Lois – proudly holding her tabby cat – had posed for a photograph, was smashed to splinters. Then, as the juggernaut settled down to work, it lowered its huge arm and a bite of earth the size of a small car was torn from the ground. Frightened and feeling slightly sick, I retreated to the rear of the house to brood on the frailty of living things.

The wildness here wrapped its arms around me. Once, there had been a patchwork of small lawns here, sewn together with low stone walls. In the upper corner, near the pantry door, stone steps rose diagonally to the smokehouse. I had not yet been inside it, but I looked dreamily on at its chipped red paint and whitening old boards – looking for all the world like a speckled hen. Two small lawns dropped down below this, and I sat disconsolately among the weeds on the low retaining wall between them. In front of me was my beautiful black maple tree, with its vast green leaves as heavy as canvas and as big as my two outstretched hands. On my left rose another small walled plot, that Sadie had devoted to her own favourite flowers. Now, in the late-summer light, their own frail great-grandchildren bore themselves defiantly among the thistles and bearded dock leaves. Above me, and shading my meditations, stood the high tangle of the grape arbour, with its rampant spindling tendrils and sereing leaves like stale bread. Swinging slowly among the stiff whir of honeybees, there were tight bundles of bittersweet black grapes, from which Charlie had made a brandy-like wine.

As the air rang with the hollow chesty clank of machinery, I could contain myself no longer. I simply *had* to explore…something. I decided to climb the higher stone wall bordering the smokehouse, and then toil up the steep bank towards the old kennels. My heart was beating with the expectation of mystery, and I plunged my fingers into the yellow-flowered ivy on top of the wall. As I buried my toes in a crevice between the stones, a voice sprang out over my left shoulder. It was my mother, shrieking.

'A copperhead! A copperhead! Run! Run! A copperhead!'

I flung myself backwards as if my hands and feet had caught fire. There was a dangerous poisonous snake lurking somewhere close to me and I had to think fast to avoid a terrible fate. (It wasn't that I feared being bitten, but I had heard that the antidote was injected through a long needle pushed into the navel, and that thought terrified me.) I ran for all I was worth towards the front of the house, cascading down the stone-bordered lawns like swift water. As I rounded the front of the house I came in full view of the battlefield. A hideous brown gash six feet deep and five feet wide now dug its jagged way from the wall of our house to the hill behind the barn. Its eastern flank, on the side opposite me, was protected by an earthwork nearly four feet tall. The monster itself had now advanced to the vicinity of the wellhead, and continued to batter the ground in its wake. I was forbidden to go towards the road, my way across the garden to the fields was blocked, and I was being hotly pursued by a killer serpent that had probably already eaten my mother. There was only one thing to do: I dove into the great trench.

What a magnificent cold wormy smell. The coffee-coloured soil took the imprint of my hands, the hard minty stones flew from my feet. The roar and shuffle of the grim machine was stifled. The sky above held no horizons. I rested and caught my breath wonderingly. After a time, the world above me fell still, and I came to myself. I was suddenly flooded with shame. I had abandoned my mother to die in the cruel jaws of the snake.

What could I do? I pawed feverishly at the earthen rampart, and gradually dragged myself to the surface. I looked fixedly at the ground, but nothing was moving. I crept slowly forward, cautious lest the demon lay in wait somewhere, hidden by the tattered bushes. When I neared the perilous corner of the house I armed myself with a sharp stick, and sprang forward violently. No one else was around and the air was disturbed only by the grating hum of the locusts. I pictured my mother lying somewhere in the undergrowth, a mere swelling in the copperhead's midriff. At last I gave up my reconnaissance and sought help by going around the back of the house, east of the Great Divide and towards the barn. There, to my relief and astonishment, stood both my parents, watching as the menacing JCB exited through the gate behind the barn where it was loaded on to its trailer. For no good reason other than filial piety, I ran to join them. My father looked at me and I looked at myself. I had the appearance of having been dragged on my chest for a mile through an open-cast mud-mine. Having been a boy himself once, he said nothing. Neither did I.

The new pipe for our water supply was laid in place and attached in less than half an hour after the machinery was taken away. It was two-and-a-half inches across and looked hopelessly insignificant at the bottom of its vast ditch. I cannot recall how long it took to fill in this immense cavity, but I do know that the task fell to one man with a spade who seemed to have a limitless capacity for hard work.

While this went on I was allowed to sit in the semi-darkness of our cellar and watch the plumber at work. The pipe from the well was coupled to a tank as big as four stout men. From here, a maze of copper tubes fired off in all direction – towards the rooms upstairs, towards the shiny new grey furnace, and thence upwards into the hollows of the walls overhead. Six feet away, on a raised platform was the silver-black oil tank that fuelled the new heating system. Otherwise the room was empty except for my imagination.

The walls were three-foot deep and built of mortarless stone. On top of these, and running unsupported for the entire width of the cellar, were flatted oak logs, still with their bark. Everything was powdery with an expiring lime whitewash, and heavily swathed with dust-laden spiders webs. White porcelain insulators, remnants of the original wiring, dotted about the floors, walls and ceiling. As the plumber finished each of his chores he ran up the curving stairs to the ground floor, dodging the low beams that spanned just above my own head. Upstairs, the work went on rapidly. Rotten plaster was replaced, broad wooden panelling spread over the walls of kitchen, sitting room and parlour. New front doors were shaped to fit both the trapezoidal holes of the two originals – one to the sitting room and one (for special guests) that led straight to the parlour. The stairs, hallway and bedrooms, with uneven plastered walls faceted like diamonds, were covered with new wallpapers. The cast iron claw-footed bath was fitted with gleaming new taps, and all the fixtures were made bright. But one curious aberration in this plumbing defied remedy. That is that the drain from the bath could not be connected to the main waste pipe, but instead proceeded solitarily outwards through the wall, under the garden, and emerged like an artesian well to fan itself out beyond the stone-walled embankment between the house and the field below, where it could be heard by listeners on the front porch. In times to come, this arrangement would mock me more than once as, like all boys, I shied away from washing. Each time, after a suitably tedious splash and feeling myself thoroughly steeped, I would pull the plug only to be greeted with shouts from outside of, 'Not yet! You can't be clean yet.'

The former sitting room was converted into a kitchen, and Jane laid out her pattern for the hand-built birch cupboards. She also sewed from morning till night, making curtains and blinds for every window, cloths for every table, along with aprons and shirts for her small band of workers. Paint and varnish was spread by the lakeful, wood cut by the forest, nails hammered by the freightcar. Outside, the weak and downcast were heartened, the sturdy and brave made to know their places. The split maple tree by the smokehouse was halved, with its peeling limbs like an old man's arms shorn to the trunk. Stone walls of all dimensions were painted white, and a graceful black iron-and-wood swing was hung from the rebuilt front porch. The walkways to the rear of the house, with their delicate stone drains laid by Charlie Ford, were cleared and swept. After the broken earth of the front garden reknitted, the beautiful nut trees were pruned. Charlie loved these trees and had bought them as saplings from a far-away merchant, and planted them himself. One was a curved and achingly brittle English walnut, whose ripe fruit – smooth and soft – was more prized than the stinging sharp and shingly barked American black walnuts. Beside this, squarely in the centre of the garden and nearly twice as tall as the house itself, was the only pecan tree on Catoctin Mountain. Pressing my face against its bark and stretching my seven-year-old arms out in both directions, my hands did not even begin to curve inwards towards one another. The easy strength and long-summer friendliness of this noble tree still lingers warmly in my recollections, steady as a faith long-proven.

The garden was fringed with dry wary clusters of green and brown, whose work of gladness was still many months away. Six feet from the walnut tree, in the direction of the pig pen, was a medium-sized tight vertical bundle of shoots that, in time, would grow heavy with the dipped olive-hued leaves and rich indigo blossoms of lilac. To the right, on the low rise towards the barn, was the silver-barked ghost of the magnolia, whose green-on-yellow-on-green leaves and musky aroma would colour the evening light next summer. Nearer the house, guarding the curving embankment that rose to the kennel, was the barbed wire mesh of Sadie's old-fashioned rose. When June came round, those gripping bare tines would burst into second youth with scented flat red blossoms, indolent in themselves and a comfort to the aching senses of their attendants.

But the work of preparing a home for ourselves and an abode for our prospective livestock went on through the winter. The shed nearest the road, originally built to house the waggons and once home to a legendary Model-T Ford, was re-roofed and its floor, eight inches deep in feather-white dust, was cleared in expectation of our first tractor. The ground floor of the barn and the old milk house were emptied, swept and whitewashed, in readiness for the new stalls that would be built in the spring. The pig pen, for thirty years home only to rats, was scrubbed and made wholesome. The rusted padlock on the smokehouse was knocked off, revealing a glorious tunnel of timbers bright and glistening with rainbow-black soot, like silk to the touch, and high empty hooks still sharp and strong enough to suspend whole hams and slabs of bacon. The springhouse and its annexed washhouse, long past hope, were dismantled, and their sandy-mortared foundations swept and cleared to form a patio in the shade of the black maple tree. On the hillside behind the vegetable patch, once the scene of the dreadful end of 'Sally Caxton's' dogs, in the midst of a virtually impenetrable jungle of multaflora briars and honeysuckle vines, a crisp winter day echoed with the jolly shouts and commotion of friends. Four giant men – three brothers and their father – all with round, red, smiling faces, crossed Catoctin Mountain from Shookstown, bringing with them axes, scythes, chainsaws, and the goodwill to help my father clear his land. They were all Jane's cousins and as children the three brothers had been among the little host that Dutch raised in exchange for her livelihood. Now grown men, they swung about them 'like hickory', roaring with high sprits and wiping out the dense undergrowth in swathes. The huge vines, some as thick as my arm and with thorns an inch long, were dragged into piles where on another day, when the ground was frosty, they could be burnt.

Among the merriment of the working men, I walked remote in my childhood. I watched as my father, bone-tired and feverish with thoughts of the work still to be done, grinned and grew happy in spite of himself. I sat down on a damp and newly-uncovered ridge of earth, looking right and left. This ridge – three feet deep, four wide and five hundred long, ran like a belt around the middle of our largest field, steeply propped against the mountainside. When he first bought the farm, Charlie Ford had dug it himself to act as a breaker against the run-off of rainwater that poured down the old farm lane. Now, free of saplings and weeds, it would come again to its original use. In a triangle, at the very top of the hill, were three tall apple trees that Charlie had planted as much for their beauty as for their fruit. The bottom of the hillside flattened into a small, gummy, green swamp, beyond which was a loose stone wall, bordering Floyd's meadow with the baseball diamond. Following this wall around the swamp, you come to the smaller of our two streams. Jump over the narrow breach between the wobbly green stones, and there is the corner of our smooth back field. Now, like all of the other fields, it was covered with medium sized trees: hickory, locust, poplar, oak, elm – impassable with scrub and briars. In the centre-left of the field was an enormous greenstone boulder that still showed a neat round bore-hole that Charlie had drilled half a century before. The hole, only half of which remained visible, had held a charge of dynamite that Charlie hoped would shatter the boulder into manageable chunks. Instead, the explosion succeeded only in lifting up a large slab of stone that slid downwards, increasing the unusable area of the field, as well as scattering shimmering green shards over a forty-foot circle.

Wedged between these two large fields was a heavily-wooded parallelogram called The Hollow. Steep leafy banks fell away to the muddy borders of the stream, where the tracks of racoons were refreshened every night. Small trees – sumac, locust, pine and paw-paw (with its blue-skinned banana-yellow fruit) swarmed beneath a towering canopy of elm and tulip poplars. These poplars formed a crucial part in our farm economics. The barn needed to be resheathed, stables and stalls for the cattle needed to be built, the pig pen had to be strengthened, the farmyard re-fenced, new gates were needed for every field, and boxes built for the chickens and fowl. For this the majestic poplars, silver-barked in winter, white-flowered in summer, would be sacrificed.

Now if you have never stood close by when an awesome and truly mighty tree is felled, then you have missed one of life's most stirring moments of sadness. It begins with a twinkling in the uppermost branches as the base of the tree – representing decades of struggle against drought, storm, disease and marauders, is pulled asunder and mixed indiscriminately into a soft tawny pile of dust. Perhaps the cruellest injustice to a great tree's strength is the very softness it becomes when it can no longer defend its heart from the use of steel. The shudder spreads down branch and limb, and a breaking yearning crush, like the cry of a wounded deer, booms forth. This is followed by a silence – breathless, yielding – then the accelerated rush of a wind passing downwards, as the uppermost boughs, once bordered only by the sky, speed to the ground. Here a shaking, growing, loudening crack as the branches splinter before the clumsy thud as the trunk itself is at last run to ground. Then the sadness – the sorrow of knowing that no one can ever restore this monument to hours of sunshine and a moment of chance.

The great logs were laid side-by-side, file-on-file, like the fallen columns of a temple, until they were taken away in small bands to be sawn by the old mill up in Fisher's Hollow. When they returned, processed into wide sweet-smelling planks, Moose piled them in an orderly fashion inside the barn, whose new skin they would become. The multitude of limbs and branches, literally acres of twisted fibrous green-grey wood, were carefully sorted. Everything usable was sawn into firewood, the crooked stumps split and piled into dry corners among the surviving trees. The millions of small branches and twigs, scrappy with old birds' nests and pocked by Time, were drawn together into thirty-foot mountains to be burnt in their turn.

And so we were provided for. We were safely housed, our fences were satisfactorily propped up, our outbuildings cleared and safe, our fuel supply secure. Without really knowing when, and scarcely knowing how, I found myself moved to this special place. How much help I had really been I shall never know. I certainly carried the graceful headcase of my father's hand-built grandfather's clock across the threshold (sitting room, not parlour), and I personally put the angel on what must have been the house's first Christmas tree for many years. We were tired (our legs dragged); we were broke (our clothes were thinning); but we slept peacefully at night. So much so, that it was months before I

45

noticed that my own was the only room in the house without a door. Outside, more work waited only for the return of fine weather. But inside, as the nights drew down, we came once again to believe in ourselves. For myself, I even had a new ambition. One chill day, as Jane tightened the tentative grip of kitchen-window-to-window-frame, I beheld a miracle. As the frame pulled inwards, a tiny crack opened between the boards. Out of this crack, white and flashing, sprang a little disk of silver. It rolled across the floor under its own momentum and bounced to a stop against my shoe. I bent over and picked it up. It was a solid silver quarter – worth twenty-five cents in 1896, but priceless to a small boy at any time. For me, it was evidence that untold riches lay buried in the new world I lived in, in the old world of my family's past. From that day, my quest became to dig up those riches one by one.

CHAPTER FOUR

I Danced in the Morning

In the Appalachian mountains April drops like music through the pines. The flour-thick March mists scatter under the southwind's broom, and clearing skies darken from hazel to sapphire. The chocolatey smell of newly turned earth mingles with the rusty, tongue-swelling fumes of freshly spread manure. All around you silences deeper than those of winter, the pauses in a large life awakening, swell upwards from pasture to woods. The clattering arguments of birds, toiling for home and melancholy with love, weave themselves with the pillars of sunlight that plunge through the trees. Watch for the cobalt flash of bluebirds, the flame-centre red of the cardinals and the daisy-eye prink of finches. The crisp carpet of oak leaves opens to the burst of new ferns and the forsythias' hot glow. Under Charlie's tall apple trees the dogwoods whiten and the greening grass parts to the rush of daffodils, crocuses and hyacinth-blue cornflowers. For you I gather these days in my hands, as then I gathered flowers in an Easter gift that brought tears to Dutch's eyes.

If you can keep a secret, I will take you mushroom hunting with me. What we want is a day like today: last night's soft rain lies drying in the hollow palms of the new-budded leaves, and a creamy, warm sun is just growing round in the East. We'll go up the Coxey Brown Road past the sharp turning and, if no one is about, climb the low bank on the left, beyond the slipped boulder, but before Fisher's Lodge. We'll cross the overgrown fields, marked out now only by the round-headed stone walls, and carry on till the old blue shell of the Fisher House appears. We'll keep to the right and jump into the three-sided field. There in the north corner is the marker we've been looking for. Only a foot tall and green like ocean spray, there is a twenty foot pool of mayapples – little plants shaped like palm trees that often act as the herald of the new year's mushrooms. Morelles – wrinkled and fleshy, small as a coat button or as round as a baseball; keep your eyes on the leaves and walk very slowly. There! A whole family, yawning themselves awake under an elm leaf. Take out the pillowcase you've brought along and break them off one at a time from the crumbly soil. We'll go on in a line towards Fisher's Hollow, looking for more mayapples and sunny shoals and the damp dust of fallen trees. With our pillowcases full we'll go back along Fisher's Lodge. Hold on…I hear a shuffle in the leaves. There he is, it's Hank. We'll wait here until he gets a bit closer. Don't be put off by the tobacco stains on his bristly chin. Although they look old, they're renewed everyday through leaks around his toothless gums. Look at that sackful he's carrying!

'Morn' Hank.'

'How do.'

'Any luck today?'

'Not a damn thing.'

'No, us neither.'

'How's at daddy uh yourn?'

'Alright.'

'Got is hogs yet?'

'Nope, not yet.'

'Whar se gonna gettum?'

'Don't know. You got any?'

'Might.'

'How many you got?'

'When se wunttum?'

'Don't know. Soon as the pigpen's done.'

'Uh huh.'

'Want me to tell him to come and see you?'

'Naw. I speck I'll see im.'

'Alright. See ya.'

When we get home, we'll wash these up, melt some of Florry's freshly churned butter, and have ourselves a breakfast.

What about those pigs? I told my father about what Hank had said, but he wasn't interested. 'We don't want any uh Hank's pigs.' Why not? 'Because they all know each other like Adam knew Eve.' I didn't know what that meant, but he made it up to me by taking me to the livestock auction at Woodsboro.

Woodsboro is a town on the opposite side of Catoctin Mountain where every Tuesday morning farmers gathered for six hours of slow-moving barter. Using our new poplar boards, Moose had built us a new pig crate. It was so heavy that we could barely lift it on to the truck, but at least its sliding door worked and I could hold my head up high when we joined the other 'farmers'. You see, on these occasions, as in all social intercourse, dress and composure are paramount. We had flannel shirts like everybody else, we had leather boots with red laces, our truck had rust, we walked slowly, smiled seldom and gave every appearance of having driven thirty miles with a pig crate for no other purpose than to take a morning constitutional.

The first stages of a livestock auction are equally vital. Begin by walking around the junk sale, where it's possible to buy half pairs of rusted scissors, hand-spooled balls of baler twine in six foot lengths (suitable for string beans), Smith Brothers' tin cough-lozenge boxes, greasy carriage bolts, toothless augers and damp copies of *Progressive Farmer*. The goal here is to be seen as serious. Consider things. Imagine uses for them. Excite the sellers to a froth of anticipation, but then withdraw your conviction at the moment of truth. This way people will know that you have money in your pocket, but ought not to be taken as a fool. From here there is the Farmers' Market with honey and jam, sausages and scrapple. Buy a heavy sandwich with yeasty home-made bread, and a thick pink slice of brown-sugary hickory-smoked ham.

But for me the real excitement begins as I draw near to the animal sheds. Like everyone else, I walk with my hands buried in my pockets, but I cannot resist stroking the rug-like winter coats of the mute and pensive rabbits. My heart breaks when I look at them in their doweling cages, piled like cord wood. Beside them, even more crowded into their wooden cages, frightened and singing like prisoners, there are hundreds of chickens: tiny yellow chicks, pullets just beginning to lay, young roosters throwing themselves about defiantly, and old hens, fat and worn out with a lifetime of work. Sitting on the ground, tied up with burlap, sit half a dozen laconic geese. How I want to stroke the short neat feathers of their long necks! But I am forbidden on account of the danger posed by their powerful beaks.

In my father's footsteps I bow into the sudden darkness of the holding pens where the larger animals wait their turn to go into the ring. My feet scuff in the sawdust and straw and I blink into the anxious bovine eyes that peek through the boards by the door. The air is rough with the brutalised voices of cattle, sheep and pigs, uncertain on their feet and unused to darkness at mid-morning. I run my thumb down the bumpy spine of a black bull calf that steadies himself against a wall. We go left, through the cows, towards the high squeaks of the pigs. (Watch your step, as some have gone this way recently.)

In the pens all around us were the long, highly-arched black saddlebacks, gingery Cheshires, and every other noble variety of pink and white porker. But what we sought was that most ancient of breeds, the nondescript – that myriad mix of genes, redolent of a carefree July romp in the straw, sturdy, robust… and cheap. Hope existed in the form of three separate pens, each housing three or four parti-coloured shoats. They were short-nosed, long-eared, unevenly, black, red and white, and not knowing a pedigree from a corn cob. What we needed was one male and one female, not related, and likely to take an interest in carnal relations. Though my father could not help licking his lips at these good prospects, we both studiously made it apparent that we despised these reprobates as unfit for our company.

We seated ourselves on the varnished wooden benches that surrounded the auction ring like an amphitheatre. I was under the strictest orders not to budge, flinch, or make any sudden hand movements. I watched as under the rumbling mutter of the auctioneer the handlers led in animals of all species, breeds, ages and conditions for our delectation, all of which appeared to be sold without my having noticed anyone offer a bid. I scanned the crowd closely, but waiting for a farmer to bid is like waiting for a shooting star. You can guess what happened. Maybe it was the dusty air, maybe it was the barnyard smell, maybe it was for a reason known only to the Maker of all children, but my nose began to itch. I was lost. I could do nothing to help myself. I twisted it round on its spindle till the cartilages ached, but it still tingled with a low burn. I decided at last upon a manoeuvre. First I slowly sat up very straight, then I carefully slid my right hand out to my knee. By bending in imperceptible stages, I gradually brought my nose to my knee and found succour.

Meanwhile the last of the sheep and cattle had been sold and we were waiting anxiously for the dry parade of trotters to emerge from their pens. I was not disappointed, as among the first entrants were our own preferred candidates. My father grew tense and, three sharp nods later, we were the owners of a frolicsome young boar. When the next pack entered, we abandoned our caution and, disregarding all notions of accomplishment or fortune, chose his future bride on beauty alone.

When we arrived at the farmhouse with our impatient grunters it was like a homecoming. The young couple found themselves the sole possessors of a tidy spacious pig pen, a vacant farmyard, and a trough of syrupy corn mash. Never was such a look of gratitude and relief seen to cross two porcine countenances.

They got on well. They strutted, they swilled, they scratched, they sunned themselves. When they were bored with other pursuits, they took to excavation. Their first major achievement was to re-locate three large chunks of loose concrete from the area nearest the farmyard gate. Though each one of those pieces must have weighed at least two hundred pounds, the young pair of engineers deftly pried them out and sorted them to one side, uncovering a ten foot area of soft earth. Like the pillows of fussy sleepers this earth was prodded, fluffed and re-arranged to suit each day's mood.

One day, the couple were unusually restless in their sleep, and we noticed that two new objects had appeared in their muddy divan. One of these was a smooth-backed brass ring, centred by a turquoise-coloured stone. The other was a heavily corroded horseshoe, nearly ten inches from point to point. Suspecting something of their origins, we took both finds to Charlie Ford. The old man took them in his knotty hands and turned them over slowly. His throat tightened and a warmth spread over his cheeks, as the shadows of seventy years fell from his eyes. For a glittering instant his legs grew strong under him, the fine light muscles spread out over his back and chest, and he felt the sun of Aprils long gone dancing in his hair. When at last his voice came, it was lingering and low.

'These belonged to old Tobe.'

Tobe was the largest, steadiest and most widely praised shire horse in the valley. For twenty-four years he was Charlie's companion and co-worker, labouring beside him in all weathers and at all hours, wherever there was work to do. He walked or stood, turned left or right, trotted or paced at one call of Charlie's voice. Few farmers could afford one such noble animal, and practically none could afford to keep the three necessary for spring ploughing. Instead, families banded together, loaning their horses to one another until everyone's fields were turned. No horse was so much sought after as Tobe, and wherever he went he pulled the lead, as guide for his two fellows. Charlie was immensely proud of his horse and even proud of his devilish intelligence. For instance, Tobe was notorious for having taught himself to open stable doors, as well as feed bins. Lowering his great head through the stable door, he would seize the large iron pin that coupled the hasp and pull it out. He then spat this on to the ground, bumped the door open, and strode across the farmyard. At the other stable door he repeated these actions and got inside among the feed bins, the lids of which he learned to nuzzle open. When he was, at last, no longer able to work, Charlie put him out to pasture, despite the expense of having to feed two horses. On the day Tobe died, Charlie wept bitterly and, against everyone else's advice, he dug an immense grave for his old friend in the high ground above The Hollow, where the cherry blossom still falls softly.

Meanwhile, our pigs prospered. When they were not luxuriating they were fornicating, with the result that in a few months' time we became the owners of nine new baby pigs. Mama and Papa Pig were very proud. My own mother and father were very proud. In complete sympathy with my home circle, I too was proud. I showed them to everyone.

One Saturday afternoon, when the piglets were about a month old, my sister came home with her new boyfriend. It was his third visit. Moose was still wearing the politeness that all fathers wear on these occasions, but I was adamant that our visitor must see the pigs. Perhaps because he was the soul of good manners, I couldn't see what was obvious to everyone else. That is, this young man – a native of the hard streets of Frederick, who since returning from Vietnam wore his hair long and dressed in Roman sandals – was the last person in the world to look with interest on a litter of pigs. But either as a result of my urging, or through love of my sister, he was prevailed upon to have a look. As we all stood gazing over the low gateway into the pig pen at the prone and sighing body of Mama Pig and her nine offspring happily snorkelling against her belly, Satan laid his cold hand on Moose's shoulder and whispered to him an idea:

'David, have you ever picked up a baby pig?'

'No, I don't think so.'

'You ought to go in and get one and bring it over here for Audrey to see.'

Although this was neither the Halls of Montezuma nor the Shores of

Tripoli, the ex-marine's honour was touched. Smiling weakly, he crawled very softly over the plank wall, and with his practically bare feet sponging gently on the straw, he drew up close to the little family. He extended his hand soothingly and rubbed a comforting rub on Mama Pig's flank. Unperturbed, she chortled softly and stretched her neck out in full repose. Flexing his fingers slightly, David grasped a small plump quadruped and raised it to his chest. Then, without further adieu, the infant raised its tiny dull eyes upwards and emitted a scorching 100-decibel scream of terror. In a flash Mama Pig sprang up and swung round like a dreadnought. It was the first and last time I ever heard a pig give a battle cry, but just then she opened her mouth widely and let out a bubbly, growling moan. A certain piglet fell instantly to the floor, and I doubt whether a pair of Roman sandals has moved that fast since Caesar crossed the Rubicon. David dove over the wall just in time to hear the slam of Mama Pig's great bulk as she pounded into the boards behind him. A moment of silence followed, then an explosion of laughter and the joining of hands in a lifelong friendship.

The pigs were not our only tenants for very long. They were soon joined by a motley collection of shaggy, knock-kneed calves. All of these calves represented types least useful to profitable farmers. We bought bull calves from dairy farmers who had no use for cows that did not produce milk. We bought heifers from beef farmers who preferred the larger size and weight of steers. All together they formed an oddly sorted little band of hopefuls, led by a very feminine young heifer that we named Elsie. Elsie rose to power by virtue of her short pointed horns, and she gained everyone's affection through her mild intelligent manners and sweet looks. She was delicate in a bovine way, with long white lashes and a strange, almost lavender-coloured coat that betrayed her uncertain heritage.

The kennels had by now all been altered from their original use. The three large rooms nearest the farmhouse had been converted to a workshop, and most of the rooms adjacent to it were used for storage. But one room at the far end of the building was fitted out with new poplar boxes to suit a flock of chickens. These boxes were sturdy and snug, open at one side and filled with clean straw. Whenever the birds felt convivial they could assemble freely on the roosts that projected in front of the boxes. Moose built a long, skilfully demarcated feeder that allowed everyone a fair chance to eat in company without disturbing one another's repast, and Dutch gave us some ingenious, century-old pewter waterers that used upturned Mason jars as reservoirs. The chickens themselves arrived from three different sources. Moose got a bargain on half a dozen speckled hens from an old acquaintance in Wolfsville. They were reputed to be 'guaranteed layers', but I doubt whether these venerable sisters had seen any eggs since Mrs Noah made the omelette. Another bargain came in a flat-ish cardboard box, delivered by Junior Wheeler after a visit to Woodsboro: fifty little yellow chicks – called peepees because of the sound they make. They were adorable and gadded about all day under their sun-dappled canopy. But the third lot came with the best references: six mature Rhode Island Reds and a fine young speckled rooster. Dutch got them for us from an old friend of Annie Waterman's, and the six hens quitted themselves like professionals. Within two weeks of settling in they began to lay big brown eggs, smooth as acorns and warm as pebbles.

The rooster, on the other hand, proved to be a bit more problematical. He was, no doubt, a handsome piece of work. Black and white, like a knight in full livery, he was over two foot tall and carried a steep red comb on his manly brow. Dignified and confident, he was also heavily armed with inch-long spurs. As a private fief for himself, his wives and his dependents, my father had cleared the entire area formerly occupied by the long runs attached to the kennels. Both for shade, and with a view to the future, the large, level, grassy yard was dotted with apple, pear, cherry and plum trees. No finer home could be imagined, and for a while everything went smoothly. I, for one, learned a lot of important things about chickens. To start with, no chicken with an ounce of sense (and no chicken has more than an ounce of sense) will be content to eat from a wooden feeder, be it never so cleverly carpentered. Instead, Epicurean hens prefer to climb into their feeder and, sinning like Onan, cast their seed upon the ground, where sweetmeats like grubs and worms are plentiful. Another interesting observation is a demonstration of the etymology of the expression, 'Are you a chicken?' I am here to tell you that chickens really are 'chicken'. If they escape their bounds they stare at you quizzically, one eye at a time, without acknowledging their own guilty deeds. If you make *any* move, towards them or away from them, they fluster. Try and touch one, and she will simply go beserk, wild and with utter terror, too panicky to make good an escape. Secure a hold on her and she will fall silent in an infinite decline of spirit, with a resignation to imminent death as pathetic as any Victorian lady expiring from the vapours.

But our majestic rooster was made of sterner stuff. He certainly never lowered himself to the shame of attempted escape. He had no reason to. All of his needs – I mean *all* of his needs – were amply surfeited inside. As he matured in his…duties…he came to believe himself irresistible. Every morning at approximately twenty minute intervals he drew himself up to full majesty and crowed with riveting, ear-splitting power. He made himself heard as a fecund father and boastful lover for half a mile in any direction. This proved to be his downfall. On a warm mid-morning, as I went about my chores, a stranger dropped into the orchard from the hillside near Charlie Ford's old pear tree. The stranger, about ten inches tall, bright as polished copper and with a stride like Gary Cooper's, was in fact a young Bantam rooster, belonging to our neighbour Obidiah Taylor. Now despite their diminutive stature, Bantams are known for an inverse proportion of nerve. Certainly on the day that I looked at him, although I weighed about eighty pounds, he probably weighed four and his manner convinced me that had I chosen to rumble with him the outcome would have been doubtful. But I didn't choose. In fact, there was hardly time. Standing as discreetly as possible among the hens and wishing myself up a tree somewhere, I watched as, perfectly oblivious to his new spectator, our mighty rooster composed himself for his next oracular delivery. As his speech began, the little Bantam found his target and sped towards him. Just as the speaker reached the dying fall of his third trill, there was a scudding growl as the little bird threw himself, spurs first, at his giant adversary. The two of them tumbled into the dust amid the scattering, dismayed shouts of the hens. What followed was both a shock and a disgrace. After a few half-hearted attempts to bring his powerful weaponry to bear on his attacker, the once-grand black-and-white gave in to fear and tried to run away. But his huge strides, double the length of the Bantam's, were not enough to save him, and as the two of them repeatedly drew circles around the perimeter of the orchard the Bantam triumphantly plucked out our rooster's grand tail feathers one-by-one. When at last I could no longer bear the shame of our hero's defeat, I pulled together the puny bit of courage I had and waited for an opportunity to intervene. As the racers drew near the hen house I saw my chance. Loosening the door with one hand, I waited until the black-and-white came into range. As he was about to pass, I kicked him in through the opening and pulled the door shut in time for the Bantam to speed past. The little victor skidded to a halt, then rounded sharply to have a look behind. Being the only other male in the immediate vicinity, and totally without tail feathers, I besought myself of a means of escape. As the Bantam stood between me and the gate to the farmhouse, the only other option was to leg it to the far gate into the field beyond. I made it just in time as the little fireball pulled up to a stop by the gate. Thinking fast, I did a quick change by opening it for him to pursue me, then, as he did so, hopped back over the fence, closing the gate to shut him out. But mine was a pyrrhic victory and both of us knew it. If he had chosen to, he might simply have jumped in again beside of the pear tree. But he didn't. Satisfied with his conquest, he puffed up his Lilliputian chest and crowed a tiny crow. Then, without looking back, he marched home. I need hardly tell you that old black-and-white *never* crowed again.

As a kind of gypsy cousin to the chickens, we also bought a half-dozen guinea fowl. Rugby-ball-shaped bundles of grey feathers, guineas fly much too well to be quartered, but rather prefer to range freely over the entire farm. They are known for two peculiar traits. One is the possession of a voice like a klaxon horn, and the other is of an IQ half that of a chicken. For instance, they will try to eat anything. I watched one day as three of them laboured to eat our truck. They also try and raise enormous families. I say 'try' because usually they fail. We once had a guinea hen lay a nest of thirty-two eggs, of which twenty-two hatched. As the days passed, this little flotilla shrank remorselessly. Many were simply lost as the hen refused to limit her foraging expeditions to conditions suited to her minuscule charges. A few appeared to have drowned in the tall dew-soaked grass. Three tiny tragedians were only just saved when their doting mother led them for a walk over a fresh road repair, failing to notice that a handful of her offspring remained stuck in the gluey tar, cheeping piteously. In fact, only four survived to adulthood. Out of pity for their misguidedness, we allowed generations of their descendants to live among us, taxing them only occasionally by the loss of a few fresh eggs.

In the years that I lived in the farmhouse we had a succession of four dogs. Three of these were named by Jane (Prince, Duke, Duchess) and one was named by me (Spot). I shall leave it to you to ponder over the theme of my mother's musings. My own inspiration, I need hardly tell you, came from Spot's sole distinguishing feature. Otherwise, although he bore some resemblance to a Jack Russell, his parentage was as dubious as that of all our other retainers. At peak times we also had about ten cats. They were not only good pets, but they are indispensable on a farm where the likelihood of rodents is quite high, because of the large amount of grain and hay stored outdoors. I was given the honour of naming the first kitten, and I settled upon 'Ralph'. Ralph was a real charmer, and never more so than when she had three kittens of her own. She was the last cat I was allowed to name. The duty of naming cats then fell to my father. Besides the usual run of Toms and Maurices, he also gathered ideas from a variety of sources, all connected with each cat's particular background. For instance, one that fell asleep on a packing box woke up to the name Noodles; another, given to us by a supermarket employee, became Safeway; and one that followed his mother about in the way a chick follows a hen, was christened Peepee. Through their combined efforts we were kept totally free of rats, and only occasionally bothered by mice. An added bonus to a young boy was the succession of small corpses that regularly appeared on our back porch – untouchable, but each worth an anatomically curious stare.

Spring time is also the season for planting, and for this we were not prepared. For my own part, I had answered a small ad in a magazine and undertaken to be a door-to-door salesman of 'Reliable Seeds' – flowers and vegetables. By doing so I earned $15.00 as well as stored up enough 'credits' with my employer to receive a mail order croquet set, the first one I had ever seen. But more importantly, we needed equipment. We had a tractor. It was a lipstick-red forty-year old model, called a Farmall B. To give you some idea of its size, you should know that Farmall tractors run in ascending order from A up to M. Anyway, we also had a plough. Originally, it had been designed to be pulled by horses, but Moose adapted it to fit the tractor. We also had an old harrow, suitable for giving a fine finish to newly turned earth, but not large enough or heavy enough to crush the big clumps left after ploughing. For this I learned we needed a contraption called a disk.

The best source for equipment like this was a public auction. Indeed, short of any attribute you might be born with, a public auction is the best source of everything. These auctions were a strange and sometimes haunting mixture of private family matters and public holidays. Each began with a sale 'bill' published in the local newspaper. These 'bills', with an unvaryingly black-bordered, two-columned format, ranged from a few inches in length to nearly a foot. They always contained three essential types of information: the reason the sale has come about (nearly always a death or severe disability); the date and time of the auction, together with directions to the farm where the sale was to take place; and an itemised list of particularly sought-after goods to be offered. This last was a plain list, without any qualifiers to indicate the age or condition of the merchandise – but as everything represented the holdings of a single household, it was possible to build up an approximate picture. That is, if the list included a six-gang plough, four tractors, three oak dressers, seven Dutch ovens, forty pieces of Blue Willow china, and a full 'quarter section' (160 acres), one could infer that all would be in tip-top shape.

On a typical Saturday, business commences at ten o'clock. Arriving early for the traditional walk-round, we park our pick-up truck in a meadow alongside fifty other pick-up trucks. A pinewood sun lights the fresh southwind, catching its breath in the budding apple trees. What we see is the extraordinary scene of a life turned inside out. For days, sometimes weeks, children, family and friends have worked to make virtually the complete set of a lifetime's belongings portable. Everyone present has been to an auction like this before, and as a result they are always set up in the same way. Long columns of furniture placed side-by-side run like spider's legs from the house, mingling with the shade trees and climbing roses of the garden. Whole rooms are arranged adjacently outdoors. Beside the handbuilt cherry bedstead, given as a wedding present, lay the naked and sagging mattress and frame. There are two chairs that don't match grouped beside it. On one is a cardboard box full of magazines and books on fishing that used to lie on the floor beside the bed. Wardrobes and chests of drawers are propped about among the early spring irises. Children play hide-and-seek among the kitchen furniture, lining the gravel walk to the springhouse. Cluttering every flat surface there are the huge crocks that once held sauerkraut, the Mason jars that had been full of golden sugary peaches (whose blossoms begin to tremble in the trees behind the porch). There are crates full of cutlery, blades worn hollow by too much sharpening, and smoothed by the hands of five generations. Quilting frame, plank-bottom chairs, wooden dry sink, marble-top washing stand, and a pile of the traditional black-edged multi-coloured 'granny-square' blankets, circle the rusty porch glider that eased the aching backs of the farmer and his wife. Near these, on the sandy patch where the grandchildren used to play, is a 'Steiner' chair. With its heavy rockers, wide arms and trademark acorn finials, these massive chairs were each hand-crafted by Dutch's cousin Steiner Hunter from the oak trees surrounding his house. They have fetched four-digit prices for decades.

Inside the hollow house my footsteps ring dully on the floorboards as I wander from room to room. I count seven dry, swept fireplaces and find a sixty-year-old subscription form for *The Saturday Evening Post*, and two copies of *Grit*. Back downstairs, three tables have been pushed together in the kitchen to form a counter. Behind this, volunteers from the Brethren Meeting House are selling sausage sandwiches, kinklings and shoo-fly pie. If you're thirsty, there's hand-mixed Coca-Cola. Otherwise, the kitchen is empty, its tall ceilings – built to dispel the summer heat – echoing with the gossip of old friends.

As we walk down the rain-washed ditch towards the barn, we see everyone we know. Hunter, Waterman, Winters, Taylor, Ford – names I have known as neighbours all my life. There is a mood of melancholy merriment when a community comes together to witness the dispersal of one of its member's goods. We look at one another, speculating on what each other's interests are, whether idle curiosity, a replacement lamp for the parlour, a fine piece of carnival glass, a working draw-horse for carving axe handles, a Farmall L, or simply a matter of goodwill towards the old folks, now gone.

We go on to the farmyard, and it's now as silent as a ghost town. A hundred cows and forty chickens left for Woodsboro more than a week ago. I open the little hatch inside the huge sliding barn door, and run with scattering scuff on to the padding-hay floor of the barn. Transparent pages of light stand in rows, as the sun comes in between the cracks in the sheathing. I climb the wooden ladders above the empty hay mows to read the Roman numerals carved into the beams, to look for swallows' nests, and to dream of a walk in the rigging of a tall ship on a storm-broken sea. I push open the narrow door leading on to the feeding platform above the farmyard. I sit on the end, ten feet above the dry manure-plastered woodwork, and listen to the proceedings in the old hay field beside the lane. Things go on unexceptionally:

Who'll-give-me-four-bits? Eight-bits-in-a-dollar. Give-me-thirty-dollar-thirty-dollar-thirty-dollar-for-the-disk. Give-me-thirty-dollar-for-the-two-gang-disk…

After one nod of the head, our ploughing could continue.

There were three pieces of ground that needed to be ploughed. The largest of these, totalling about three acres, was our back field. One of Moose's first outdoor chores after moving house had been to clear the tangle of seedlings, vines and bushes from this field. In midwinter he had then gone among the more substantial trees, six to ten-year-old ones, and cut deep rings into the bark about a foot above the ground. Then with the spring sap rise, as the low bordering grey-green stonewalls were overspread with peach blossom, these unlucky orphans quietly haemorrhaged. The trunks were cut down and shaped into long poles for bar gates, and the brushwood dragged to The Hollow and burnt. After this, we only had to clear three acres of stumps.

Few agricultural pursuits can be more demoralising than pulling up tree stumps. After the spring thaw and the ground became workable, we spent countless hours at this task, disengaging the finger-like roots. As we worked every evening in the dim rum-coloured light, the soft earth was rapidly torn and mashed to the consistency of wet plaster. There was no one to help us with this one, and to me the whole thing seemed hopeless. My father would reverse the tractor as near as possible to the largest bit of the stump, while covered with pastey mud from my fingertips to my elbows, I dragged a six-foot log chain from the tractor to the roots. I passed this round and round the largest bit as tightly as the huge links allowed, then with numb and inflexible fingers dropped the chain through the tractor's link-up, hooking it underneath. I then had to run backwards quickly, to be out of range while the tractor heaved and grunted, pulling desperately at the immense spindly network. As often as not, the chain links simply gave way and slid off, or shattered with a fine ping. If we were lucky, there would be a ripping crack of roots and a cascade of earth falling like shrapnel as the stump gave way. There were more than fifty of these stumps and it took weeks of drudgery to remove them all.

At last the field was cleared, and when the soil had dried, the plough, disk and harrow did their work. Using a borrowed planter, several hoppersful of corn went in after the last threat of frost. This is a difficult business to judge, and no one's advice is reliable. The only sure guide is eventual success and the praise of one's neighbours who smile and repeat the formula, 'knee high by the fourth of July.' For once, we were lucky.

The second piece of land we ploughed was the field immediately in front of the house. This field covered about two acres, and as the season wore on it would be filled with potatoes, tomatoes, sweet corn, French beans, lima beans, cucumbers and pumpkins. The remainder of our vegetable supply would come from a quarter acre patch separated from the farmhouse by the grape arbour, flowerbeds and lawns. This patch had served my family with food for five generations, and it was the third and last to be ploughed.

All at once, Easter came, dropping a cloth of repose over our lives. After the magic of the silver quarter find, I spent the whole of the school holidays sticking a long thin table knife into every crevice in the house. I crept painstakingly over the corners of attic and cellar, looking for loose boards, or disguised panels that might be concealing a hidden trove. Apart from a gold-spined edition of Edgar Allen Poe's poetry, with a moth-eaten end sheet, I found nothing except my own growing imagination. I convinced myself that every wall that held some unexplored portion, contained something to be uncovered. One day, I even tried to persuade Moose to replace each of the wooden stair treads. Finally, without ever actually abandoning hope, I was won to the idea of extending the search to the immediate vicinity outside the house, where I felt certain that the Sheriff's people would have had no time to pry.

Meanwhile, Easter Sunday brought new ambitions. Sitting beside the wood stove was my large wicker basket full of sweets – more than enough to make me queasy before church – and my new suit. In my family, Easter is a time for new clothes. Dressed in my finery, I sat impatiently through sermon and hymns, anticipating the afternoon. Then running out of the church clutching my Sunday-school gifts of an orange, an apple and a small china dish, I made promises to meet my friends at Floyd's meadow for the great Easter Egg Hunt. All over Harmony Easter Saturday was spent in dyeing eggs to be donated for a community egg hunt. Then, while the faithful were at their prayers, a squadron of The Loafers patiently hid hundreds of eggs in the tufty grass of the baseball diamond's outfield. When the moment came, the village children sprang over the wooden footbridge and charged wildly into the meadow, filling their wicker baskets. My best return was fourteen eggs, all of which I ate within the following four days. This peculiar form of gluttony had two strange side-effects, one surprising, one not. Of course, I felt miserable, as anyone who eats 3.5 hard-boiled eggs per day deserves to feel. But there was also the baffling symptom of memory loss, which allowed me to repeat my actions year after year.

CHAPTER FIVE

Jericho, Jericho

May came, and we were undefended. I was the only one to notice that our left flank was completely exposed. If anyone had seized the high ground in the woods above the apple trees, we would have been utterly at their mercy. With my natural military instincts, I realised the only thing to do was to build a fort among the cluster of trees that stood invitingly on a precipice of rocks, giving a view of several miles over The Hollow, Floyd's meadow, above the Meeting House, and all the way to South Mountain.

It took a great deal of wheedling at Headquarters to be allowed the necessary pioneering tools. When these tools were at last forthcoming, they consisted of a single implement. I was given careful lessons in the use of a small hatchet, so dull that it would have taken three blows to cut through a lump of coon cheese. After this, I was coached in methods for determining the criteria for proper building materials. These materials were two in kind: any stone I could lift, and any dead tree that I thought I could fell with my hatchet. The first of these materials presented few problems, and I quickly scraped together enough stones to make a foot-tall, three-sided enclosure among the trees. With this as the foundation, I planned to build up walls with the trees I felled. (How noble are the dreams of youth!) As I looked around, there were plenty of trees for the taking. What I wanted particularly was the tall straight model, so long dead that all of its branches had fallen off. There were fine examples all over the hillside.

What I hadn't reckoned on was the amazingly resolute way dead timber can resist the invasion of a dull hatchet wielded by a small boy with unsteady aim. Nothing daunted, I set-to with a will. My father was too amused to be very angry with me for making cuts at elbow height – which was easier – rather than ground level, which would have showed better woodmanship. An hour of pounding on a six-inch trunk tended to produce work reminiscent of something done by a tall, inept beaver. At this point, my stamina generally gave out, and the threat of hatchet-elbow loomed large. My way around this was to attack the tree with plain brute force. By this I mean getting up a good running start, then throwing myself like a chimpanzee at the tall slim tree. Usually, I then swung about for a few minutes, as might a pole-vaulter stuck in the mud, before the crippled trunk snapped off with a dull crack. Dragging myself and my victims to my small building site, I gradually built up three low walls, log-cabin fashion. When it was finished, or rather when I was nearly finished, the walls were about shoulder-high, and the fort commanded a panoramic view in three directions. I later stocked it with lethal projectiles, like dry clods of mud and exploding sycamore pods. I patrolled the surrounding area regularly, and stood sentry duty as often as I could. I was certain that my diligence, and the obvious impregnability of my handiwork guaranteed our safety. In any case, we were never assailed.

I had many reasons for developing this militarily over-active disposition. Evidence of war, even memories of war, were all around me. In fields east, west and south of our own there were granite monuments to men from all over America who had fought bravely and died tragically in the Civil War. Fifteen miles away, in a cluster of immaculate farms, the battle of Sharpsburg was fought in 1862. In terms of casualties, it remains the single worst day in United States military history. As a boy I wandered over these still achingly beautiful fields, alert to the haunting stories of the Miller Cornfield – where the Texas Brigade was virtually annihilated; Bloody Lane, where whole regiments from the Great Lakes states were smashed in wave-like assaults; and Burnside's Bridge – where a single company of Georgian sharpshooters stalled an entire army corp. There were places of great enchantment, like the Mumma Farm, where a regiment of new recruits was driven back by a column of honeybees, angered when a shell burst open their hives. There were places of great horror, like the Dunker Church – a tiny white building, sister to my own Meeting House – that formed the cusp of half-a-day's attack, where thousands of young men struggled in hand-to-hand combat, until they were decimated by the artillery of both sides. And there were places of heart-rending pathos, like the Turner Farm, where the owners lost two grandsons within sight of their own home, each man fighting for an opposing cause. Nearer to home, there was the battle of South Mountain, a vicious rear-guard action fought over Turner's, Crampton's and Fox's Gaps. Strangest of all, both of these battles were precipitated by a lucky find. When Robert E. Lee's Confederate Army left its camp near Frederick, one of his generals made a present of three cigars to a colleague. That colleague wrapped the cigars in some paper, and stuffed them in his pocket. A few days later, when the Union Army camped on the same fields, a private soldier was very pleased at his good fortune in finding the tobacco – an extremely rare commodity for northern soldiers. As he looked at the papers in which the cigars were wrapped, he recognised their significance as an official document. He passed the papers to his sergeant, and they rapidly made their way to the commanding general. They were in fact an official copy of the southern army's troop dispositions. The immediate results of the discovery were the battles of South Mountain and Sharpsburg, the defeat of the Confederacy's first major invasion, and ultimately, the opportunity for Abraham Lincoln to issue the Emancipation Proclamation, freeing the slaves.

Harmony was not untouched by these great national events. As the armies pursued one another up and down the mountainsides and in and out of our valleys, squadrons of soldiers passed through the village as foragers, and occasionally as would-be raiders. Locals recalled that when the impoverished southern army arrived, although they behaved themselves with unlooked-for decorum, they commandeered blankets, clothing, shoes, firearms, chickens, vegetables, firewood and flour. More disturbing, with the late-summer harvests coming on, was the soldier's forcible exchange of their worn-out horses for those of the local farmers. Less than a month later, after the farmers had carefully doctored these broken down animals back into a fit working state, the Union Army marched through and repeated the whole exercise.

Maryland was one of the three slave-holding states that did not secede from the Union and, as such, was unusually torn by divided loyalties. Even within a village the size of Harmony, folks held opposing sympathies. The Hunter family, up in Fisher's Hollow, were Confederate supporters. When the southern army passed through, Steiner's grandfather was a young boy. When a squadron camped in one of his family's fields, he got so excited that he badgered his parents to let him camp out with the soldiers. The men were jolly and agreeable, and his parents were reluctantly persuaded. The next morning the boy's mother was horrified to find her son crawling with lice.

On the ridge opposite Fisher's Hollow, just above Russell Waterman's farm, the Miller family were Union supporters. After the battle of South Mountain, three of the Miller boys helped to clean up the battlefield, and in return, they were allowed to collect as many abandoned rifles as they could find, to be sold later. Shortly afterwards, when the battle of Sharpsburg was over and the Confederate Army was dragging itself homeward, a party of raiders got wind of the fact that there was a cache of arms at the Miller Farm. Warned of the raiders' approach, the Miller boys barricaded themselves behind a stone wall that bordered the open field in front of their home. They had loaded as many rifles as they could – hundreds so the story says – and laid them out in rows behind the wall. As the raiders drew near in the hot evening sunlight, the Millers kept themselves as well-concealed as possible, to hide their small number. Then, when the enemy came within range, the farmers laid down such a rapid fire that the southerners beat a hasty retreat.

As a boy, it was C.E. who gave me a feeling for these times, and tales of bravery and terrible hardship rang in my ears as I walked over my beloved hills. I stood on a pinnacle of stone, looking out over the plough-striped fields, listening to the spatter of thrushes, and pictured in my mind the grey passing of armies. As I walked down the gritty dirt roads, I heard the tramp of feet, the clatter of hooves, and the laughter and shouts of young men. My imagination was fed further by a growing library of history books that I bought with my pocket money. In these I could see streets that I knew well pock-marked with shell-holes, and fields where on summer afternoons the tin whistle of grasshoppers played, once covered with corpses and the debris of war. But these things grew out of a head well-tuned to fancy. Most stirring were the realities that C.E. placed in my hands.

Among C.E.'s many pioneering electrical contraptions was his set of hand-built metal-detectors. He began to build these just after his return from the navy, and they gradually came to be not merely a pastime, but a source of real income. In over thirty-five years of active detecting, he reckoned he had found more than 22,000 bullets, plus large numbers of other relics. One morning on South Mountain, he found the leaf-covered remains of an old trench, which in a space of six feet, yielded 300 bullets. Another hot summer afternoon he had been searching in

Crampton's Gap when he decided to rest under the shade of a large oak tree. As he sat down on the ground the detector gave a sharp pip-pip, indicating that there was something under his feet. He was somewhat confused to find that whatever it was that lay in the ground, it formed a long thin T-shape. Digging very carefully with his pointing trowel, he slowly uncovered a curved row of coat buttons, with cuff buttons on either side, and a brass breast plate slightly off-centre. C.E. guessed that on one of those hellishly hot afternoons in 1862 a soldier had thrown down his jacket under the shade of the tree, and simply never picked it up again. A hundred years later, driven to shelter by the same scorching heat, C.E. uncovered a part of that unknown man's story.

On another day, C.E. scaled the side of Maryland Heights, above the old national armoury at Harper's Ferry, and came home with a twelve-pounder cannonball. He also found two live shells on farms owned by his friends at Sharpsburg. One of these he donated to the National Battlefield Museum there. The other he kept on the floor of his workshop, both as a doorstop, and as grim shrapnel-loaded amusement to be passed around to reluctant onlookers.

Some of these mysterious artefacts passed to me. C.E. made me a present of twenty different kinds of bullets, and a fine brass US beltplate. I held these in my hands and tumbled them through my fingers for hours together, trying, trying to conjure a reality out of them. How, I wondered, could violence ever have grown from the soft soil and feather-white sunshine of my world? What did men see in one another that made them so disturb this peace? As I looked on the hard bits of metal that had broken through the void of Time between our separate lives, I came to believe that if I knew more of the things themselves, I might come to know more of the men who made them.

And so I came to read less of deeds and more about things. I walked through the same fields and forests, the same orchards and valleys, my head full of how metals were made and wood was shaped, how water was harnessed and how crops were grown, trying, largely in vain, to grapple method on to motive. In this, C.E. was my guide. With typical thoroughness, he had written to the U.S. Geological Survey Department and bought the highly detailed contour maps of the entire area. He compared these to their nineteenth-century predecessors and recorded the differences: where houses had once been and now vanished, where mills, or stables, or roads had been moved or demolished. He spoke to all the old-timers, and noted down what they said in the form of tiny coded symbols directly on the maps. Then in private, always in private, he visited these places, coming home with brass buttons, lead bullets, silver and gold coins. To be sure, it took an astute combination of technology and psychology to uncover them, and in this C.E. re-worked the patterns of human behaviour with what he knew about local customs. When he learned of the existence of an abandoned cabin, he made a careful survey of the ground. After this, he traced out the approximate line of the foundations, before beginning a search in each of the building's four corners. People always hide things in corners. Sometimes, he found a few coins, sometimes jars full. Other favourite hiding places were chimney foundations, and the ground under hardwood trees. The area around the front door was a good place to look, as people often drop coins while rooting change out of their pockets.

C.E.'s maps were dotted with places like this, but he also noted places where people met in past times: groves where parties or festivals were held, fields where livestock was exchanged, or roadside businesses long-since disappeared. Then on warm May-bright Sunday mornings, before Dutch left for the Meeting House and before The Loafers convened, he would begin the ritual. I sometimes watched in wonder as he prepared himself with care. The day began with a bowl (well, nearly a bathtubful) of cereal and fresh fruit, and a scalding shave. This was generally carried out to a vocal accompaniment, begun by Dutch:

N'I ain't gonna be late.

I knaw.

Gasey said 'roun one.

I knaw.

En don' you be down nare wi them ole loafers.

Whowelp…

Where you goin? Clarens! *Whare ya goin*?

I'm goin ta hell.

Whowelp!

Aw, I'm goin upta ole Henry Umphersock's place.

Whatinee hell ya goin up air fer?

Gonna do some detectin'.

Waal, you jis git down air after church.

Uh-huh.

Gasey said 'roun one.

Uh-huh.

Don't you 'uh-huh' *me*. You gonna put gas innat machine?

Naw, I'm gonna push it.

Yawlta takuh toot along'n seef Seymour's got any taters.

He ain't got no taters.

You gonna take 'at radio a'hisn back?

Naw.

Ain't chew don nat yet?

Naw.

Whowelp.

Then turning to me, with his eyes sparkling with mischief,

Bub's gonna fix it.

Aw, yer fulla bug-juice. He ain't gonna fix it nuthin uh-the ki-und.

You comin long Bub?

Sure Pap! Can I?

C.E. never invited anybody but me, and he seldom invited me. So when he did, I jumped at the chance. Going anywhere with him was always an adventure for two reasons. On the one hand, he always did some things in exactly the same way. On the other hand, for me every trip was to someplace new, to see someone new, and to find or find out something new.

On this particular day, C.E. was dressed as usual in the forest green canvas trousers he always wore, and a bright red-and-white checked shirt. He always wore shirts in bright red, blue, orange or yellow, and he always wore a 'cow-turd' cap. This was an ordinary flat cloth cap, so-called because the locals reckoned that it looked like a cow pie that someone had stepped in and slid to one side. We loaded up the car (or 'machine' as they called it) with the metal detector, the bag ('toot', rhymes with 'foot') for the potatoes and the radio (which was of course fixed). I gave Dutch a big resoundingly wet smack of a kiss – because it was fun and it always made her crumple up in mock terror and giggle – and we set out. After teaching himself to drive, C.E. drove for forty-five years without a license, never scratching another car. But driving with him was unlike going with anyone else for the simple reason that it was plain that Fortune doomed him to frustrations barely surmountable. The space behind us was always threatened by wild-eyed drug-taking maniacs whose great speed promised to capsize us. Very often he patiently pulled over to let these menaces overtake us. But cars waited at junctions for the precise moment of optimum awkwardness before pulling out in front of us. If we were at a junction, oncoming cars slowed down imperceptibly, to lengthen our wait. But while all of these things provoked four-letter responses, C.E.'s special brand of swearing – a rich, succulent blend of mouth-filling, lip-smacking, throat gurgling roar – was saved for traffic lights. These demonic contrivances held special C.E.-cameras that deduced his approach. They knew exactly how long to remain green, favouring miles of open road, before clicking to amber at the exact instant when braking is a nuisance. No traffic light was ever an exception, and I looked upon them as cues for outbursts of Jesus-goddam-christ-that-goddam-shitty-light-saw-me-comin-goddam-it-shit-arsey-lights-wait-all-damn-day-son-of-a-bitching-lights-no-goddam-good…

This was diverting stuff for a small boy playing hookey from Sunday school. But C.E.'s other marvellous driving habit was coasting. Whenever we topped a large hill, he turned the engine off and we drifted pell-mell to the bottom. If no one else was around, he'd let the car roll on to an almost-complete standstill. If anyone asked him why he did this, he would say it was to save fuel. But I knew better. He did it because it was playful. So little in an adult world is suspenseful that C.E. loved to turn bits of that world into a game of chance. How far could we roll? Would anyone see us? Would the Machine ever start again?

The journeys themselves were always familiar and always new. Up the valley past the Wheeler's Farm, and by my friend Paul's house. Paul's father was a great hunter. He killed at least two or three deer every year, sometimes hunted bear, and also held the dubious distinction of killing the last known bob-cat on Catoctin Mountain. I only saw him occasionally, and was glad enough not to.

A little further on and the road bends into what the more prosaic locals call a kiss-your-arse-curve down to the bridge at Ellerton. On the corner opposite was a large unpainted clapboard building full of coffins, belonging to the funeral parlour in Myersville. The road straight ahead is called Harp Hill, and climbs its way sometimes vertically to Wolfsville. But nearly everyone turns right, towards Crow Rock, taking the low swinging road beside of Middle Creek. On the left is my friend David's house. He was the oldest of five brothers, born to a very musical family. David himself sang tenor, played the trombone, cello and piano. With his father and brothers, he staged private concerts for his mother, and they were all regular performers at their church.

At last, with the debit of one radio and the credit of a toot full of potatoes, C.E. pulled the machine up on to the side of the road, overlooking a wide hillside field. A gentle breeze, like rainfall on deep water, pattered in the trees beyond us. The foxtail grasses along the stone walls wagged, and tall orange cow-lilies shook their brown tongues at the bees. Butterflies battled about the dandelions, and there was stillness except for the distant hum of cow for calf. We scrambled over the wall and dropped down on the margin of the field. While C.E. assembled his kit, he explained the circumstances. It seemed that the last time he saw Dutch's cousin Seymour Winters, Seymour told him that when he was a boy he had heard that a regiment from the Union army had camped for a night on the Umphersock Farm. This sent C.E. to the history books, where he found that the regiment had in fact been from Michigan. They had formed part of the famous Iron Brigade, and had spent only one night on the farm before marching off to Sharpsburg. Now the Iron Brigade was known for only two things. First, they were mostly huge burly foresters recruited from the settlers in the great north woods. And secondly, they had unshakeable courage, always walking into battle wearing distinctive wide-brimmed black felt hats.

As the bluejays courted in the blackthorn tree, I remembered what I knew about them. On that terrible summers day a hundred years before I was born, the Iron Brigade went into action against Stonewall Jackson's Virginians. Advancing through rolling fields towards the Dunker Church, they were aiming for a crossroads on the Hagerstown Pike. As they neared their goal they were caught in a murderous crossfire from Bloody Lane. In the ensuing slaughter the Northerners refused to retreat and, as a result, they were practically wiped out. Eyewitnesses remembered that the dead of the Iron Brigade lay in long curved unbroken rows across the sloping hayfields, their formations still intact. The photographs of the battlefield confirm this.

When at last he was ready, C.E. pulled his cow-turd cap over one eye and sauntered with a slow side-to-side gait along the wall. The field itself was a glossy green carpet of wheat, but the edges were unplanted, leaving access for machinery. This was perfect, because C.E. reckoned that the men were likely to have camped near the road – more wood for fires, slightly sheltered, not as far to walk, easy to defend. I waited expectantly, following at a short distance as he panned about with the great detector. The yellow-jackets purred in the daisies, and the drum-tap of swallows clicked in the scrub oaks.

I was watching the shifting crescent of a high cloud when C.E.'s footsteps stopped. We had gone about thirty feet and he stood rigidly, waving the detector about in gradually reducing strokes. He pulled the trowel from his belt and stabbed it into the ground to mark the spot. Then he lay the detector down and dug a small hole about eight inches deep. Sure enough, it was a bullet. But the bullet had a tiny gimlet hole bored into its nose. C.E. explained that when soldiers came off guard duty, they had to remove the charges from their rifles by manually pulling out the bullets with the screw-point end of the ramrod. This meant that we were on the right track.

Three feet further on and he called me over to listen to the pu-wing of the detector as it signalled another find. In a short while, we had found half-a-dozen bullets in this manner, one of which was smashed by a heavy blow. All of them had been dropped in a semi-circle about eight feet across, probably grouped around the site of a campfire. This idea was corroborated further by finds of little shapeless gobs of lead, all extruded from a bullet mould.

As I held these relics, the May sky darkened to the blue sheen of September. I saw the footsore men, hot and weary, sitting at my feet, cleaning their rifles, moulding bullets, drinking coffee, writing letters. I looked to my right, at the far away prospect of South Mountain, purple-blue under a film of opal-white cloud, and I thought that this spot might have seen the last night's sleep many of these men ever had. How foreign these small drops of lead seemed! I knew then that whatever I found in the past, whatever ghosts I might call up, I would come to know nothing about them except for the simplest habits of their humanity. A few men had sat here around a fire before going to their deaths just beyond the mountain opposite. Nothing more remained. Yet somehow it was this touch, this ability to feel something, to see something that others had left in my path, that became the most important element in my search. It was the small things that connected us, however little those small things might add up to.

I came to believe that the earth held stories, and wherever I looked at the farmhouse, this proved to be true. I gave up stabbing knives into the woodwork – though one day Moose found a trove of marbles that a boyish C.E. had hidden in a corner of the larder, (proving C.E.'s own theory of hiding places). Instead, I began to dig holes. Sometimes idly, sometimes purposefully, I found things. Crouched under the gorey stalks of the poke bushes along the farm lane, weeding potatoes, I collected shards of bone china – snowy white and printed with pink and gold flowers. On the bank below the old springhouse, littering the ground among the cucumbers, were thick grey shards of broken crocks. They had been used to store food in the cold shallow pool of the springhouse floor. As they gradually broke with use, with carelessness, with severe frosts, Sadie Mae threw them out into the field in successive fits of pique. Sitting among the buzzing leafy arabesques in the vegetable patch, I gathered little lumps of coal – an alien substance to my woodburning world. I learned that they had been brought in by Sally Caxton, who insisted on burning a fuel that she knew from long use.

Sometimes I challenged the earth to prove me wrong. It never did. Once I volunteered to extend a flowerbed on the southwest corner of the house. Given my general aversion to work of any kind, Jane was pleasantly surprised, having no real notion of my motive. I dug enthusiastically, and was not disappointed. Ten inches into the earth I uncovered a long black-lace scarf, dotted with turquoise sequins, much decayed, but still holding together. It could only have belonged to Sally Caxton. Some time later a friend of mine disputed the universal applicability of my theory. I invited him to choose any spot he liked, and he selected a bare patch under the black maple tree, waiting to be re-seeded with grass. We sat toe to toe, bashing at the ground with trowels when, at a depth of six inches, my trowel hit metal. It proved to be a ten-inch iron wheel. Another time, as I stood listless under the hollow apple tree, rich with boyhood ennui brought on by potato weeding, I thumped away aimlessly at the ground with my hoe. A little hole gradually formed, and all at once there was the ping of metal against metal. This time, it turned out to be a find of more worth. It was a small iron sphere, about two-and-a-half inches across, known as a grape-shot – a kind of mini cannonball used as shrapnel during the war.

There were also natural wonders to collect. Finger-like smokey-glass quartz crystals grew out of rocks in The Hollow, and purple cuprite pebbles washed down the lane after storms. One day I burst into the kitchen, red-hot with the discovery of a small orange-black square, about a quarter-of-an-inch on each side. The little cube was disproportionately heavy, very, very smooth, and obviously stone. I was shocked to discover that this surprised no one.

Yeah, atsa jackstone.

What's a jackstone?

Iron.

Where's it come from?

Dohn't know, issisuh only place outsida Rook's Farm whereya can git um. I gotta whole box um some air. So's yer grandaddy, an so's is.

I gathered them by the score and kept them in an old French sweets' tin. Some were the size of a pin head, and others nearly an inch square. After a little rain, they glistened dully on the workshop path. But my real goal was to find something to boast of in family circles. Charlie Ford had found a tomahawk in the vegetable patch. C.E. had found an extremely rare pre-Revolutionary Virginia penny in the onion square beside the Mary House. But I found nothing of note. I was a disappointment on this score…

Still, I shone in others. My books made me proficient in mechanics. Moose found me very useful in that I developed astonishing accuracy in estimating the board-footage of timber that might be gleaned from a standing tree. He began to exhibit me in the same manner that Mozart's father exhibited his own prodigy. On one occasion we visited a farmer nearby who had installed his own sawmill to supply his farms' need for timber. Local farms consume a lot of wood, used mainly for fences, cladding and repairs to stabling and machinery. But for this farmer, unused to the processes of nineteenth-century technology, things were going badly. The trouble was that the huge belts used to transfer power from engine to saws gradually, but inevitably, worked their way loose and fell off. This was bad for two reasons. First, flailing ten-foot belts are extremely dangerous and, secondly, if the belt came off midway through a log, it was very difficult to extract the massive steel blade firmly gouged into the wood. I listened as the men debated the subject, and stealthily waited for an opening. At last there was a silence and I spoke up:

'The difficulty is that the powershaft from the engine is incorrectly balanced with the take-up wheel of the saw mandrel. What you need to do to bring them into sync is to have them balanced in the same way that wheels on your truck are balanced.'

Judging from the looks on their faces, you might have thought that I had suddenly dropped down like rain from a clear sky. Their embarrassment was delicious, and proved to me that I was right. Anyway, the saws were fixed in no time…

There was no limit to my mechanical aptitude. No limit, and no direction either. I amused myself by designing entire nineteenth-century factory complexes. I worked out water resources, rail connections, layouts for workers' cottages, mining codes of practise, output regulations, distribution channels and stock ratios. Using an 1896 J.C. Penny catalogue, the 1860 Patent Office Report, and reprints of *The American Agriculturalist*, I even designed and built working copies of machines and handtools, mostly using wooden blocks, card, brass wire and pins. Most worrying to my parents was my dedication to a Confederate Ordinance Manual detailing the manufacture of fireworks and explosives. They knew already that I had made my own charcoal, and they certainly saw me saving morsels of the bright yellow sulphur given to the cats as a cure for 'distemper'. The fear was that one day I would stop believing that saltpetre was a chemical only available from caves in Tennessee, and learn that it was readily available as simple preserving salt. Had I done so, I have no doubt that a short walk to the smokehouse, followed by a rustle in some small blue bags, would have resulted in the manufacture of enough gunpowder to blow myself to the moon before my tenth birthday.

My father decided it was time to divert my attention. Looking around for a means, he took inspiration from the dedicated way I stood to the ramparts of my fort, defending us with a pop-gun and a store of vegetative bombs, and bought me a B-B gun.

This was a hopeless affair. Relying on compressed air, this miniature shoulder arm fired, or rather lobbed, a minuscule copper-coated projectile half the size of a petit-pois. It was woefully inaccurate – a tendency which exactly suited the deep-down pacific leanings I immediately realised when a live firearm was put into my hands. Still, I carried the burden of belonging to a family of good shots, who lived in a world where hunting was a way of life. I was strongly influenced to shoulder this weapon as a part of my growing responsibilities.

I did not get on well. For one thing, I am impossibly short-sighted.

Add to this the fact that I am right-handed and left-eyed, and you can guess the reason why Moose once measured the distance between the tree-I-hit and the tree-I-aimed-for as fourteen feet. It was C.E. who pointed out that the left-eyed problem could be solved with an eye-patch. The result was a wad of folded kitchen towel stuffed between my face and glasses. Thus armed, I was teasingly cajoled, not to say bullied, to go out and kill something.

There was certainly game enough. Racoons washed their food in the streams and groundhogs sat wringing their little black hands like shopkeepers among the cabbages. Squirrels knocked about the nut trees at sunrise every morning, looking for last year's harvest buried deeply in the tight grass. Rabbits gorged themselves to obesity among the carrots and lettuces, and muskrats paddled about in the pools by the old mill bridge. Still, I simply couldn't bear to harm any of these creatures, even if I could have hit a moving target (which I couldn't), or even if a B-B had been lethal (which it wasn't). What I needed was small stationary game.

Finally, hounded to assert myself, I went out in the late tawny light of evening for a walk in the forest. In the woody ground above the barn I found a tall dead elm tree where, near the top, I could just make out a tiny silhouette. Gritting my teeth, I took aim (not actually at the target – that *never* worked – but rather far wide to the left). I pulled the trigger and there was the familiar pulsing thud of the gunstock against my shoulder. There followed a swift borrow-borrow-tumble as the small feathered animal plummeted to the ground, landing two feet in front of me. Filled with horror, I stepped up to its crooked brown body and turned it over. It was a robin, and he was stone dead. I pressed a trembling finger against the unbelievable softness of his orange breast, lifting the feathers slowly, with awe, in a way I would never be able to do with a living bird. So this was killing. I now knew that for its victims, death could be random, unjust and cruelly irredeemable. Stunned into automatic behaviour, I buried my first prize in a makeshift stone sarcophagus, my heart too full and my soul too ashamed even to mention the deed.

So the pressure to prove myself went on unabated. Every so often, conspicuously under Moose's eye, I stood beyond the farmyard fence and pounded away at the barn roof. There, arrayed across the summit like a shooting gallery, was a host of pigeons. Far from driving them away, I am sure that the strange spectacle of a small boy pointing a stick at them drew in many newcomers out of mere curiosity. I am certain that I fired hundreds of shots at them, each one pinging harmlessly on to the tin roof, and no doubt raising an amused chuckle among the birds.

Then one day tragedy struck. Bored with the sing-click of pellets on tin, I aimed a bit higher, in the hope that perhaps gravity might drop a B-B on to some unfortunate head, causing a concussion and thereby freeing me of this odious hobby. To my astonishment, instead of a commotion at the far left (where I had aimed), there was a wild flustering clatter at the extreme right as a bird disappeared down the back of the barn roof. Relieved that I was at last finished with this business, I ran for all I was worth to claim my trophy. What I saw terrified me. As I rounded the corner of the barn, thirty feet in front of me, limping and struggling, the pigeon was running for cover. It had no real direction, but appeared only to be trying to get as far as possible from the scene of its injury.

I knew what I had to do, and I followed my prey as quickly as I could. At last, the exhausted bird gave up its efforts in the shade of Charlie Ford's pear tree. My head was pounding and my lip trembling and what I did I did without hesitation or thought. With my eyes riveted to the quivering black bead of the bird's own eye, I lowered the barrel of the gun and carefully lifted the pigeon's wing. Pressing the muzzle to the animal's chest, I believed the pellet would puncture the bird's heart, and end its suffering instantly. With my vision clouding over, I fired. The quick thud on my shoulder was answered by a startled reverberation from the pigeon. To my extreme dismay, it simply trembled and looked more miserable. I had missed my mark. Here, trying desperately to end the suffering I had wantonly brought about, I succeeded only in adding to it. There was nothing else to do. Thinking fast, with my heartbeat roaring in my ears, I lowered the barrel once again to the animal's tiny head. With a sickening shudder, I fired again. Instantly a drop of watery blood crept upwards from an invisible wound, and the pigeon closed its pallid eyelid.

It was over. Breathless and bewildered, I staggered backwards and sat against the grassy, honeysuckle-sweet bank. My face was uncontrollable with repentance, and I prayed harder than I had every prayed before, beseeching God that He might give rest to this innocent soul that I had tormented uselessly through a selfish concern for my own esteem.

That afternoon, I quietly buried the pigeon under the pear tree, amid a scatter of drying creamy white blossoms. It was the last death I have ever knowingly brought about, and the lesson it taught me was a bitter one. My family, assuming logically enough that I stowed the B-B gun under my bed as a result of frustration and boredom, said no more about it, and the issue was dropped. But for my part, as the decadence of May was shorn-up by the hard hours of June, I looked out upon the living things around me with utter sympathy and wonder. How susceptible it all seemed to the pain of our own making. Yet how like us in its fears, its fragility, and the mutual need to guard the unity that is Living.

CHAPTER SIX

Peanuts and Crackerjacks

The army invaded in June, and along with eleven other boys, I went out to face them. We had drilled almost every night for more than a month, but when the vans disgorged them into Floyd's meadow, it was obvious that we could do little to prevent ultimate defeat.

The story really begins at the end of April, when the Community Club voted to re-found the long defunct little league baseball team. Because of the shortage of cash, every boy who was interested had to go out and find a sponsor to pay for his kit. The pay-off for the sponsors was to have their names emblazoned across our backs, just above our numbers. After a lot of fruitless searching, I finally persuaded a merchant in far-away Frederick to fund my grey flannel uniform, green socks and green cap. Shortly after, we assembled on the benches alongside the old diamond to be assigned our places, see our equipment, and agree on times for practice. By virtue of its having been my father's old position, I was to play first base. This, as I knew, was a 'hot corner', and would mean that I would be in on nearly every play. It also would give me plenty of opportunities to appear really foolish. The equipment consisted of a heavy leather catcher's mitt, mask and pads, half-a-dozen Louisville sluggers in various weights, and three batting helmets – large, medium and small, in red because that colour was cheapest (never mind that our uniforms were grey and green). The boys all voted that so long as the weather was fine, we'd practise every night from supper until sundown.

And so we did. Night after night we spent hours batting, fielding grounders, handling fly-balls, learning signals, warming up pitchers, practising every scenario. The air rang with the shouts of boys:

Get-one-get-two-get-three!

Comin'-down!

Heads up!

Hey-batter-hey-batter-hey-batter!

Now-atsa-crackerjack!

Time passed and we felt good about ourselves. Our legs strengthened, our backs straightened, our chests deepened and our aim improved. We were ready for Opening Day.

Then the worrying news came. In the lottery that decided the line-up of team-against-team, we drew as our first opponents the team from Fort Ritchie. The Fort was a huge army installation, located about twenty miles further up the mountain. It was staffed by army personnel whose chief criterion for this duty (as far as I could tell) was the possession of genes that fostered superb baseball-playing progeny. Besides a huge pool of human resources to draw upon, added to this was the vast wealth that the U.S. government lavished on its sons' athletics. My first glimpse of the invaders was that afternoon in Floyd's meadow when the six matching white vans pulled in. Out of these vans there piled twenty-seven boys – enough for three complete teams. While our uniforms were of the sort unchanged since the days of Casey Stengel, and carried our sponsors' names in two-inch letters above our shoulder blades, our visitors wore the latest design. Their jerseys were a light blue, stretchy summer material, pricked out in yellow, and their trousers were snowy white. Each boy brought his own individually numbered helmet, and had his own name across his back. Their equipment, including the newest lightweight aluminium bats, was carried for them by a squad of second-string bat-boys. The players themselves were an awesome set of impressively symmetrical Greek heroes. I doubt whether there was one whose shoulders were not above my head. They were beautiful, like spoilt disdainful young gods. But even their starry gazes of unperturbed superiority could not help registering the surprise they felt at seeing their vans pull up to stop in the middle of a cow pasture. The sniggering started in earnest when they strode single file over the narrow log bridge leading to the diamond. In front of them was the three-tier tin-roofed bleachers, full of local fans. To the right and left, the open benches for the teams. Dotted randomly around the outfield was a series of about 100 round, greenish extra bases, left by the cows, who peered inquisitively over the farmyard fence.

Amused and nonchalant, the visitors spread themselves out long their benches. At their backs, along the stone wall that separated Floyd's meadow from our own swamp and Hollow, they laid out their 'bull-pen' to warm up the pitchers. There seemed to be a whole cast of extras brought along to set up folding tables with cold drinks dispensers, first-aid supplies and clipboards with which to plan strategies. Bat boys polished the shiny metal bats, oiled the gloves, and buffed the sky-blue helmets. Meanwhile, behind our bench, we too warmed up. My friend Paul was to be starting pitcher, and we were relying on his curve to baffle the opposition. Using my first baseman's mitt, I caught for him, while beside of us (using our only catcher's mitt) our third-string side-arm pitcher doubled as catcher for our second-string fast-ball pitcher.

At last, the Umpire's voice thundered, 'Play Ball!' and the Harmony side took the field. You would have thought from the professionalism of our chatter that we were veterans of fifty years.

C'mon Paully-boy, get this one outta there!

Hey-boy-hey-boy-hey-boy!

Looks like my grandmother!

Swing-batter-swing-batter-swing-batter!

C'mon Paully!

But all of this staunch banter did little to ease the trepidation we felt as the first son of Achilles ambled from the on-deck circle to the plate. With our voices cracking all around him, Paul bore down with a whistling curve that sped straight at the visitor's heart before pulling away at the precise moment, clipping the inside corner.

Stee-rye-hike One!

A visible sigh of relief went through the boys, and our manager signalled for the fielders to shift left, expecting the batter to pull the ball down the left-field line.

C'mon Paully, Give'im another!

Letterip, Boy!

He couldn't hit a watermelon!

Hey batter, hey batter, swing batter!

Paul spread his knuckles over the laces and gave him the full wind-up, repeating the last pitch exactly. But this time there was that high sound of a rifle shot, and 100 heads turned upwards, losing sight of the ball as it travelled back over the left-fielder's head. I felt the breeze as the huge champion jogged by me, even before the ball plopped over the old wooden snow fence that marked the boundary for a home run.

Things went from bad to worse. As the top of the First wore on, batter after batter got Paul's number, and connected for singles and doubles. But there were no more homers. Our manager, with only two more pitchers in reserve, was reluctant to take Paul out so soon. Besides, we all knew he was giving the boy his first chance to pull us through. When at last the inning finished on a fine double play, the visitors took the field with a lead of 23-0.

We now faced a jubilant, not to say exultant opponent. Their grinning little side-arm pitcher saw our first batter ground out to third, and the second struck out swinging on a low-and-outside slider. As our third batter stepped slowly to the plate a light titter went up from the opposite bench. Tom Fox was the best-looking boy on our team. He was the youngest son of Dutch's friend Gaetha, and his mysterious quiet ways made him a favourite in the village. Thick brown curls spiralled under his cap, and our visitors mistook his reticence for fear. But when the pitcher dug his toes into the mound and lay out with a hissing fastball, eleven little hearts soared. There was a dull whack as Tom dropped a line-drive over second-base, getting himself a double.

With one man on, our second-string pitcher Albert Waterman came up to bat. Albert was the biggest boy on the team, and he batted clean-up. Like all his family, Albert had the distinctive Waterman walk – a kind of rapid sidle, like a man walking on a ship during a storm. But with a two-and-two count, this big South-paw smashed a long fly over the right-field fence, bringing Tom and himself home. The first inning finished with our side trailing 23-2.

When we took the field for the second inning we had made a few changes. For one thing, Paul and Albert had changed places, with Paul behind the plate as catcher, and Albert on the mound. By coincidence, the visitors were now back to the top of their line-up, and Albert faced the giant who had hit the first homer. We chattered like hickory for our man, and the two of them looked at one another. A little flicker of anticipated joy pursed the batter's lips as he lifted the bat off his shoulder and tapped the plate. Albert wiped a great shock of wavy hair off his sticky forehead and pulled down his cap. Paul pointed three fingers – this inning's signal for a fastball – and Albert rocked back into his heavy wind-up. There was a whoosh as the bat pummelled the empty air, and the Umpire bellowed,

Stee-rye-hike One!

In a few more minutes it was a full count, and both sides grew tense.

Paul dropped two fingers and Albert nodded. There followed a long low slider, and another whoosh.

Stir-rike Thur-ree! Yer outta here!

We could hardly resist cheering, but with a stern effort to save face, chattered feverishly.

Atta boy, Albert, ole boy, ole boy!

Atsa crackerjack, hey boy!

Albert looked downright ashamed of himself for being so happy.

The next two batters got on base, one on second and one on third. After a full count, Albert walked the next one and loaded the bases. With only one out, things looked bad. The next man up was a tall right-hander, and the infield shifted left to check the threat. I hovered about, loose footed, ready for a possible double-play, when I saw Tom – my opposite number over on third base – step down the line towards homeplate. This was a tremendously dangerous, even foolhardy thing to do, given the stature and physique of the batter. You see, if that model-of-comeliness had put the wood on one, pulling the ball tightly, Tom would have had half-a-second to react before a lump of horsehide and cord crashed into him. The rest of us stood dry-mouthed, too full of admiration to tell him to back off for the sake of his health.

Albert's third pitch ended as a terrible volley, driven foul down the third base line, four feet from Tom's right shoulder, and narrowly missing the third-base coach. The visitors' bench was emptied in a moment as their team leapt to its feet shouting mock-warnings and whistling hoarsely. The batter grinned fiercely and pointed the heel of the bat towards Tom, knocking it twice against his helmet as a gesture of what Tom could expect.

The next pitch fell low and outside, and all of us smacked our fists in our gloves, full of nerves, full of fears. And then it happened. Albert laid down an inside curve that that son of the army converted to a scorching line-drive which barrelled straight in Tom's direction. Fortunately, the ball came in at about four feet above his head, and Tom got a glove on it like lightning. He jumped, and there was a whip crack of leather as he came down with the ball. Almost before his feet touched the sandy infield he whirled round and tagged out the third base runner. The inning was over, and we had held.

Yeeeeeeee-ha! Atsa boy, Tommy!

With that show of courage, the lads caught fire. Every inning we bore down on them hard, holding the lines, running down the lead-off runners, picking them off first base. We showed ourselves as stalwart young men and would have gone on with unbroken dignity but for a few little incidents. In the fifth inning, the visiting team's manager appealed for an Umpire's decision after one of his demi-gods lost a fly-ball to centre-field after slipping in a cow pie. The Umpire ruled that the cow pies were a threat to all of us, and that the play should be marked down as a fielder's error.

My own chance came in the bottom of the ninth. The score was now 23-4 and it was our last chance. There were two outs and two men on, and I came to the plate for the fourth time. On my first two trips I had struck out, and on my third I had flied-out to left field. Although I was a good fielder, my poor sight meant that I simply couldn't see the ball's path rapidly enough to react properly. By now, this was obvious to everyone, and it looked a sure thing that the game would end with me left ignominiously at the plate. The visitors' bat-boys even began to pack up their equipment in readiness to load the vans.

As I looked at the mound I met the pitcher's eye. There was no amusement there and no pity either. He, like everyone else, was tired and wanted me out in three pitches.

I took the first pitch high and inside, just under my chin. I was relieved to hear the words, 'Ball One' from the Umpire. This is called 'brushing the batter back', and it worked. I was so nervous that I let the next pitch, a fast ball, roar down the centre of the plate, where any good hitter would have leaned into it.

Stee-rye-hike One!

There was a shuffling of feet as people prepared to leave, and a slurping on straws as they finished their Coca-Colas. The pitcher smiled in spite of himself.

I bit my lip and steeled my nerves for the next one. Obviously pleased with his last effort, the pitcher laid down another fast ball, a little higher up than the last one. I pulled sharply and felt the ringing in my hands as bat met ball. Unluckily, I was a little late in my swing, catching the ball a bit too low. It spun upward violently, and whirled off foul, dropping over the stone wall along right field, thudding into the swamp.

Strye-hike Tuhoo!

So this was it. The agony was nearly over. I looked to my left, where my team-mates, worn-out, trampled and soundly beaten, looked at the ground in front of their feet. Saddest of all, Tom Fox, his sweaty face caked with dust, stood placidly, his head leaning on the wire mesh fence.

With the lightest of twitches round my eyes, I stepped back into the box and tapped the bat on to the corner of the plate. A bitter moment approached and I was determined to face it. The gallant Assyrian Prince, high on the pitcher's mound, his eyes twinkling with certain victory, twirled the ball in his hand and dropped his arms to start the wind-up. Then from some remote corner of the visitors' quarter, adding insult to injury, a waggish eye read the label on my back, and a voice cried out,

C'mon Watson's-Ice-and-Beverage, get a hit!

When the pitch came in it proved to be a curve that got away. It found its mark just under my lowest rib. I dropped the bat in a spasm of pain, and my team-mates, screaming 'Bean ball!' charged to the third base line ready to draw blood on my behalf. Our manager pushed his way through, and rubbing my back grumbled, 'Walk it off, walk it off.' Over the tumult, the Umpire's voice resounded,

Take your base!

Striving hard against the burning sensation surrounding my kidney, and the flood of relief I felt to be out of the box, I hobbled to first base. My part in the debacle at least was over, and I had quitted myself well.

The rest? Ah, well, the dreams of boys are many, the triumphs few. Harmony lost 23-4, but we shook our opponents' hands with the pride of equals.

And so the summer days swelled wider at my fingertips. Hollow white clouds, like scallop shells washed backwards and forwards on the sea-green skies. The pale sunflower shade of the hardwood trees ripened to a velvety lustrous purple-green. The breezes of sunrise, flushed like wind-over-water, and the evening air splashed heavy with lilac, honeysuckle and the aniseed taste of lilies. In The Hollow, the green tangle of ivy and sumac hung like tapestries, dividing the forest into a cluster of streamside rooms. The stream itself, round, fleshy and sweet-smelling with the spring rains, roared and bounced around sudden tree-studded islands into wide shallow pools. Here, on Sunday afternoons or in the hours between school's ending and baseball practise starting, I sheltered my imagination from responsibilities. My habit was to collect dry branches and sort them into two kinds: five-foot long 'rudders' and one-foot long 'boats'. At the top of The Hollow there was a deep pool where the stream burrowed through the stone wall before plunging over a low falls and into the rapids below. I collected my 'boats' here before leading them one by one on the perilous journey towards Carroll's pasture. With my head full of stories about Confederate gunboats running the treacherous gauntlets of the Louisiana bayous, I ran along the stream bank using a 'rudder' to steer each dead stick through the fast waters. Sometimes I lost them in the overhanging bushes, sometimes the waterlogged wood simply sank. Most made it triumphantly through the last wide pool before the drop into the pasture below. For me, as captain, the problem was the almost-constant exertion. From the time each 'boat' left its first anchorage, to the final plunge to safety over the rocks at the bottom, I was on the run. There were piles of stones to scale, swamps to avoid, gullies to jump, briars to dodge; at one point I had to swing on a locust tree branch across the water, because the bank was clogged with scrub. What I needed was a backwater or two where my boats might ride at anchor while I caught my breath.

I decided to provide for these backwaters by damming the stream.

It's possible to learn a lot about Life by attempting to dam a stream. My first plan was to create a shallow lagoon on the level space one notch above the drop to the final pool. This was a low-lying area with a narrow entrance and a wide tumbling drop into the main current. My plan was to lay a low stone wall along the lower edge of this pool, deepening the water slightly, but really aiming to slow it enough to widen the backwash and create a wide shallow. Although I collected and piled up dozens and dozens of stones and arranged them prettily along the ridge, I succeeded only in covering my hands, arms and clothes with a semi-permanent green moss, and forcing a lot of water to propel itself in little spumes into the current below. In any case, my whole development project vanished a few days later – scattered by the cows, as my father said.

My next civil engineering work was to dig a canal around the shallows on the stage above the last failure. The purpose of this canal was to give me freer access with my rudder and to slow down the rush of water that made this area most dangerous for my boats. Using Moose's shovel –

the handle of which reached above my head – I dug a gentle curve from the high point to the low one. I learned immediately that without a lock system, I had to start in the middle of the projected watercourse and dig towards both ends, otherwise the channel filled with water faster than I could dig. Unlike the last effort, the canal was an immediate success. For a whole afternoon I boated contentedly on its muddy waters, basking in my achievement.

Now although I considered my earth-moving work complete, the next evening I discovered I was mistaken. Overnight, my gentle shovel-wide canal had widened to a two-foot current, with a three-foot shoal. I told Moose about this with some consternation, and asked for his advice. He had no advice. In fact, he said nothing at all. But he plainly shared my consternation. Anyway, the whole matter was resolved by the next evening when I found that those pesky cows had trampled the whole area to a uniform flatness. With impressive bovine skill, they had even piled up a low mound of earth at the canal's opening point.

I resolved to make one more attempt, if, for no other reason, to outwit a herd of mischievous cows. I looked at the whole area carefully, and reviewed my previous mistakes. I determined that the best thing to do was to build a high tight dam at the narrow gap between two boulders, through which the water roared like a steam engine before dropping to the pool of my former shame. I knew that the walling would have to be deep to withstand the pressure of the stream, but luckily the gap was only a few feet wide and the boulders were worn to a Y shape by centuries of the swift current.

I began by tumbling in some very large stones, on top of which I plopped medium-sized ones, and so on to the top. I plugged the gaps between the stones with rotting leaves from the stream banks. I even deposited an extra supply in the deepening water in front of the dam, just in case the originals washed out. The effect of this work was tremendous, and its subsidiary influences unexpectedly diverse. Within minutes a pool of water six-foot across formed. This spread out gradually to form a shallow puddle about twenty feet across, spilling through a host of little drains back into the main channel. I was jubilant. This was more than boating, this was practically yachting. In an exultant mood, I brought down stick after stick, allowing them to bob about freely before making the final rush over the dam itself, and into the current beyond.

Moose did not share my high spirits at all. If anything, the forces of reticence contracted his jaw even tighter than last time. He managed to struggle out a warning that cows like to wade.

Unluckily, he was right. By the following night, nothing remained of the vast underwater garden I had created (and which had grown exponentially in my absence). Nothing, that is, except a lot of soggy earth, wash away sticks and leaves, and some puckered and yellow grass. The marauders had even kicked or nuzzled out the large stones I had moved, dextrously lifting them on to a pile of rocks beside the boulders. To this day I remain in awe of the physical prowess of our hoofed neighbours (not to mention the taciturnity of fathers).

Cows and water formed an integral part of my June experiences. After the calves were fully weaned, they were put out to graze in the fields across the road from the barn. This was a large, rather rough area, bounded by the road on one side, a neighbouring pasture on another, and dense bird-ripe woods on the other two. In the centre of the field was a cluster of apple and walnut trees giving shade, and in the Northeast corner were two sheds with bedding. The only thing missing was an open supply of water. What there was, was a well-head with a pump, a garden hose, a cast iron bath, and a small boy.

I don't know whether *you've* ever watered half a dozen thirsty cows on a hot June day with a low-pressure garden hose, but even if not, I'll bet you can guess at the situation's potential for excitement. For one thing, a cow's naturally slow-moving curiosity was so stimulated by my appearance, that they lost all summer shyness and proceeded to take turns drinking off the water as fast as I could pour it into the tub. If it hadn't been for their sheer size and endearing timidity, I might have run amuck and attacked the lot of them for this little act of precocity. My responsibility towards them extended only to filling the tub with water. For a boy to stand about in the hot sun, clutching a feeble garden hose only to watch his best efforts vanish down the whiskery rubber-lipped minty-grass muzzles of his protégés, was barely endurable.

I tried any number of lethal experiments with the water itself. I tried to bring down the host of flying insects that buzzed round about us. I discovered that it's almost impossible to drown a water spider. Spray does little to hamper the business of flies. Wasps get mightily annoyed if dampened. Bumblebees are rather more fleet of wing than they appear. Eventually, when the tub was at last filled, and the eighteen various stomachs were awash, I had two choices. Either I could assist with weeding the vegetables, or I could assist with work on the barn.

Weeding the vegetables was hellish for a number or reasons. Aiming at self-sufficiency, my parents had planted vast quantities of everything. There were four two-hundred-yard rows of French beans. There was an acre of potatoes. There was a six- by two-hundred yard jungle of pumpkins, watermelons and cucumbers. There were serried ranks of tomatoes, lima beans, and sweet corn, to name only few of the more expansive items. Boyhood impatience with repetition notwithstanding, these crops entailed an immense amount of work. Being too small to wield a hoe really effectively, my job was to burrow delicately among the prickly white-downed leaves and uproot the weeds closest to the plants. The stationary nature of this handiwork left me prey to every sort of insect. Besides the eleventy trillion stinging species that inhabit the Appalachians, there are others whose habits or physical characteristics are infuriatingly troublesome. There is a small grey-black spider that carried a kind of studded woolpack on its back. If you accidentally try to brush this one off, it sticks its little thorns into your hand. There is a gruesome variety of smooth-bodied armadillo-shelled caterpillar about the size of an adult's index finger. These creatures, known as 'tomato caterpillars', were so repulsive to me that I once lost all moral compunction and trapped one in a packing-thread noose and hung him up on the workshop door as an instruction to others. There is also a species innocuously known as 'bean bugs', to whom Nature has awarded a defence mechanism that can only be described as disintegration. Lacking any visible signs of eyes, limbs or locomotion, these pitiful droplets mysteriously appear on skin or clothing while you work. If you should touch one, its little baked exterior vanishes, and what you are left with is a quarter teaspoon of liquid egg-yolk.

But large insects, *really LARGE* insects, make me panicky. Once I was so insulted by the indecency of a yellow and black spider as large as the palm of my hand, that I stood at a safe distance and threw a bushel full of stones at it, until I was satisfied that I had conveyed the degree of my displeasure. But my special loathing was awakened by the evil spectre of a praying mantis. It's no good telling a boy about the utility, friendliness and overall serviceability of a grey-green dinosaur-like monster, with a goat-like head and a foul unoiled walk. If I saw one in

89

the open air I was content to lift it on to a forked stick and launch it into a low orbit round the sun. But on one occasion my personal space was invaded too nearly to allow for such restraint. One of my bedroom windows faced the vegetable patch, and one evening as the katydids chirruped in the maple trees, I climbed wearily up the stairs to my room. As I flopped heavily, not to say dirtily, on to the bedspread, (my hands and shirt dotted with bean bug juice, my arms popply with 'sweat bee' stings), I saw him. Propped above my doorway, grating his massive shoulders together, was a six-inch praying mantis. Without patience and without mercy, I took off my heavy shoe and planned an assault. But no matter how warily I proceeded, as I moved my right foot, he moved his two left ones. At last I lunged, and with one tremendous whack I produced an enormous greeny-yellow stain on the wall. Thirty years later, after scrubbings and repaintings, a certain diagonal, shall we say 'lustre', remains.

In preference to this, while it lasted I opted to help with the barn repairs. The great piles of planks that had been cut and stacked last autumn, had been carefully cured through the winter and were now ready for use. Little by little we knocked the old sheathing off, exposing only as much of the interior as we could re-cover in an evening's work. My jobs, as principal assistant, were many and various. As each piece of wood came down, powdery light with age, or spongy with retained damp, I had to collect them and carry them to the open field above the well-head. There I had to pile them (not too tightly) for an eventual bonfire. When the section of wall was cleared, Moose gathered together a number of the newly trimmed planks and propped them against the building. When he was ready I had to shove these (I couldn't really lift them) upwards until they were within his reach. When they were in place, I had to lean my back against them until he nailed them down, each blow of the hammer sending shrill vibrations through my shoulders. In this way a two storey barn large enough to hold 1000 bales of hay was covered with new timber.

When it was finished it shone like a flesh-pink beacon for comment. Word of a newly finished barn got around quickly and we were not short of volunteers willing to paint it for us for a nominal fee. With so many other things to do, my father was willing to listen to these proposals. There were plenty of offers to finish the building in red-trimmed-with-white or white-trimmed-with-green – the only two combinations locally acceptable. As the farmhouse was white, it seemed best that the barn should be white also. The best quote came from a group of young gypsies passing through the village on their way to the orchards above Catoctin Furnace, where the soft fruit picking was about to begin. These fellows were desperate for work and they agreed to paint the barn for half the price anyone else could name. They would also supply their own materials. Reckoning that a large unadorned rectangle wouldn't require great skill as painters, Moose agreed to the proposal.

The day came and the four men arrived with a pick-up truck load of strange gear. There was an air compressor, yards and yards of rubber hose, a water tank, some cans of fluid, several sacksful of powder, some smallish ladders, and not a single paintbrush. Jane was the only one at home, and not being fully conversant with the means of large-scale exterior decoration projects, she was reluctant to comment. Imagine her surprise when less than three hours later there was a knock at the door, and she opened it to find a wide-eyed ghost grinning expectantly. Behind his white-speckled black hair there was the shimmeringly brilliant aura of the newly whitened barn, radiant in the crisp sunlight. His three colleagues were loading the equipment into the truck, as astonishingly, the work was finished. My mother handed the man an envelope and without opening it, he touched his imaginary hat and joined the others.

A few hours later my father came home and discovered just how much more than we bargained for we had actually received. Not only was all the woodwork painted, but so were the stone foundations. Indeed, they had also painted the ground floor windows, all the fittings, and about six feet of grass surrounding the building. Anyway, the job was done and the barn sparkled.

The next surprise came about a week later. A low-lying afternoon sky gathered itself into bundles. A breeze, aromatic with pine and the gingery sharpness of newly cut hay brought the clouds over slowly, and by evening a soft rain settled in. After the short summer night, we awoke to find that our once gleaming barn had faded somewhat to a light silver. After two more days of rain, this colour wore down to a bluish-grey – a tint it levelled off at. Whitewash, as we discovered, is not really suitable for new wood. No more than bargains are suitable for new agriculturists.

But other work went on. The school holidays came on at last, giving me my first whole days of freedom. But my waywardness was not total, for I was placed in Dutch's care. In her household, the pace of days was unvarying. Up at dawn, she began the tremendous cycle of laundry that she undertook for three households – Charlie Ford's, mine and her own. This laundry was sorted out on the floor of the long galley kitchen. From here it passed through a series of wicker baskets until its turn came to be carried outside to the back porch where the washing machinery was kept in summer under a canopy of deep purple flowers. This machinery included a huge white Maytag washer complete with wooden 'wringers'. The tub on this machine was filled with bucketsful of hot water carried outside from the kitchen. After a load was washed, the wringers were swung back over the machine and each piece pulled out of the steaming pool and passed through the rollers, after which it plopped into a galvanised tub. The water was then drained out and a rinse 'cycle' poured in. The washed load then passed through the machine for a second time. Very difficult to clean items, or heavily soiled clothes, were washed by hand on a ridged wooden 'washing board' propped up in a galvanised tub. When all the tubs were filled, Dutch tied on her bonnet and carried them one by one up the steep bank to the rear of the house, where the clothes would be pegged out to dry in the burning midday heat. To cope with this amount of laundry, C.E. had built four clothes lines, each over 100 yards long. Like all village women, Dutch's goal was to be the first out with the day's washing. She seldom failed.

Meanwhile, I gathered strawberries from the patch behind the clotheslines, picked young dandelion leaves for supper, snapped off asparagus shoots, or dirtied my hands abominably by climbing the tall pine trees.

Yu-hoo b'ur gid in ere boy, er ull fan yer boddum!

At lunch time, C.E. came home for the beginning of his siesta. Packed full of his favourites – ham, cheese, bread and fresh fruit – he lay out as nearly prone as possible on his wooden Maine deck-chair with its iron slip-cog recliners, and tried to have a nap. I say 'tried' because everyone in the county knew about C.E.'s siesta and thought it an opportunity to throw a little business his way. As regular as dew on a daisy, from 12:00 onwards the telephone bombarded him with stories of dysfunctional televisions, gasping radios, moody blenders, unmusical stereos, and a host of other electronic disorders. Although these calls were a lifeline to his business (he had no workshop phone), each in turn was greeted with a familiar snarl,

Ooooh! That god-damned bitchy-assed telephone, always god-damned ringing off the bitching hook. I'm gonna rip that shitty bastard off the god-damned wall…

But then a miracle…With his hand on the receiver, C.E.'s face composed itself. The hard lines softened. The burnished blue veins faded, and his voice transformed itself to a chocolatey sweetness,

Good mornin' Mrs Miller…Has it?…No picture at all?…Just a hum, but no sound?…Welp, I spec' Toosduh's alright, say roun' Two?

Seated again comfortably, lemonade in hand, the episode was repeated at intervals for more than two hours.

God-damned miserable phone…

Towards the end of the month, with the lavender skies hardening to a smooth deep blue, C.E. took me, along with Dutch, in The Machine as part of an afternoon working party for Dutch's brother George Ropp. Great Uncle George lived about a mile from his parents' former home. Behind his house, a smooth tapering field sloped upwards against the Southwest side of Catoctin Mountain. George covered this field – all in all about four acres – with neat rows of black raspberry canes. Every June these canes were covered with a deep purple-black fruit, sweeter than a blackberry, but richer and fuller than a red raspberry. When C.E. dropped us off in the hottest part of the afternoon, George always greeted us with the stern unmoving smile of a mountaineer, and laid his callused hand warmly on Dutch's shoulder. There was no other outward show of emotion between them, yet it always seemed that however long it had been since they had last seen one another, their present conversation took up where the last one left off. George himself was a tall robust man who wore a wide-brimmed straw hat with a black band, and always carried his hands on his hips. His face resembled Dutch's not at all, but instead he had his father's hard blue eyes, softened by kindness and glinting with merriment.

When at last we had fortified ourselves with lemonade, we set off to work. George led the way followed by his small wife Fanny, dressed like Dutch in a gingham print dress and bonnet. Being the smallest, I followed, carrying one punnet only, and not a tray of twelve like the others. As we entered the long columns of plants I caught my breath.

The mid afternoon sun made the sky over my head feel like liquid crystal. The air, unstirring, hung weightily, aglow with the violet and honey smell of ripe fruit. Above me towered the simmering green-black flanks of Catoctin, luminous and silent. Burrowing my way among the scented leaves I confined my labour to the lowest vines, nearest to the ground, so that Dutch would have to bend over as little as possible. The fruit was less opulent here, and it took a long time to fill a punnet. Although I can say truthfully that I was much too conscientious to eat any of the soft warm purple berries, none of the adults believed me, and all attributed my poor show to wanton rapine.

As the afternoon wore on, and the sweat circles on our clothes gradually became joined up, the women replaced their bonnets with folded up squares of water-soaked cloth. Trayload after trayload of brimful punnets of bulbous black globes lined the paths leading to the field. By evening these were arranged in tiers in the cool shade of George's workshop. Then, as the evening sun fell in orange and black spirals over the ground, people began to collect under the trees around George's front door. Although he never advertised his merchandise, and I never saw money exchange hands, custom brought 'custom' to his doorstep.

My own day concluded with a special suppertime treat. I watched with eyes as round as pennies as Dutch's heavy, work-worn, blue-black stained hands scooped a palmful of dark berries into a white china bowl. Then with a spoon small enough for my mouth, she mashed the fruit, still warm with the rays of a high June sun, into a coarse puree, stirring in a trickle of cold fresh milk. Hours later, with purple fingers and purple tongue, I would fall asleep, dreaming of the purple-black skies of an early summer night.

CHAPTER SEVEN

Like a Fox on the Run

July begins in the fast-drying dewfall lying grey-white on the fading grass. As sunrise flecks the mountainside with foamy yellow mists, the stillness grows pungent with the fumes of warm wet vegetation. In the lull between the pre-dawn finish of birdsong and the bright-winged commotion of their daily work, the sparrows, thrushes and blackbirds sit on the fence-posts in languid repose. Light pours like water down the tree-tops, emblazoning the heights and drawing long shadows from the cedar-fringed forest to the rock-strewn Hollow. In the farm garden, turtles push their heads through their black and yellow shells, and the cannonball splash of bull-frogs is lost in the freedom of silence. In the cockle-blue light of the kitchen I look round at the sturdy, highbreasted rows of Mason jars, lining tables and covering the floor and kitchen worktops.

These jars, like the hundreds that succeeded them, were Dutch and Jane's handiwork. They represented hour upon hour of gruellingly hot, back-stiffening labour, undertaken to provide a winter's worth of fruit and vegetables. Afternoons spent in the ember-raining sun, picking bushels of French beans, resulted in olive-hued quart jars stuffed symmetrically with tiny bean-furrows. A parade of enamelled buckets full of scarlet ripe tomatoes now cooled, packed whole, or juiced, or pureed. Pint jars of yellow sweet corn blossomed on the windowsill.

When breakfast was over, I helped my mother carry these supplies down the winding stairs to the cellar, where they filled a host of wooden racks that Moose had built from leftover poplar boards. While we were working, Dutch arrived with a small bundle of time-hollowed knives wrapped in a dishtowel, ready to begin another all-day session. This day's materials, buckets full of cucumbers and trays full of black raspberries, were piled in the pantry. While Dutch prepared the workstations, Jane went around the house opening all the windows as wide as they would go, and setting up fans to dispel the heat. Besides the kitchen cooker, my parents had bought an enormous black secondhand professional cooker that C.E. had wired up in the cellar. As the day progressed, both would be used to prepare the food and sterilise the crateful of jars.

The black raspberries, now cool and with rose-like breath, were carefully spilled into an enamelware colander, and washed with cold water. Taking them out in handsful, Dutch slowly crushed them with Sadie's potato masher, before straining the pulp through a double layer of muslin. Mixed with sugar, tasted, cooked and stirred with experience, this purple work of two summers days would solidify into a fine jam that, topped with wax and gingham, won blue ribbons year after year at The Great Frederick Fair.

Meanwhile, Jane prepared the savoury food. A score of cucumbers were washed, topped and tailed and cut into wafer-thin slices. At the same time, an exotic brew of vinegar, cinnamon, cloves and allspice bubbled in readiness. Then, with a steamy hiss and eye-stinging rush, the pickling process got underway. By evening the entire house was richly clotted with the succulent odours of cooked fruit and hot crushed spice.

Once outside, I listened for my father's voice. It would come, as it always came on July mornings, beckoning me to work I did not love, drawing me from amusements I was certain I might discover. Today, I knew without being told that he was in the barn tidying up. With all the resources of boyhood's Thespian arts, I sought him everywhere. I looked slowly around the workshop, where of course there was a vacant silence. I visited the chicken coop, though I knew the hens had been fed hours before. I looked in the sheds and the pigpen, I oversaw the gardens and the lawns. Then as I made my way reluctantly towards the barn, I heard a rustling in the hayloft. I ducked quickly into the groundfloor stables, giving every appearance of undertaking a thorough search. At last, his head poked downwards through the hay-hole:

Hey! Where'nee hell ya been?

July was the month for the first cutting of hay, and I hated it like cats hate water. For amateurs like us, it was hot, filthy, tiring work, that left us scratched, blistered and hardly able to see or breathe. Besides our tractor, we had a waggon that Moose had built himself. But we had no other haymaking machinery – mower, rake, baler – for three reasons.

For one thing, our fields were not yet in a suitably smooth state for haycutting. Likewise our tractor wasn't big enough to power the heavy baler. And lastly, we simply couldn't afford the equipment we needed.

Instead, we trawled the local farmers who we thought might have a surplus. Sometimes, we were more successful than others. In our first winter, we relied on an old friend of my father's, who lived far up on South Mountain. This old man had some bales of dry dusty grass packed into an open-sided log-cabin-style shed, that he let us have at a greatly reduced price. The real problem here, apart from the low-quality of the hay as feed, was in getting it home. Because of the great distance and the roughness of the mountain roads, we had to bring our purchase home on the pick-up truck. Despite tying each load down very carefully with ropes, the winding bouncy roads meant that we often lost bales over the side. Whole ones could be re-loaded, but broken ones had to be abandoned. Similarly, a near neighbour sold us the leftovers of a two-year old crop, which he described as 'better than snowballs.'

So having learnt our lesson, when summer came Moose negotiated with a farmer up in Fisher's Hollow to get a bargain rate on new hay, where the deal included our own labour in helping to bring in the whole crop. This farmer was named Hoover Kenwood, and he was one of the best-known characters on the mountain. There were a few reasons for this. Hoover's home and farm resembled Russ Waterman's in terms of neatness and overall comprehensiveness of junk collections. More interestingly, he had an invisible wife. Everyone knew that Hoover was married, some people even recalled that his wife had been a schoolteacher. But no one remembered her looks. She was certainly still alive. If you sat in the fly-blown morass of the kitchen, there was plainly someone moving about in the next room. Once, I even caught a glimpse of a skinny arm retrieving a glass of iced tea. But like everyone else, I certainly never saw her, nor ever heard him speak to her.

I would have remembered it if I had heard him speak on the subject. It was impossible to forget or ignore anything that Hoover said. This is because Hoover never spoke without shouting. Habitually. No, really shouted. The logical inference was that he was deaf, but he wasn't. Perhaps his wife was. Anyway, his voice could be distinguished in any assembly he attended. He made particularly awkward company at public auctions where his voice rang out even above the auctioneer's.

Heyare em far ingins las night?

Yep, two'uh'um.

Whar'd a' go?

Deed I dowhn know.

I spec a wen up air ta Gracen's.

Naw, coun'be. A' wuz gohn purt'ner haf-nower.

Wellsir, en. Mebbe Dutch'll know.

But there was still another characteristic that made Hoover's manner of speaking notable. That is that he had a vocabulary that made C.E.'s look positively austere in its restraint. When provoked – and he was easily provoked – a voluminous string of expletives, delivered with ear-splitting power, would burst forth.

On a typical day of haymaking, my father and I would pay a mid-morning call on Hoover, to make sure that his plans hadn't changed. He was a somewhat mercurial character who might, without explanation, decide to sleep in late, go fishing, or forget us altogether. If things went exceptionally well, we would tumble along the ruts and craters of the long track to his house and find the farm utterly silent. There was no point in knocking on the door because if Hoover was home, he'd be outside before we got close enough and, if he wasn't home, his invisible wife would be no help. The next thing was to find him. Generally, we walked along the thick-dusted bramble-edged lanes that led upwards to the high flat fields. The morning air, always fragile in summer, was beginning to pick up the low whirr of blades and ting-ting of tynes as Hoover raked over the hay. By now, the hay had lain cut in the hot sun for about three days to cure, and Hoover was busy raking it into long columns, known as windrows. Moose would confer with him about the best time to come back for the baling. A certain amount of chin-rubbing and sky-reading went on, before some hour in the hottest part of the day would be agreed upon.

As that hour approached, my heart grew heavier. My work began with opening up the gigantic barn doors while my father reversed the tractor in to collect the waggon. I then had to raise the heavy steel waggon 'tongue' and aim its forked end over the tractor's 'hitch'. When the two were aligned, I had to drive in the steel pin that held them together. I jumped back as the waggon was pulled away, closing and locking the huge doors behind him. After this, I had to run to the gate that connected this field to the open road, and open it to let the tractor out. Once it was out, I had to close the gate behind the tractor and jump on to the high waggon, the sides of which were nearly eye-level for me. I rode this way for about a mile to Hoover's house, feeling my bones knock together inside me as we drove along his deeply-pocked lane.

When we reached the hayfield, the atmosphere had been transformed to the density of boiling water. The cooked-mint smell of the hay went some way towards drowning the heated throb growing inside my temples, which I could feel slowly mapping the contours of the underside of my face. The penetrating roar of the empty fields and empty sky surrounded us, broken only by the pat-pat of the tractors and the furzing clatter of locusts. When Hoover was ready, he coupled the first waggon to the rear of the baler and took the driver's seat. Moose rode on the waggon, standing nearest the baler, and I stood at the rear. In this manner we rattled on to the first windrow.

Now Hoover's farm equipment mirrored his whole outlook on life. The baler itself was an enormous old-fashioned model, built sometime near the close of the Second World War. It, like the tractor, had once been red, but both were now faded to a uniformly pinkish rust. Its mechanism included a tremendous lever on top which appeared and disappeared with rhythmical regularity. Each time it leapt upward, aiming to ram the hay backwards into the boxed bale-making chamber, it looked uncannily like a prize fighter delivering low upper-cutting punches.

As the trio of machines and trio of operatives shunted along, the work began in earnest. Hoover's job was simply to steer the baler's large spinning rake evenly along the windrows of hay, ensuring a regular supply got into the machine and that none was left over for picking up later. He also had to guard against going too quickly, in which case the power-take-off supply to the baler, running in co-ordination with the engine revs, would force the hay through so fast that the bale-tyer would fail to work, and the result would be a waste of hay and twine. My father's part was to lean over the space between the waggon and the baler's tail chute and lift out each bale as it formed. He then had to pass these backwards to me. My business was to pile up the bales tightly at the back of the waggon.

As each load began, I found the work fairly easy. Although the rough twine cut into my fingers and palms, I didn't have to lift the bales very much and, as each one weighed from thirty to fifty pounds, this meant a lot to me. Gradually though, as more bales came my way, I had to begin piling them up like bricks. This process was fraught with difficulties. For one thing, I was performing on a moving stage. Also, given the ratio between my size and that of the bales, I found piling them a bit of a struggle. As they mounded up, my father lifted them up into my reach, and my working platform slowly rose farther and farther from the ground. Sometimes, if we hit a bump, bales tumbled off the side and there were shouts and countershouts as we came to a halt. If the bales were intact, I merely had to climb down and get them, lifting them over my head where Moose could reach them and tuck them snugly in. Stern looks were generally enough to suffice as punishment for my part in this affair. If, however, a bale broke, making it necessary to move the scattered hay forward to another part of the windrow, I was forced to suffer the bravado-rich rebukes of my mentors. Fortunately, I never committed the ultimate folly of falling off the waggon myself.

Anyway, there were some highlights. Occasionally, if we passed through a low spot in the field the hay would be so wet that the bales were practically immovable. In these instances, everything came to a halt as the two men negotiated about the saleability of this merchandise. Hoover always maintained that it wasn't that bad, and that it would dry out in no time, while Moose inevitably claimed that in this humidity it would either mould before it dried, or spontaneously combust and blow up his barn. The end results were always two. We bought more wet grass than we really wanted, and I got a breather during the period of the Summit Talks.

Another happy moment often came at windrow corners. As the tractor and baler swung round on to the next windrow, the gap between baler and waggon would widen so far that Moose couldn't reach the hay, with the result that bales fell off to one side, once again giving me a breather. But best of all were the frequent mechanical failures. Sometimes the baler's fierce punching arm failed to raise itself. Other times the tying apparatus refused to work, sending out helplessly collapsing squares of hay. For me this was a blessing. Not only was there the certainty of a temporary adjournment, but the accompanying fireworks were spectacular. Sitting on the high green-yellow mountain of hay, under a pitiless, bald-white sun, I licked the salt off my lips and watched the comedy.

Responding to my father's shouts, Hoover whirled around on the steel tractor seat and let the engine idle down long enough to hear the explanation. As an acknowledgement, Hoover tore his wide-brimmed straw hat off his head and threw it as far away as possible. He then leapt from his perch and buried his sweaty grey head in the tractor-side toolbox. Now the contents of this toolbox were widely known. There were two screwdrivers, a massive adjustable wrench and six hammers. For this particular repair, Hoover brought the wrench, a screwdriver and two hammers – one huge and one small. Before beginning the repair itself, he laid down all of the tools except the large hammer. Then, jumping up and down like a bear with a burr under his tail, he commenced pounding on the steel flanks of the baler, screaming obscenities with colossal vigour:

Jesus-god-damn-Christ,-this-shitting-god-damn-arsehole-of-a-god-damn-machine-ain't-worth-a-god-damn-shit-holing-piece-of-shit.-Goddammit-I-don't-know-why-I-fart-about-with-this-god-damn-son-of-a-bitching-bastard…

Meanwhile, the baler looked as though it had withstood this concentrated machine-gun fire on many previous occasions, and its durability was a credit to its makers. These tirades re-surfaced with each outburst of frustration throughout the repair process, and even carried on when we were back underway – the sound muffled only slightly by the roar of the equipment.

Things went on in this manner until three waggons were filled; that is, until about 200 bales had passed through our hands. At this point, the tractors were disengaged, and re-hooked directly to the waggons. Hoover took one straight to his own barn for unloading, and, with me clutching the rear upright of our waggon, we lumbered home. Once again there was the to-ing and fro-ing with gates and barn doors, as Moose reversed into the barn. Inside, the broiling midday sun had pushed the temperature to over 100 degrees Fahrenheit. The actual working style was similar to the previous one. Moose unloaded the hay backwards, one-by-one, and threw it to me overhead in the hay 'mows' (rhymes with 'cows'). Once again, my job was to stack the bales like bricks. In this case my work was even more hampered by circumstances outside my control. In the intense heat and blinding dust, I simply couldn't work at my father's pace. As time wore on, the bales seemed to grow heavier, and I had to cope as best I could with the fact that the unevenly-sized bales did not fit tidily into the available space. Very often small gaps were left into which I sometimes slipped up to the armpits.

As the depth of the hay increased, the difficulties mounted. For one thing, Moose had to throw the bales higher and higher. Eventually, we could not see one another, and the heavy bales often landed on me. Also the nearer I got to the tin-and-shingle roof the hotter it became – so much so that I could actually feel the breath passing in and out of my lungs.

As each load was finished, we returned to the hay field for another. A good day's work might see 600 bales stored away – perhaps 200 for ourselves – with work finishing at sundown. We never ate while working, and we only had water to drink, and that only when at home. By evening, underneath a coating of grass and seeds, I had reached a light crimson hue, my head pounded, my hands bled, and I could turn a handkerchief black. Sometimes, we could not get such a large amount of hay at one time. This meant that more days would be required to fill the barn. All in all, we aimed to have around 800 bales to see our livestock through the winter.

But not all days were this rigorous, and few nights were. Evenings not spent in watching the playfulness of the swallows against the citrus-coloured skies, might finish in the breathtaking spectacle of the ten thousand yellow sparks of lightning bugs against the blue background of the forest. The air was musical with the songs of mockingbirds, and drenched with lilies, roses and honeysuckle. Sometimes we went out to play parchese with Charlie Ford. On the Fourth of July we would all sit on the front porch and watch the fireworks launched from South Mountain. The creaking chains of the porch swing set the accompaniment to the display, faintly audible, even at a distance of six miles. The show itself was put on by local patrons, and the activity centered on the old Washington Monument. This monument bears no resemblance to its famous namesake in the nation's capital. Instead, it is a three storey, greenstone cylinder, slightly tapered at the top, giving a panoramic view over the surrounding mountains. It was built by a handful of patriots a generation after the Revolution, and it is said to be the first large monument built in honour of the country's first president. Once in a while, the larger towns sponsored parades. At these events every high-school and village band in the county gathered to march for their respective honours. Most brought baton-twirling majorettes, some had a rousing drum corp. We certainly always attended to cheer on our own venerable scarlet-and-black-clad Harmony Band. Interspersed with the musicians were the 'floats'. That is, there was a series of hay waggons (like our own) got-up by local charities in the guise of a weird and wonderful interpretation of the work they did. There were giant papier-maché cows for the Future Farmers of America, pink dining room tables with roses for the 4-H, a green miniature homestead for the Ruritan Club, a living model of the Iwo Jima Monument for the Veterans, and a host of others for the Eagles, Moose and Odd Fellows Clubs. There were strolling clowns, and highly polished fire engines, topped by their volunteer crews and their Dalmatian mascots. I truly loved a parade.

The only thing grander than a parade was a carnival. Every town large enough to maintain its own Volunteer Fire Department sponsored a week-long summer carnival. Near every town of consequence, these Fire Departments owned a bit of land set aside for these once-a-year extravaganzas because, not only were they great fun, but the profits contributed significantly to the Departments' upkeep. There were, of course, certain essentials for these events. There was always a Ferris Wheel and a merry-go-round and, depending on local affluence, a few other rides as well. If you had a steady hand, you could throw darts at balloons. If you broke three in a row, you won a small prize. You could then hazard this on three more throws for a larger prize, and so on until you owned the most expensive teddy bear at school. If you had a strong back and arms, you could use a sledge hammer to send a leaden projectile twenty feet into the air where it rang a bell to salute you. If you could throw a baseball with any skill, you could chance twenty-five cents on three pitches to try and hit a lever that dunked a man into a huge tub of water. If you had good co-ordination and a powerful grip you could climb a smoothly-peeled twenty-foot pole, shiny with fresh lard. Less athletic spirits could throw wooden rings around green 'deposit' Coca-Cola bottles, or toss nickels into glassware, trying to win prizes. There was always a large tent with long parallel benches, set up for bingo. At one end of the field, a waggon would be drawn up as a makeshift stage, from which, as the darkness deepened, a local band would give forth. Generally, there was a permanent structure with a kitchen and drop-side doors, where you could buy ham- or sausage-sandwiches, french fries, hot dogs, hamburgers and Coca-Cola.

For my part, I loved carnivals. I always brought a bit of pocket money, and usually I could coax an extra dollar out of each of my parents. Although my lack of sporting prowess meant that despite years of trying, I never brought home a really respectable prize, I seldom returned without a bagged goldfish in one hand, a plate or vase in the other, a ham sandwich in my stomach and a dizziness in my head – leaving behind me a trail of cast-away nickels and dimes.

But I also loved carnivals for another reason. Like all children, I was eager to take everything apart to see how it worked, and to me a carnival was no different. I was given a rare opportunity to do this by the fact that C.E. was often called in to rig up the show's necessary wiring. As sorcerer's apprentice, I was allowed to run about carrying bundles of wire and canary-coloured light bulbs. I watched with ringing admiration as my own grandfather pursued his mysterious craft of connecting loudspeakers to poles, microphones to school-desks, and strings of lights to the trees. No one could have been prouder than me to see crowds of people with their faces lit and their music played by means of wires that I had helped to lay.

Harmony could not afford a Fire Department. Instead, the Community Club sponsored a two-night Festival in Floyd's meadow. The preparations were many and various, but volunteers were plentiful. Fore more than a week, the village women cooked and sliced whole hams, patted out hamburgers, chipped potatoes, polished kitchenware, sharpened knives and laundered aprons, tablecloths and dishtowels. Meanwhile, Club officers booked a few bands to provide the entertainment, shored-up the plank stalls and food stands, arranged for delivery of paper plates, cups and plastic knives and forks, and attempted to cleanse the meadow of cow pats. C.E. and I busily strung wires, hung speakers and tested lights, making everything tip-top for the big weekend.

At last the night came, and how strange it all seemed. At work, and now at play, how remote, how alien seemed all the adults that I knew. How altered were my constants, how distorted were my certainties. In the glittering yellow light of the lamps, C.E. was all smiles and laughter in the company of his friends, his mind and his attention unreachable to the claims of boyhood. My father, likewise ensconced in a group of after-shave-cloudy men, became someone foreign – a young man again, bad with stories, winking with humour, serious with plans. My mother too, grouped with old school chums, church choir singers and little league mothers, was carried far away on a tide of the singleness of adulthood. Even Dutch, my mentor in all things, was lost in the alternating cycles of the food stand. I was unable to speak to her or even gain her attention as she hurried from cash-taking to order-filling, from cooking to soap-suds-up-to-elbow work.

So I wandered about on my own. On the ridge behind me there was the sagging pale white back of Floyd's barn, its crooked roof cutting a jagged outline against the moonlit sky. Beside it squatted the little workshop where the Club met, and between us the low board fence of the farmyard. I climbed up two planks to look into the inquisitive round eyes of Floyd's cows, mystified at the noisy human invasion of their grazing rights. Holding out my hand in the darkness, I drew the attention of one young steer, that lifted his head and straightened his neck, trying to determine whether I was friendly and whether I brought food. There was nothing else here but the steamy cooked-grass smell of cattle-breath, the hum of flies, and the rhythmical whoosh of hairy tail against flank. Turning back, I skirted the edge of the festivities, and looked down at the stream that divided the meadow from the field with the baseball diamond. So much had happened here – yet night made all things indistinct. I could see nothing of the diamond except for the grey moonlight against the empty scoreboard. To my left was the log footbridge, and at my feet the crackling batter of the stream sounded invisibly. Looking back, how strange it all seemed: little islands of golden light and human voices teased by the dry herb-filled nightwind, all in the vaster darkness of the field. There was no danger and there was virtually no temptation. Like all gatherings of this sort, alcohol was taboo. Indeed, what other communities adopted on principle, we were forbidden by law. That is, ours was a 'dry' district, where the sale of liquor was banned. So the villagers and their neighbours mingled, forgetting their feuds, forgetting their labour, but never forgetting themselves.

And I joined them, preserving my detachment. Nothing is ever frank among people who gather at night, and I was no different. With vague dissatisfaction, I tried vainly to blend, merge or fold myself into the pages of the crowd, but I couldn't. I broke balloons, I threw wooden rings, I tossed nickels and I chewed a ham sandwich while listening to a band that played no song I didn't know. Yet I came to see how distinct, alone and separate everyone in this group stood from everyone else.

Before, I had known them all as a whole: working, eating, praying, even hating together. But now, all at once, this new context made each one single, each one alone. I too felt alone…

But the evening finished and I dreamt no dreams. There was nothing in my life to remind me of these feelings for more than a week, at which time I made a discovery. I had been playing a version of one-person catch with a rubber baseball and the workshop wall when the ball, for the thousandth time, took a bad hop and jumped the retaining wall at the bottom of the garden and landed in the honeysuckles. Mindful of snakes, I leapt in as always and was dragging my feet around the brown-spaghetti tangle of vines when my foot turned up a piece of blue plastic. It was in fact a document wallet issued by Farmers & Mechanics National Bank in Frederick. Inside, there was a dingy folded piece of paper, with a pencil-drawn map.

The blood pumped into my head like a geyser. I simply couldn't believe it. It *must* have been Sally Caxton's. My first instinct was to shout with jubilation and run into the house to tell my mother to put aside her apron as we were all rich now. But then I was seized with an awful panic. What if she didn't believe in it? What if no one did? Would such a hope of good fortune prove to be childish and land me face down in a pool of guffaws, or an even more bitter indifference? And so, without meaning to, I found myself grown-up enough to doubt the efficacy of my hopes and to recognise that in this world emotional secrecy is sometimes necessary.

So, I hid the map in my room and set about deciphering it in private. I turned it round and round, and held it under different lights, but the faint scratching became no clearer. I was convinced that the sketch of interlocked squares represented the fields and lawns around the farmhouse, and the fact that it was in a banker's wallet lent support to my belief that it was the key to the whereabouts of Sally Caxton's fortune. But try as I might, I could find no X, nor any thinly veiled symbol indicating 'look here for loot.' Though I struggled mightily to read this precious document, I got no further in unravelling the mystery.

Then one afternoon, as the pheasants crackled in the briars by the stream and the humidity blew like a wet curtain on the breeze, my father had a visit by old Clarence Farley. We were standing in the shade of the hollow apple tree. Moose was drinking a glass of homemade root beer that I had fetched for him from the house. I was always volunteering to bring him cold drinks regardless of the distance to the house, because on days like this when the sun made the earth smell like burnt leaves and spread creeping fires from the base of the neck to the temples, the coolness of an interior, however briefly enjoyed, was always as welcome as rain. Although guessing my motives – he generally rejected my offers in the hope that by doing so he was discouraging my latent tendencies to moral weakness – on this occasion I was allowed to go so that I might put a dressing on my hand. (In our continual efforts towards economy, Moose had thought it wise to use barbed wire leftover from fence repairs to mend the bean supports, with the result that the immense tensile strength of the wire when cut snapped, scoring my left hand badly.) As Moose drank his root beer, Clarence pulled in to ask about our prospective crops.

How do, Moose?

Hey.

At at boy uh yourn?

Yep.

How's em taters uh yourn?

Need rain.

Yeah. Ain't gohn git none oh.

Suwhat dey say.

Gonna have any ta sell?

Oh, myut.

Uh huh. How much ya reckin?

How many ya wunt?

Olh, 'bouta bushel er two.

Uh huh. Well, five dollarsa bushel.

What kinder they?

Kinn-e-beck.

Uh huh. You say um fer me, un I'll git um.

Arright.

Then things took a more interesting turn. Clarence rubbed his unshaven chin and pushed back his straw hat.

You gittna Dawg-Walman's house done nen?

Welp, wer gittin nare.

I usta do work ferrer yunno.

Didja?

Yep.

Wudja do?

Mosly heavy stuff ferrer. Diggin inaw.

Now this was my chance, and I took it:

Ever bury anything…?

At first he couldn't have looked more surprised if I had spat on him. Boys simply *didn't* speak up to their elders, let alone virtual strangers. He thought for a moment, weighing up the options, deciding at last that the story merited telling, regardless of the listeners. His damp, mossy brown face widened into a grin, and his green eyes twinkled. He lifted up an old vinegar jug, full of clear corn liquor distilled up in Spruce Run, to wet his whistle. Putting his cracked and calloused hand on a fence post, he looked straight at me.

Shur did. Usta berry em god-damn dogs awl la time. Sep air wuz once was strange inn. Shad me down one mornin an said air was a biggol dog atad upin died un she wandid im burred. I said, 'Whar ya wun im? Up inna field back air?' An she said, 'Naw, thissis a special un. Ni wun im inna garden back yeer.' 'Wool,' I says, 'Whatnee ell you wanna digupta gardin fur?' An she din say nuthin'. So I says, 'You jis show me the dawg so I know ow bigta make the hole,' an she got funny. 'Naw Clarens,' she said, 'I ain'ta gonna. He's a real big ole feller, ni wunna real big old, ni wunnit deep. Six feet deep.' Ni said, 'Wull, fees at big, hown na shit you gwona gid eem in na ole?' She says, 'Doln you warry non 'bout dat, nat's my bisnis. You jis dig at ole.' So, I dugger. God-damn six foot olen six foot wyud. Ni sez, 'You shurr yuh doln wan me to burr at dawg en?' An she says, 'Nossir, I'um shurr. Neuw jis git on olmen lee me be.' Suh I wen olm. Wull, nex day I wen rounan, dohlncha know she'd fillt in nat ole gawd-damn thing! Wull, I nerer seen nuthin lyuhk it. An she wuz real liddle like. Swo I recken, wull, know what a say…

He looked portentously at my father, who said nothing. So I offended again.

Where *exactly* was this hole…?

He got serious and gave Moose directions. I listened, dry-mouthed, and pictured the entire plan.

I was astonished at my father's complete show of indifference to this scarcely veiled suggestion that a fortune lay buried in his vegetable patch. Clarence, his transaction complete, left us. It was then that I realised why my father was a good poker player. Although he said nothing on the subject, I could see he was plainly agitated.

By the following morning, the die was cast. As luck would have it, the lettuce patch had had its day, and the spring onions and carrots were already over. The day dawned hard and clear, with a sky damp and fresh as a new cornflower. There was a mouth-watering coolness in the shadows, making every muscle loosen in anticipation of a fine dry day. My parents and I were up early. After a review of Clarence's directions, we settled on the spot, and Moose set-to with a will. The first part of the digging, through the light soil used for more than a century and a half to grow food, went very smoothly. Our energy was high and there was no cause to expect anything. Still, I looked closely at each spadeful, ready for a stray coin or fragment of a greenback. I listened intently, anticipating the chink of spade against strongbox, or the clunk of a wooden chest, or even the crunch of a quart jar.

But there were no sounds except the grating of stones and the dull heavy rush of soil over soil. Sadly, very sadly, we realised that the earth had the appearance of never having been disturbed at all. Hours of sweaty exhausting labour had given no riches and settled no dreams. But still, it had suggested several things and proven at least one. Either we had been taken-in (which wasn't really likely) or Clarence's memory was incomplete or fuddled with moonshine, or Sally had in fact buried a dog. But what we knew for certain was that, like the farmhouse itself, desire and illusion, need and imagination, can combine to make the improbable worth a little faith. And ready to laugh at ourselves, we lost none of that faith.

CHAPTER EIGHT

Sixteen Tons

Hard as ice and hot as a welder's flame, the August sky lays a hand upon your shoulder. Pressing like wet fingers, the humid wind draws down and runs up your neck and into your hair. As you walk through the funnel of pines that rests against the hillside above the Mary House, you have to pull tightly at small uneven breaths as the changing weight of perfume-rich air enfolds you. There are no sounds except for your knees against the leaning silver-green foxtails, and your feet in the plush of bread-coloured pine-needles. Sometimes, a stiff dry ping-hizz of a grasshopper bounces off you, leaving a trail of 'tobacco juice.' The birds have hidden themselves against the swelter, and not a human sound disturbs you. A storm is coming and an invisibly complex world steadies itself with tense alertness. For hours in the growing quiet white flakes of cloud have piled up in the void over South Mountain. The old-timers, tasting cold water in the air before sunrise, know that a cruel and powerful tumult is brewing, and will arrive before sunset. As the white flakes pile to form a mountain in the sky, their base pushes lower to the earth which, like a burning fire-brick, scorches them to a cindery black. Hours pass, and in the plague-silence of the afternoon the mountain of shadows detaches amid the faint echoes of distant thunder, groaning like torn damp wood, and filling the chest cavity with an aching hollowness. Slowly, echoes re-echo, and you have a taste of warm steel under your tongue. The atmosphere levels into a thickening yellow, and the pressure of stillness runs through your joints like sand. The thunder grows, each rumble as stern as iron chains falling from a great height. As you sit down on the unpainted, age-blue bench on the Mary House porch, a tinkling of small leaves fringes the shade around you. Without real gradation, the breeze is stronger, and heat-ruined branches of the walnut trees shake loose and clack downwards on to the roof, the iron bridge and the stream below. A trembling whirl of shadow-over-shadow runs towards you, and the gongs of thunder begin to overlap. As your face dries utterly in the stinging wind, the first heavy spoonsful of rain smack on to the road, raising startled columns of dust. The drops bang harder, bulleting into the empty briar rose, ricocheting off the tin roof, bouncing in little pills from the surface of the stream. The thunder connects now, but the rain does not speed. The air, wallowing and gloomy, purple as a bruise, swings about noisily, stitched with rain. At last the tearing and shriving of the skies draws closer, and the glittering indigo sprays of lightning pierce the horizon. Like geysers of molten metal, the flames pour downwards through the cracked black clouds. The rip-bang of the near-misses shakes the ground under your feet. For the next ten minutes, all the dangers of the world surround you. Fire and flood co-mingle to wrap you in thrilling vulnerabilities. So charged is this moment with uncertainty that the passing hinge of the storm awakens you to a happiness lost. Though the pounding of the rain lingers, the crashing stones of thunder now fall behind your back. All sounds have joined into a single death, sweetened now by a jasmine-white glint of light and the raisiny taste of clear air. As the rain thins into a pattering splash, the tentative voices of birds rise up from the pines and honeysuckle banks surrounding the Cider Press. Within minutes, a chorus is joined and the air is enlivened with a lush prayer of thanks, as moving as the spectacle of a high-summer storm.

Twice, in summers long past, lightning struck the farmhouse. On the first occasion, as the afternoon wore away, Dutch was on the front porch busily working to catch-up on a backlog of laundry built-up during the harvest. Ignoring all the signs of the impending storm, the wringers ground on and the water sloshed in the tubs. While the heavy drops pounded against the pepper-black earth of the flowerbeds, and the shrill crack of thunder vibrated against the windowpanes, she raced on to gather in her work and to empty the rinse-water down the drains. All at once there was a piercing whistle, and the bang of a thousand rifles as a white strip of lightning leapt on to the northern gable, ran down the tin roof, followed the iron downspouts, and made a hideous arc into the swirling laundry tub, pouring itself out on to the ground with the cascading water. All the while, Dutch stood two feet away in utter bewilderment, only slowly regaining enough composure to run into the house without even the luxury of a scream.

The second time, four summers later, was a cruel mockery. The pattern of the storm was unvarying, and with the wisdom born of experience, Dutch secluded herself in the remotest corner of the kitchen. Creaking softly against the floorboards, the gentle swing of the Steiner rocker balanced a comforting melody against the wild fury of the storm. My mother, then a girl of six, sat on the floor watching Dutch mend an apron. As the violence of the storm surrounded them, Dutch finished her last stitch and laid her work in her lap. Just as she was reaching for a pair of scissors that hung on a hook by the window overlooking the grape arbour, lightning struck the southern gable of the house. This time it followed the newly installed lightning rod and plummeted down along its heavy wire towards the huge iron stake buried in the flowerbed. But along its way, the shock was so great that it snapped all the metal utensils off the wall, sending the whirling scissors on a two foot spiral where they finally gouged out a part of Dutch's upper arm, leaving a scar she bore the rest of her life. Then, with a child's lack of compassion, Jane ran up the two flights of stairs to the attic, which she found cloudy with blue smoke and reeking of brimstone. (Still, we were lucky – a farm one field away from ours was struck nearly every summer, often having trees split or cows exploded...)

For me, the storms of that summer were dramatically apposite. School started again in only one month, and I was in turmoil. In the months since moving to the farm, I had aged rapidly into an individual. I had learned to work hard, sleep deeply, eat lightly and relax as often as possible. I had learned to hope for much, expect little, trust people and doubt things. Most importantly, I had gained self-reliance – the one true blessing of a childhood spent in the countryside. Now, with so much to savour, my heart ached with the knowledge that I lacked a companion who, from having shared similar experiences, might share my emotional eminence. Therefore, taking inspiration from the wars in the heavens, I did what all sensible boys do: I resolved to fall in love.

The finding of an actual love-object proved to be no real obstacle. I made a mental calculation of the suitable candidates within my range of experience, and at last settled upon a girl I had known for more than two years. I tried to remember whether I had ever spoken to her, and finally decided that on the balance of probabilities, I had. My next chore was to set about making myself worthy.

I made poetry my means of doing this. Throughout the rest of that month, I painstakingly re-wrote all of the songs I knew. Every free moment I had was spent in replacing the lyrics of popular tunes with woeful ballads of my own making. Like an August sun breeding mosquitoes over stale water, my fertile pen multiplied its achievement exponentially through the passing weeks. Decades later, I found that these summer extravagances numbered 250 lyrics. Thus when school started that September, my arsenal of romantic utterances was fully prepared.

Meanwhile, the quotidien affairs of farm life carried on as a kind of comic sub-plot to my lofty undertaking. For one thing, having now birthed and weaned their calves, our own and our neighbours' cows got flirty. Through no fault of my own, I was made a reluctant spectator to these operatic spectacles of bovine courtship. Despite the violence of the summer storms, the intensely dry August sun had drunk up much of our smallest stream, and the cattle had to be moved frequently from field to field. Always recalcitrant on a hot afternoon, passion did little to improve their spirit of co-operation. As a result, my work on their behalf took on several new dimensions. First, mindful of snakes, I had to dip under the high magenta towers of the poke bushes, and see whether the small stream was running. Not fully cured of my first obsession, of course this also meant inspecting sandbars on the off-chance of finding a gold nugget. If the stream was running – not just standing in steaming pools, but actually running – I could return to the shade of a tree somewhere and dash off a few quatrains. But if the water wasn't moving, I had to find my sun-drunk charges and escort them over three fields to the largest stream, which itself bordered a pasture too small for continual grazing. Led by the hum of flies and the switch-swatch of tails, I could always expect to find them in a cool dense jungle of undergrowth, grassy breath, and the boiled pottage of fresh faeces. Rousing them to their feet could take a few minutes and, despite its strict prohibition, the temptation to hurl a stone or two at them was always strong. Gradually, a dim familiarity with the situation began to settle on them, and they obliged me, marrying their will to mine and allowing themselves to be led to the goal of fresh water. I remember even at the time being impressed by the docility of creatures, each of whose weight and strength was at least ten times my own, that allowed themselves to be force-marched for half a mile in the midday sun, marshalled only by a small boy who lacked all true incentive.

Anyway, every few days the head-count I made of them came up one or two short. On these occasions, I had to shut the cows I could find into the small pasture with the stream, while I sought their companions. Now a cow gone AWOL is not as easy to find as you might imagine. For one thing, when the mood strikes them, they can force themselves through the tiniest gap in a fence, dragging their immense leathery bulk unflinchingly against the barbed wire. My problem was to find which gap had been the scene of the most recent exit. For this, I turned Tuscarora. I began with an attentive patrol of the fences nearest to the spot where I had found the others, looking for tell-tale signs of escape. These signs might be loose or wobbly posts, stones tumbled off into the grass, crushed branches or battered weeds or briars. The real giveaway was a tuft of wiry hair on a stretched piece of barbed wire. Day in and day out, the number of these tufts increased, but I kept a mental diary of where and when I found each, so that any new find could be registered instantly as the latest. Once found, I climbed through the same opening, keeping my eyes and ears open for some sign of the fugitive's whereabouts. Sometimes in the distance there might rise the demented throaty scream of a coitus-crazed bull. In these dangerous cases I immediately abandoned the search and sought adult help. But more often than not, I simply looked around for the hoof-beaten paths that were sure to lead me to the gossipy, rowdy little herd where our own stray would be prancing provocatively among, or mounting shamelessly upon, our neighbour's beasts. Once found, the escapee usually would resign himself/herself to being led homeward peaceably, albeit with a mysterious and sly look. Often they would be content with no other return journey except to smash once again through the fence they had originally crossed. While this didn't bother me – in fact, I liked it as it saved me the trouble of a long walk through gates and around crops – Moose frowned on it. This was because it was the job of the offending cow's owner to mend any fences that his cows had damaged. By summer's end, our fences looked like the pallisade walls of Andersonville prison, and our wire consumption kept the Pittsburgh mills turning.

We hatched a number of plans to try and get round the August water crises. Our back porch, which for some reason that I cannot remember was left without a rain-gutter, formed part of an interesting experiment. By mid-morning, as the clouds began to gather in portentous lumps, we collected every bucket we owned and lined them up in a long expectant row. The number of these buckets was sufficient to form an unbroken chain for the porch's entire twenty-five foot length. When the inevitable downpour started there was a raucous batty-batty-batter as tiny streams, like Andean waterfalls, jumped from roof to empty buckets. Gradually these streams turned to rivers and the rattle of drops was replaced by a constant drabble of water into water. If the storm was of typical fruitfulness, we could net about twenty half-bucketsful. I could then carry these over the short level walk to the barn's watering trough, under the grateful eyes of the herd.

But of course this bounty was unpredictable. What we needed was an open source of fresh water as reliable as our own well, and in a place reasonably convenient to the livestock. Such an opportunity appeared to reside in a marshy patch of ground about five yards to the right of the farm lane separating our field of potatoes from the small pasture bordering the stream. Every old-timer in the village spoke with confidence of the powerful springhead that lay somewhere in this sweaty, air-curdling, dragonfly-launching morass that stayed wet through summers when even the fish in Middle Creek had to swim sideways just to stay wet all over. Our only trouble was how to spot the exact point where the spring surfaced.

You see, springs are imperiously temperamental. It's no wonder that the Greeks believed that they were the habitations of peevish and unpredictable divinities. Having been a part of a working party of two charged with the task of finding one, I too came to believe that the place was somehow sacred and infernal. Under a pitiless blood-drained sun, capable of giving a reptile heat-stroke, I crept around in knee-deep – and when I slipped, waist-deep – water that smelt of last summer's stewed lettuce and was regularly patrolled by squadrons of top-gun mosquitoes. My job, among the more ludicrous in my chequered history as a farm boy, was to move about without disturbing the water (?), keeping a close eye out for the tiny puckers on the water's surface that might indicate that the water was being pushed upwards at just that point. I was not to be misled by the little gasps of noxious fumes that fermenting weeds sent bubbling to the top, nor by the obvious (!) low spots where water was simply draining away.

After more than an hour of being subjected to this murky boiling, with my ears humming to the tunes of insects rich with my blood, and so dizzy that only the threat of imminent extermination in Davy Jones' Locker kept me standing upright, I was convinced that a pattern of three six-inch chain-like self-repeating ripples marked the site of the god's lair. Pushing a stick into the mire, I whispered a few words of gratitude for my deliverance.

But my sojourn on dry land was, alas, to be but a temporary one. With our target clearly marked, my father made it our next task to gather together a fine pile of flat stones with which to house the newly-discovered spring. These flat stones came predominantly from our own dry stream bed, and we hauled them by the cartload to the nearest piece of terra firma adjacent to their destination. Ironically, many of the stones had once been part of my maritime engineering projects, and I had a secret desire to see whether our four-footed dam-busters would carry out their work on this new project with anything like their former skill.

With the stones in readiness, work began in earnest. Although we started at that hour when a feather's-weight of dew still lay in the long shadows under the elm trees, the sun was already powerful enough to penetrate bluntly into our skulls, making all thoughts a blank. We started by shovelling the vegetable muck away from an area about ten feet across. Although the smell was of cosmic proportions and lay like a worm on the soft flesh above the hard palate, I was relieved to see that after an initial 'scrape' of earth about a foot deep was removed, the ground was somewhat firmer everywhere except for a circle three feet in diameter around my marker. At this level, most of the light mushiness in the soil disappeared, and it resolved itself into a blue-veined butterscotch clay. Slowly and painstakingly we opened up a funnel of earth six feet across at the top, narrowing to just over three feet at the bottom. Every few spadesful we stopped to check our progress. Sure enough, while we watched, a little mouth or two would gradually open up in the clay, and the hole filled with water.

By this time there was no longer room for us to work side-by-side, so I was put in charge of bucketing out the water. This was a much more slowly-paced occupation, and it gave me plenty of opportunities to observe the world I had invaded. Sitting wearily in the mud, I became a spectre to the curiosity of passing dragonflies. One by one they came along, hovering in confusion, no doubt with pity and shame for my appearance in comparison to their own vibrant turquoise and black-winged elegance. There weren't any flies – presumably the frogs had eaten them. Likewise, bees and wasps were unlikely to risk soiling themselves in this unwholesome jungle. I must admit that I was somewhat dismayed to find that I was no longer delectable to the mosquitoes. Perhaps, I smelt off.

Anyway, what I found most amazing were the creatures from the Land that Time forgot. Several long blades of grass were weighed down with spittle-like clusters of larvae. Black beetles, as round and hard as nickels, sprang out of the mud and crashed angrily into the surrounding frontier. But most spectacular were the lizards. Now as far as I, and indeed anybody else in the village knew, there were no lizards on Catoctin Mountain. Yet, like the stuff of legends, from under the occasional spadeful of mud and clay, a wiry four-legged runner, between four and six inches long and the colour of uncooked pork, leapt out for its maiden voyage in the clear light of day.

At last, with the turkey buzzards circling wistfully above our feverish heads, my father called quits to the digging and I began to pass him stones. When the business was done, we had formed a six-foot stone cylinder in the earth. To our immense relief, the subject of our labour gradually filled with four feet of greeny-brown water that siphoned itself off down a stone-lined trough and into a deep ravine that finally connected to Little Catoctin Creek. By the next morning, the water was clear right to the bottom, where three little mouths opened and closed rhythmically, singing out streams of cool fresh water. Frogs sat robotically on the stones, or paddled across the surface of the pool, and, most importantly, cows drank deeply.

All was blissful until the angry sprites returned. A week after its completion, our little Ovidian dell began to cloud over. The cows stopped drinking at once. Within a few days, the water began to have a fermented tang, and the little mouths at the bottom hushed, making only an occasional murmur. To make matters worse, a patch of ground about thirty yards to the right, and once of comparable firmness, began to soften rapidly. Thus matters rested.

Well, it didn't take a civil engineer to realise that the springhead we had so laboriously housed, not liking its new accommodation, simply packed up and took to the open road. Perplexed and angry, my father decided to fall back upon the resources of technology, and re-engage his old friend with the JCB. Blinded by his determination, he was also deaf to any advice that suggested that these elusive water maids ought to be wooed and not bullied. A week later, a green-grey cloud of stench hung over Harmony, as our once verdant marsh was transformed to a seething copy of the Somme. In some respects, the goal was reached: the spring was, after a manner, contained. Unfortunately, no spirit trapped by an armlock is likely to look upon its besetters with favour, and ours was no different. The water ran, true enough, trickling prismatically from out of its smooth concrete cell, and washing musically along the stones. The pink lizards, stunned by their brief exposure to the open air, sank once again into their sedentary lifestyle. But still the achievement, however glorious, was in the long run futile. In his zeal to outwit Nature, Moose had lost sight of the fact that he had gained mastery of a spring that now bubbled forth less than a hundred yards away from a stream that never failed. Our cows, always in sympathy to the wider rhythms of their world, preferred to spend the rest of the summer drinking from the ice cold eddying waters of the creek, where they could sup freely and cool their hot tired hooves. For my part, I managed to disguise the depredations under a rich tangle of reedy cat-tails – a crop I singlehandedly introduced to Harmony through having picked a dozen ripe seed-pods from a mountainside pond, and scattering the downy seeds over the stagnant water.

Alongside this work, we had engaged the JCB for one further exploit. This was to rend a deep gash in the embankment separating the two levels of vegetable patch and orchard. Here, about forty feet from the smokehouse, Moose planned to build a snug cave in which to store the tremendous crop of potatoes that lay in waiting below the farmhouse garden. Once again we brought cartload after cartload of flat stones from the ruinous walls, stream beds and rubble heaps that dotted the farm. My memories of that August are tinged by the sensations of being either squashy and reeking with khaki-cream mud, or parched with the bone-meal dust of stone-masonry.

Never having built a stone structure of this scale with unshaped materials, my father worked slavishly under the torch-like skies to master this new art. The walls rose slowly amid the streams of sweat and glaring exhaustion of a man confident of his abilities, yet working under the knowledge that he is racing against a clock. Soon, very soon, the potato plants would wither, crushed by the tremendous weight of the cindery-dry air. After that there would be an interval of a few weeks before other crops would demand to be harvested. And then, the crippling first frosts of autumn would threaten to destroy the fruit that lay in readiness, as well as making the ground unworkable.

So we worked like fiends. Too small to mix cement in any quantity, I carried water and sand by the bucketful, and mortar by the bag. I carried small stones, hobbled medium-sized ones, and dragged or pushed large ones. I loaded hod after hod of mortar, to be ready when Moose needed them. All the while, both of us bore on with mouths full of grit and aching limbs. For me, the most dramatic moments came with the actual stone-cutting. Awkwardly formed stones had to be re-shaped, corners smoothed, or lumps knocked away by two hands, a hammer and a chisel. The drama lay in the fact that we had only one pair of safety glasses, and they remained firmly on the nose of the chief operative. My own safety lay in hiding myself in a remote corner until the chink-chank of the business ceased. As I bowed my head, the air filled with dangerous projectiles. The randomly mixed types and quality of stones added a further dimension to this. Sometimes a blow by the hammer was answered by a dull muddy shuffle as soft rounded particles crumbled away. Other times the stones were so hard that they failed to respond at all, until with a near-silent hunch, they simply dropped in two. Often enough though, chisel cuts ended in a jingling chime, and circular razor sharp bits took wing. One such bit, borne of a dust-obscured quartz vein, whirled eight feet and buried itself in the fleshy part of my left wrist, giving me a scar I still bear.

How foolish we must have seemed to the twenty-eight barn swallows perched observantly in the seedling maple trees above us. As the evening sky widened to a shimmering peach sea broken by fuschia islands and swept by amethyst winds, our orange-throated, cream-breasted patrons took pity on our miserable condition and took turns trying to divert us towards life's pleasures. One at a time, they hopped from their stations and soared fifty feet into the air, dancing wild silhouettes against a summer evening sky. From this height they plummeted in a stupendous free-fall, saving themselves only a few feet from the ground by a graceful arc of wings, each one returning amid the joyous shouts of his companions.

Days passed and the walls rose. Dumb and dizzy with labour, we suddenly and quite unexpectedly found the work completed. A hasty wooden ceiling was thrown up and criss-crossed with old steel fence-posts and square-wire fencing as makeshift reinforcement, before the whole structure was capped with concrete. When this dried, its ugliness was hidden by a mound of earth, richly seeded with grass. We fitted a heavy salvaged door to the front hole and built stacked and slatted bins alongside each inner wall. By month's end, we were ready for the first crop.

Certainly there was no time to be lost. The ripping August suns and humid nightwinds had reduced the once-proud rows of plants to a battered tangle of leopard-like stalks. Working delicately with rakes, we twined these withered vestiges into bundles as best we could, piling them at the field's end. As far as possible, we aimed to leave a stubbly row sufficient to mark the outlines of the narrow paths for the tractor's wheels. As the time drew nearer, we also collected our battery of buckets, including the rainwater pails from the back porch, along with an extensive range of bushel-basketry. These baskets, all slightly different, were of two main varieties. There was the short, wide clothes-basket type, bound by jaunty red or green bands, or there was a very tall conical variety, narrowing to only a foot across at the bottom. Each one had its advantages for someone of my diminutive calibre. The low model could be dragged without falling over, while the skinny ones could be wheeled about against my chest. It was impossible for me to lift either sort when loaded, and in any case, their single design-fault of wire handles made them treacherous to my boney fingers. My one real hope of carrying anything lay with the single example of a stainless steel two-gallon bucket generally used for carrying clear water, but on this occasion forced to join its five-gallon fellows in the emergency.

When the big day came at last, word got round the village almost faster than we heard it ourselves. Out of sight and out of earshot, on the sunny levels of their back gardens or in the cool shade of their front porches, our neighbours had been discussing the advent of this crop for no little while. Throughout the day, singly or in groups, they came, old and young to take up a bucket or two and empty all or part of a coffee-coloured ditch of its stock of fresh tubers. For everyone there was a spontaneous flood of lemonade and root beer, and most left with at least a small addition to the night's supper.

For us, the day began with the early morning drying of the dew. With the roadside entrance to the field blocked by our pick-up truck full of buckets and baskets, Moose brought the tractor the long way around from its home and in the barn, behind the workshop, past the orchard, over the meadow and along the old lane beside our ingloriously housed spring. As always, I rode on the back of the tractor, standing on the steel implement hitch. Swinging on either side of my hips were the steel arms of our new potato-plough, designed and built by Moose himself. This plough consisted of a re-shaped antique steel gang-arm, carefully mounted on to an angle-iron frame. On either side were long hand-shaped walnut-wood handles to be used to steer the whole apparatus along the row. In the centre was the polished silver-bright spade-type share, upon which hung our success or failure.

As we swung into the field, under the uncomprehending gaze of the cows, the duty roster was formed. I was to take the driver's seat. (Well, actually I had to stand, as it was the only way I could see the ground in front of the tractor.) My job was to propel us as slowly as possible, while keeping us as near as possible to the centre of each row. I had to be extremely careful mid-row to allow for those little crookednesses that make life worth living (otherwise the tractor would crush the potatoes), and at row-ends to go as near as possible to the boundary fences (to get as much as possible from each row). Meanwhile, my father would walk, or rather hobble, behind me, steering the plough by means of the two wooden handles, and controlling the plough's depth by his body-weight.

With my mother watching anxiously from the shade of the hollow apple tree, bucket in hand, we started on our first row. Because of the tractor's fairly wide turning radius, our plan was to make a series of large interlocking loops, starting at the top of the field, then going roughly a third of the way down, then to the bottom, then between the first two, and so on. For my part, this also gave me a bit of variety, as the soil colours varied dramatically across the width of the field, and I was curious to see how the crop fared in different places. Moose believed that the shadows cast by the walnut trees that lined the patch alongside the farm lane would stunt the produce in this area, but I was sure that the deep chocolatey brown humusy-light soil here would grow the biggest spuds of all.

Moose lifted the nose of the heavy plough and rested it about two feet behind the stubbly remains of a potato stalk. Shaking loose the muscles in his arms and legs, he looked up at me, grasped the handles, and nodded. His face was both determined and apprehensive. As ordered, I let go the clutch, and we jerked forward.

Although I did my best to concentrate my mind on holding the machine to the line, keeping the huge wheels between the crowded rows, I could not resist looking backwards. I had two motives for this. For one thing, I was eager to see the first fruits of our long labour on this field. But more importantly, I was shocked to see what the chore of handling the plough actually meant to Moose himself. Singly or in rolling clusters, the glistening white potatoes tumbled out, like odd-sized peas from a vastly long pod. Some were as small as a hen's egg, others bigger than a croquet ball. Although there were thousands of them, I looked on them with a child's greed-amid-plenty, wishing there were more. I felt a covetousness towards the world's whole potato supply. I envisaged a mountain of potatoes as a source of wealth and empire. And then I realised that it would be me had to pick all these riches up. I suddenly felt very sorry for myself.

But not as sorry as I felt for my father. Poor Moose. Although the tractor crept along at a snail's pace, every foot of ground was a punishment. With no wheels, springs or hydraulic slides, every stone sent a violent shiver up the plough handles and into his arms. The vibrations joined across his neck and shoulders, and his back and pectorals convulsed involuntarily. His lower extremities fared little better. Besides the plain struggle to keep upright while being yanked forward incessantly and vibrated ceaselessly, he had to stumble over ground that became uneven with instantaneous unpredictability. All of this he executed while holding the plough on the centre of the row, bearing down with his full weight, and trying to avoid squashing the produce. Within ten minutes of starting, his face was streaming with sweat. By the end of the first row he had reddened deeply and his cheeks and forehead were lined with plum-coloured furrows.

Not surprisingly, he called a temporary halt to operations. Weary and quivering, he carried the plough into line with our next intended row and rested while I let the tractor idle down. My mother was already at work on the row that we had finished, and Moose decided that we should keep one or two rows in hand so that as a group, there was always work to do. Accordingly, we ploughed another row. Being further down the field, the soil here was much softer and less stony, and the crop itself was larger. This time, without waiting, Moose shouted to carry on, and I chose a row mid-way between the other two. When it was finished, and the ground was littered with gleaming new potatoes, he paused. Visibly shaken but with a determination bordering on mania, he ordered me to turn the tractor down to its lowest idle, and grab a bucket. He did likewise, and we started to gather in the exposed crop.

Now this was the first time that I had ever harvested vegetables on this scale. True enough, I had helped to gather bushels of French beans, sweetcorn, lima beans and peas, but that was comparatively light and comparatively clean work. This time I felt an uneasiness akin to fear as I looked around at the hundreds and hundreds of grubby pearls that had to be picked up one by one, then lugged by the bucketful, and heaved by the baskets. But my musings were cut short, as my father's voice boomed out ahead of me. He was already twenty feet along in his row, and I had a lot of catching up to do. The first thing that occurred to my lazy mind was to start at the far end of the field – that way, as my bucket got heavier, I also got nearer to the depot under the hollow apple tree. And so I set-to quickly, losing sight of my hands under a film of soft earth. Within minutes my bucket was full, and I had gone practically nowhere. I lumbered this load towards the tree, stretching my arm at least an inch in the process. My plan was to have a bucket in reserve as soon as each one filled up, then, looking as pathetic and helpless as possible, to persuade one of my parents or neighbours to collect them for me. I only succeeded partially in this, but at least they too began to drop empty buckets around the field.

So in twos or threes the rows were finished. Or so I thought. The pick-up truck was loaded with full baskets and every shady corner was packed with brimful buckets and mounds of potatoes. Row upon row had dried emptily in the sun, our arms were numb and our backs sore. Poor Moose was quaking and feverish after his exertions, and I felt confident that our harvest was one of rich abundance. But then something shocking happened. Without waiting for me to join him in the cab – which anyway was full of potatoes – my father called out for me to meet him at the waggonshed. As ordered, I trudged up the hill and climbed over the fence. By the time I got there, Moose was already pouring out the contents of the baskets on the shed's earthen floor. As I dragged each basket to the doorway, he seized them and added them to the growing mountain within. So far so good. But then he started to re-load all the baskets and pails on to the truck.

But aren't we finished?

Huh. 'Bout half.

Confused, I rode along back to the field. All the rows were ploughed. Moose started up the tractor and lined the plough up once again with the first row.

Whatcha waitin' for boy?

We've done nat one.

We only done na middle.

What he meant to do was to plough each row twice more: once to the left, and once to the right. This way we could gather in all the potatoes that had grown at a distance from the plant-centres, as well as those missed because of the crookedness of our rows. My first thought was that this meant little enough to me. After all, I only had to steer, then pick up the few scattered strays that so much work might uncover. My real worry was that my father already looked dead tired, and two more complete ploughings might finish him. Luckily, the ground in each row was already a bit softer after the first pass, and the shocks of our second outing were less severe. Still, he had to tense himself quite firmly to keep the ploughshare against one side of the open furrow, when gravity would have preferred it to coast along the bottom.

My surprise and dismay came when I saw how many hundreds of potatoes appeared after the first right-hand re-plough. Once again, the same stages of three-rows-in-hand-then-gather-in were repeated over the field. These were then delivered in succession to the waggonshed floor, together with many of the former lot that had been piled in the shade.

At last we returned for the third and final re-ploughing. When this was completed and added to our now Himalayan scale pile, I thought happily that the day was done. Our neighbours had all gone home and the sun sat lowly on a spongy silver-blue cloud. My mother and I were exhausted, and my father appeared even to be walking with difficulty. When we returned to the field, I thought it was merely to collect the buckets and to close the gate. But no, there was one more thing to do. Faster than I could say, 'You've got to be kidding!' Moose unhooked the plough and reversed up to the harrow. Dry-mouthed, I watched as he sprang down and hooked it up, then set off at a comparatively fast pace. Round and round, pass after pass he went over the field, blending the once-distinct rows into a smooth even flow of rippling earth. Behind him, plain as the blisters on our hands, lay hundreds more potatoes. Most of these were small ones, but he wanted them all. I realised then that the momentary flash of greed I had felt at the outset, had, in the course of his day of back-splitting labour infected his judgement. Dutifully, but not without protest, we gathered them all in.

Finally, a merciful darkness fell. A darkness that was sweet to me, in part, because it thwarted my father's wish to sort the harvest before bedtime. That night, having soaped myself with excessive thoroughness, I slept the sleep of the dead. The next morning, barely able to lift my arms, I finished a breakfast of ham and corncakes, only to learn that in order to ensure the high quality of our saleable goods, I was to assist in sorting the produce, transporting it, and stowing it safely in the cave.

I shall never forget the combined feelings of weariness, hopelessness and sheer inanity that I believed must be a daily assault on the sensibilities of potato sorters everywhere. My job was to wade through tubers piled as high as my head, and to extract any defective ones. 'Defects' included ones cut by the plough, squashed by man or machine, or dyed green by the sun. These ones themselves sorted into two further piles, with the cut ones being reserved for immediate home use. The sad little pile of remnants was given to a grateful family of pigs. Gradually, the sorted stock was wheelbarrowed around the farmhouse and stowed in the waiting racks. Immediate orders were filled directly from the floor.

And me? Bone-tired and somewhat grubby in spite of protracting dousing, I saw my summer holiday out with three platesful of the finest french fries I have ever tasted.

CHAPTER NINE

The Sweet By and By

September falls in golden fruit. Lumpy orange pumpkins as big as a man's head, freshly twisted from the vine, are piled on the front porch walls. Green-and-white-striped-curly-neck pumpkins – as every grandmother knows, source of the best-tasting flesh – litter the kitchen floor, ready to be baked into pies. And gourds, dozens and dozens of gourds…

We discovered these little gems quite by accident, and like all little gems, they are only useful in the aesthetic sense. The story begins with my mother. Jane was always a keen decorator with seasonally appropriate materials. In March, every vase, and half our water glasses, were filled with grape hyacinths, gathered from the huge purple pool of them beneath the apple trees. In summer, it was roses and lilies. But with the onset of autumn emptiness, she needed something colourful to brighten up our indoors. Serendipity led her to find some bargain packs of mixed gourd seeds. As per the instructions advising that gourds are climbers, she planted them where they would have access to a pattern of baler-twine lines to grow up. Unfortunately, these lines were already in use to hold up French beans. By September, the whole area was a kind of toyshop jungle. Long parallels of greenery hung fervidly with tropical-coloured striped and spotted globes, cones and other oddities. We brought them in by the bucketful. We gave them away by the bagful. I used the poorly marked and misshapen ones as grenades. Still, they flourished. The cats toyed with them. The dog sniffed them. I put them into obscure corners of the farm, hung them from trees, dried them, floated them, peeled them and took the seeds out, and generally did everything but ate them. They were our Triffids, and for a whole month they surrounded us. I loved them.

A more sustaining September crop was blackberries. Besides the usual hedgerow crop, there was a fierce tangle of them on the edge of

The Hollow. Generally, I was forbidden to disturb them on the very good grounds that the vines were haunted by chiggers. Chiggers are a kind of invisible insect that live among brambles and prey upon the unwary. They have a revolting habit of infesting berry-pickers who go about their work in complete innocence. They do this by boring little holes in their hosts' skin, laying an egg, and then dying. The result, not apparent until the next day, is a red bubous that itches worse than ten mosquito bites. If scratched, the sore leaks a clear pus that irritates the skin all around the affected area. I was once nearly driven insane by fifty-three contiguous welts. Anyway, a proper defence is to take several rags soaked in crenolin, and tie them around your midriff before setting out. The tarry, burnt sugar fumes of the crenolin are so potent that they keep off all insects.

Typical of my family, we brought home far more fruit than we could eat. So we decided to drink some. Using three of Sadie's crocks as containers, my father used a potato masher to squeeze six gallons of blackberries into a pulp. This was mixed liberally with sugar, covered with muslin, and put on a cool shelf in the larder. Within an hour the muslin was humming with gnats. Fortunately, the muslin layers were impermeable, and by the next morning a froth-gurgling fizz could be heard inside, and the air was charged with the mouth-watering violet-blue scent of fermenting berries. This lasted for two more days before Moose decided to curtail the process by straining the unripe liquor into empty glass vinegar jugs. I can still see them, sitting side by side along the cool white window sills – four glistening jugs of lather-capped purple, delicious and forbidden. Six months later, I was given a sip. My tongue burned at the unfamiliarity of alcohol, but my palate rocked in the warm jammy taste and honeyed aroma of an early autumn day.

The cooling weather tempted us to other pastimes. All spring and summer we had attended public auctions, adding to our range of tools in anticipation of the coming slaughtering season. With butchering time only six weeks or so in the future, we were nearly prepared. All we lacked were a few pieces of ironwork, which had throughout this time seemed disproportionately expensive. These pieces were only two in type, but we needed a fair few of each. One sort was the straightforward humble meathook. Without a quantity of these it would be almost impossible to get the work done. The second item, somewhat specialised, was a kind of long two-prong fork, used for extracting cooked meat from the huge kettles. Being small and portable, both fork and hooks had by this time slipped into the realm of 'antiques' and were priced accordingly. As a solution, Moose proposed that we make them ourselves.

To do this, we had bought a really fine forge and bellows at auction. The forge, probably of army origin, resembled a large and very sturdy steel barbecue, with three legs and a circular fire pan. Attached to one side was a contraption that looked like an upside-down hair-dryer with a crank. Despite its appearance, when cranked, this little contrivance was capable of raising a high gale almost instantly. Apart from a clean up with a wire brush, the forge was ready to use as soon as it was fireproofed. We did this by digging a deep hole in the largest of our two streambeds, and extracting the blue-veined toffee-like clay. We kneaded this to elasticity, and moulded it to fit the fire pan. When it was dry, we cured it with a slowly-intensified hardwood fire. Other supplies came piecemeal. We found a small shop in a village thirteen miles away that sold the appropriate type of coal. A limited quantity of forgeable steel came from a local Middle School whose vocational training included metalwork. C.E. loaned us his splendid anvil and two hardies (wedges for cutting hot steel), and we had two old pairs of tongs, a hammer, and bucketsful of cold water…

We set up our smithy in front of the waggonshed one Sunday after church. It was a crisp clear day, not too hot, and just right for experimenting. While the coals slowly reached a bright glow, my father cut the steel rods into useable lengths. Meanwhile I turned the bellows crank. In almost no time we were ready. Plunging the first workpiece into the coals, we watched wide-eyed, like children waiting for corn to pop. Moose, having worked briefly as a machinist in his youth, knew in principle what to expect. But the combination of homegrown ingredients, not to mention the necessity for success, made him a bit nervous.

A few minutes later and the steel was a glowing red-orange. Moose drew it from the fire, laid it on the anvil and struck a tentative blow. There was a softening squeeze and an answering dull ring as the metal remoulded itself into a slightly flattened shape. It worked. Painstakingly, and with ludicrous slowness, we worked on. I cranked away, and at intervals the steel was shaped into a delicate point that carefully curved round into a lethal-looking hook. Satisfied with this achievement, my father plunged his handiwork into the water, and it disappeared momentarily in a frying steam. One after another the hooks were shaped, each one showing the marks of individuality betokening the work of amateurs. I even made a few myself, labouring artfully over the precision of the points.

Flushed with these early successes, we started on the long forks. The plan was to flatten one end of the round steel rod, lay it neatly on the hardie, and split it slightly to form two tynes. These could then be shaped separately into two points. That was the plan. We had watched skilled blacksmiths do this many times. The reality was that our powers of observation were not as acute as we imagined they were. The end flattened nicely, but splitting it by hammering it down on to the hardie proved to be more of a challenge. The upturned chisel-point of the hardie must have been too dull, because the resulting cut looked like it had been worked by a diamond-toothed rat. Not worried, we thought this could be smoothed out by delicate hammering. We thought this right up to the moment when we tried to do it. The appearance did improve, but the lumpy burred surface would have made it impossible to use. We tried to make another fork altogether, but it resembled its forerunner exactly. In despair, Moose flattened the opposite ends of both forks, and resolved to finish their shaping with the combination of an electric grinder and a box of files. THIS autumn, to avoid shame, we would use borrowed forks.

On the following Monday, school started. The run-up to school week was always the same. On the last Saturday of freedom, my father drove me off six miles to the nearest barbershop. I liked going to the barber. This was before the days of unisex salons, and the concept of hairdressing for men had not yet settled in our neck of the woods.

The barbershop itself was on Main Street, just down from the General Store and opposite the Ice Cream Parlour. We didn't come to this town very often, sometimes for grain, or hardware, or fancy wood or tools, and Moose liked to prime my patience (and his own) with an ice cream. Center's ice cream was locally made and it was certainly the finest available. The approach was down a long open corridor between two houses, and across a small garden. Inside, there was the cold clean smell that ought always to accompany wholesome dairy food. The ice cream, hand-dipped in huge dollops from out of large crocks, was incomparable. It came in a selection of flavours that changed with the fruits of the season, and the whims of the owner. My own favourite was black raspberry. Glistening chalky-purple, it fell back the throat in a creamy smoothness fringed with the soft tang of fruit.

Having done my duty by the food, I was expected to behave myself well in the men-only company of the barbershop. One of the comforts of this man's world was its unchangingness. The spinning barber-pole, the ting-ting of the bell, the smiles of the white-smocked men, and the nods of the local worthies. The shop was run by a father and son team.

Morn', Peck.

Morn' Moose. Who's 'at young fella ya got weth ya?

'At's muh boy, Jawhn.

Naw it ain't! Nod as big as 'at, izzee?

We made ourselves comfortable on the wooden bench that ran along the pine-panelled walls. While my father got on with the gossip of the regulars (none of whom ever seemed to need a haircut) I got to grips with the 'funny pages' of the daily newspapers. Overhead, a tiny speaker carried the soft tones of Gordon Lightfoot, mourning the loss of the 'Edmund Fitzgerald'. In the mirrored bright light in front of us, work went on chatteringly. Hair was snipped and clipped, hot towels applied, lather spread, and brilliant razors sharpened on leather straps. Whenever a shave began, I watched dry-mouthed with awe. My father had a gift of one of Charlie Ford's razors secreted in the medicine-chest at home. Of course, I examined it occasionally, and it was the sharpest thing I had ever seen. But here, one man, working with great speed, would lay the lethal implement on the invisible neck of another and draw it about. Afterwards, there were more hot towels, then the air was perfumed with the musky-mint that distinguished old-fashioned ideals of masculine hygiene.

When my own turn came I could count on two things. First, it was a great opportunity to examine all of the fascinatingly shaped and coloured bottles, implements and contrivances that littered the cupboards around the mirrors. Some of these were certainly older than me. The second thing I could look forward to was,

Wullsir, ham uh shave tidday?

How I blushed in my manliness. No, not today.

When the scissors fell silent and the little broom had done its work, I bounded from the chair and waited by the curtain to the adjourning room. While I waited, my own barber would disappear through the curtain and take a small box down from a high shelf, holding it down to my eye-level. Inside, there was a nest of lollipops, from which I might choose one.

When Black Monday finally came, I presented myself to the world clean, fresh and trimmed, with a new shirt, new trousers, new socks and new shoes. At home, I had four more examples of everything except for the shoes. My main project on returning to school was to gauge the effectiveness of my summer of versifying. The problem was how to put my lyrics into the right hands. At last, I concocted a plan. Looking as thoughtful and woebegone as possible, I let my beloved know that I had written a number of ditties, which I intended to submit to a major music publisher (indeed, this was true). My problem, that which forced my vexed brows to huddle, was that a publisher would demand that my lyrics be submitted as a typescript. I, alas, could not type, and had no typewriter (this was only somewhat true). To my astonishment, she immediately volunteered to type them for me. So far so good.

Two weeks later, she returned the folder to me, with each poem neatly typed and centred. Although I showed both true and alternatively-motivated gratitude, there appeared to be neither love nor longing present in my beloved's eyes. Friendly as always, she appeared utterly oblivious to the impassioned persuasiveness of my metered appeal. In short, I remained mortal.

Grieving at my failure, I sought the advice of an older woman, whose own love affair I had watched from blossom to fruition. My sister listened attentively while I explained my predicament. By way of advice, she drew from her shelf a small grey-clad volume that was to change my life. It was a tiny, one-volume edition of Shakespeare's Complete Works, and crowded in tiny double columns near the back, were the sonnets. Night after night, literally, kneeling by my bedside as if in prayer, I studied them. Here was a mode that was sure to win favour.

Over the coming months I wrote 250 sonnets to an unimpressed sweetheart. Like all boys, I trusted in my own infallibility, and so persuaded myself that my real mistake had been in choosing the wrong girl. So I promptly chose another. For this new love, I wrote 200 more sonnets. Thinking back, the wonder is not that I wrote 450 sonnets, but rather that I stopped when I did. My reason for stopping was not a lack of inspiration – an ingredient I probably never had anyway – but more of an awareness of other possibilities. I made new friends, some of whom were bookish, and who made me gifts of other poets. I discovered Keats and Shelley and started to write imitations of them. I also copied Poe and Tennyson. One thing led to another, and soon I was reading Homer, Plato, T.S. Eliot and Yeats. Awash with culture, I bought a cassette of Beethoven's piano sonatas and drowned my romantic agonies in a rhapsody of fine tears. I even came to look forward to school trips to art galleries...

These discoveries were as new to me in spirit as they were in kind. My family's tradition in spiritual matters, like that of most of our neighbours, was harboured by the plain creed of the Brethren Meeting House. There were, in fact, two churches in the village, differing little in customs and practise. Indeed, they shared one cemetery and worked together on practically all temporal matters. The Lutheran Church, opposite the site of the old schoolhouse, was a red-brick structure with a tall pointed steeple, housing a single bell. Every Sunday at 8:55 this bell, the only one for miles in any direction, called the faithful in to worship. Inside, the tall hollow ceilings and walls were painted mint green, and the nineteenth-century wooden pews were a pale yellow. There was no stained glass or ornamentation, and the altar was framed by a simple wooden railing painted black. There was no organ or pulpit, but the snowy-bright light vibrated to the tones of a small upright piano placed in the far left-hand corner. This instrument was played by Black Label's 83-year old mother Pauline, who also chose the hymns and led the singing. She always sought to achieve an artful balance of music appropriate to the season. So around Independence Day, we heard,

My country, 't is of thee,
Sweet land of Liberty,
Of thee I sing.

And in September,

Bringing in the sheaves,
Bringing in the sheaves,
We shall come rejoicing,
Bringing in the sheaves.

On an average Sunday the congregation numbered about twenty-four adults and a dozen children. At Christmas and Easter, these numbers doubled. Seating was arranged in a very strict order: women on the left of the aisle, men on the right. There was no minister – none could be found willing to journey so far for such a small congregation.

Instead, the sermon was preached by C.E.'s cousin Maynard Ford. Maynard had no special training for this job, and he received no payment for his services. Every week he received a letter from the church administrators in Ohio advising him of the appropriate subject areas for the weekly sermon, together with the relevant sections of the bible to be drawn upon. He combined these ideas with a deep voice and a commanding presence, and so delivered some truly fine sermons. While he stood, or rather leaned against a pew, one row in front of his congregated friends and neighbours, Sunday school classes went on behind him. There were two of these. The very young children were attended-to by Pauline, who arranged them around a table near the altar. These children had their own collection plate, out of which they funded their own supplies. At the end of each collection, Pauline chirruped, 'God loveth a cheerful giver.' Three pews back from the front row, the early teens had their own class. The message here was to make the Gospels serviceable to the lives of young people whose bodies and worlds were rapidly changing. Being a group of unusually good singers, these teenagers were sometimes organised into a small choir, and belted out a hymn or two:

At the Cross, at the Cross,

Where I first saw the Light,

And the burden of my heart rolled away…

On Easter Sunday, all church attenders were given an orange and a china cereal bowl as a keepsake. Afterwards, they poured out on to the road outside to mill about amiably and wait for the arrival of the Brethren from up the road.

My own place of worship was officially named The Harmony Church of the Brethren, but usually the building was referred to as The Meeting House, and most often we were called Dunkards (or Dunkers). This latter name refers to our strange baptismal practice. Like the Lutheran, Brethren are baptised by total immersion. In our own local case, this spiritual transaction took place in a deep pool of Little Catoctin Creek, just above the Shultz Farm. But an important difference between our two denominations was that Lutherans fall forward into the water (as if embracing the act), while Brethren fall backwards (giving themselves up to faith). A fully-fledged member of the Brethren may take Communion. This is done by kneeling within one's pew as the Host is passed along towards you. The Host consists of yeasty homemade bread, to which you must help yourself. A moment later, and the Blood of the Eucharist follows in a tray of small plain cups, filled with sweet foxy blue wine. Communion is only offered at holidays and in emergencies.

My sister was married in the Brethren Meeting House on Church Hill, about four miles from Harmony. This lovely greenstone building is perched on a windswept precipice, surrounded by small rocky farms. The bodies of the dearly departed are interred across the road in a triangle of (comparatively) looser soil. Her wedding itself was a wintry evening affair, and the windows sparkled with the glow of candles. Only a handful of people were present, and I was privileged to sit in the front row. There was no organ and no bells. The groom, no longer in sandals, stood by the altar with his best friend, and shortly after he was joined by my sister, all in white satin and as fresh and welcoming as the first snowdrop. I joined in on all three hymns and listened attentively to the brief sermon. There was no register to sign, and in five more minutes, the young pair were matched.

Brethren funerals are similarly low-key affairs. I can recall one at the old Meeting House above Ellerton, on the way to Ford Fields. It was a cunningly warm spring day, and the Meeting House shone pearly white against a lime-green hillside. Like our own edifice, there was no steeple and no belfry, and the long low rectangular building was entered from the narrow end. Like its predecessors in the earliest days of the faith, there were two doors: one for women, one for men. I wore a blue jacket and tie and sat with my parents. Dutch, always tenderhearted, wept profusely. Practically all of the men wore jackets, but only a few wore ties. The women wore their Sunday best, and there was no taboo regarding bright colours. I recall splashes of red, orange, yellow and white particularly. What marked the women out as Brethren was their headgear. Every female present wore a tiny white pill-box of lace. This symbolised membership of the Brethren, and was required dress for any church function. Some women extended this duty to include all business transacted outside the home, but they were not obliged to do this. In summer, older women wore it in conjunction with their bonnets, and in winter, with their bandanas.

But if the Brethren were comparatively unexceptional in conducting their sacramental affairs, their style and verve showed best in temporal matters. Inside our own Meeting House, we had a few treasures. True, our oak pews were plain and unadorned, but we did have a luxurious red carpet down the centre aisle. I used to run about here with disrespectful abandon while my mother practised the piano accompaniment that she needed to know as leader of the choir. We even had enough room to house the choir in a recess right next to the altar. On the opposite side from the choir, there was a small organ. I only heard this machine in action a few times, as the congregation seldom included a competent organist.

Anyway, as far as I was concerned, the real work of the church went on in the cellar below. It was here, among a group of other children, that Florry Waterman taught me the names of the twelve disciples, and that the shortest verse in the bible is 'Jesus wept.' We coloured in worthy pictures of the patriarchs, used mucus-like glue and magazines to make collages of scenes from the Pentateuch, and wrote letters of goodwill to children in far-away places. All this while upstairs the lay-preacher (who was also Florry's brother-in-law) extolled the virtues of patience and kindness amid the chaos of the fleeting world. On sunny days, we ran about outside, playing hide-and-seek among the gravestones that identified our forebears. When the last hymn was over, and the preacher's hand was shaken, we sallied like hot water down the road to meet the waiting Lutherans, with whom we exchanged stories and baseball cards, before running on to The Corner's store-porch to buy a Coca-Cola and wait for the arrival of The Loafers.

For the most part, our holy days were like everyone else's. Christmas, for instance, saw a parade in front of the altar by terrified children, each condemned to recite 'a piece', usually in rhymes, on some noble subject. My own favourite day was Shrove Tuesday. Week after week the black-walnut signboard beside the altar recorded the passing religious seasons of the year, all of which were a complete mystery to me, 'Fourth Sunday of Advent'… Shrove Tuesday always came as a total and pleasant surprise.

When it finally came, I went along with Dutch to the large kitchen in the backroom of the Meeting House cellar. Here, while I sat on a plank-bottom chair, miracles of flour, yeast and sugar were worked. You see, among the Brethren, Shrove Tuesday is Kinkling Day. A kinkling is a kind of square, pillow-like hole-less doughnut. It is made with a rich, yellow flour, lightened splendidly with sieved potato, quickly fried, and dusted with confectioners' sugar. From the vantage point of my chair, I watched as about a dozen broad-backed, brown-armed women, all dressed in printed calico and with their white-net hats pinned in their hair, worked and chatted in utter friendliness. Huge wheaten-beige cannonballs rolled under their palms, were twisted and re-shaped. Home-grown potatoes were peeled, mill-bright tins of flour sifted, and the banter of gossip floated on the yeast-heavy air. At one end of the table, great planks of dough were cut into squares and piled on to plates. These plates went to the enormous black stove, where pans of dough sat proving overhead, and peeled potatoes boiled. In front of me, two or three at a time, the squares were plunged into the seething fat. A moment later and they tumbled on to the table, over a snowdrift of sugar. Cooled and frosted, they lay in baskets by the slit-like window, while nearby the Devil himself squatted, tempting a small boy to mischief.

For me, the Brethren existed as a community of friends within the 'larger' community of the village. These same women, and others too, often got together for quilting bees – sitting together, drinking tea, and stitching their quiet homely masterpieces. When anyone was born, or anyone died, they sent food and flowers by the basketful. Their daylight hours, too full by half already, were given to charity fundraisers like The Festival, or public auction concessions. The men also worked side-by-side to get in one another's crops, and to provide help to anyone too ill or grief-stricken to help himself.

Once a year the Brethren celebrated themselves. While other congregations held their harvest-home parties, the Brethren had the Love Feast. This was a large pot-luck party that included a few of the vestiges from the old faith. Hours were spent in preparing favourite dishes. There was homemade bread, salads and vegetables of every kind. There was fresh bean soup flavoured with ribbons of pink cured ham, corn-bread with honey-dark molasses, and jars of sweet pickle relish. There were hard-boiled eggs dyed red with beet-root juice, steaming drifts of hominy, and sausages hot with pepper and sweet with sage. There were milk-white cubes of pork tenderloin, the savoury buttered smoke of chickens grilled over a hickory fire, and the lush brandy-like fumes of rib-of-beef stew. Sweetened black cherries were piled in bowls, lard-heavy steam bubbled off pans of pot-pie (heavy noodles cooked in broth) and golden peach pies glistened in a frail crowd upon the table cloth.

When everything was set out, the party gathered around the long trestle tables arranged in the shade of the high locust trees. Everything was silent except for the rustling of feet – bare feet. You see, the whole congregation stood waiting for a benign signal from its elected preacher. When it came, with laughter and goodwill, each person knelt in turn to his neighbour, washing his or her feet in a pan of warm soapy water. When all were washed and hands were clean and dried, a new silence began. Above the smiling bowed heads a quiet voice, a voice of centuries-old gladness stiffened by generations of hard work, raised a prayer of thanks for another year of food and good fellowship.

With the prayer over, some serious eating began. Throughout the meal old friendships were renewed and certain special relationships re-affirmed. Each female member of the Brethren had a 'secret sister' with whom she could share the private trials and triumphs of her spiritual life. No one knows when this custom began, but it seems an apt recognition of the special burden carried by women whose daily routine was one of toil and isolation in the midst of a natural world that offered little consolation to the weary of heart. The whole evening ended as temperately as it began, with affections revitalised and new promises undertaken.

In all village affairs, skills are praised and talents move people to awe. Most honoured are the abilities to grow food, provide for a family's needs and foster a community of happiness. It is the practitioners of these arts who live in a village's memory, and it is these people it finds occasion to support and protect.

Our finest showcase of excellence in these fields was the Great Frederick Fair. For one week in September, the county town hosted a fantastic assembly of agricultural and household achievement. The sheer scale of the gathering of farming implements was renowned as among the largest and richest in the eastern United States. With this at its heart, there spread out around it an array of century-old exhibition buildings, tents and portable structures, all housing a rural community's best efforts at promoting itself. Tens of thousands of people attended, and even schools closed for one day so that every child (issued with a free ticket) might attend. For the first decade of my life, this was truly the greatest show on earth.

The preparation of entries began months, sometimes years before the event itself. Anyone with three dollars might make an entry in the prize competitions. My own family's worth was pinned on Dutch's homemade jam. Year in and year out, her free tickets gained us a privileged entry, and her prize money funded our extravagances.

Fair Day began early in the morning. With me in the back seat, and Dutch (in hat and beads) sitting beside him in the front seat of The Machine, C.E. would drive us off. We coasted all the way down the far side of Catoctin Mountain, and skirted the edge of town by the old train tracks along East Street. At last, with cars thickening, we pulled into an empty field, the owner of which harvested nothing but an annual crop of fair-goers. Squeezing Dutch's stubby index finger, I walked through the iron gate into a world of wonders.

There was music and clatter and men on stilts. There were signboards, loudspeakers, pony-traps and candy-floss. I was transported. Our first stop was always the 'Chicken Building', inside the gate on the right-hand side. This was a huge, rectangular, squared-stone building, painted white inside and out. It was divided into three long aisles, the sides of which were divided into cages of various sizes. Inside these cages there was an example of every species of feathered domestic biped. They were marvellous. White, golden, russet, black, black-and-white, feather-crowned or sanguine-combed, feather-footed or yellow-scaled, I loved them all. Together, they set up a cacophony of unbelievable proportions. Mighty roosters bellowed furiously, extolling their virtues, defying all challengers and attempting by voice alone to outshine their peers. The hens, all of one temperament, endured their bondage stoically. Some were so relaxed that they laid fine brown eggs. Still, the prize for nonchalance went to the po-faced army of rabbits who, outside the society of their feathered fellow citizens, lolled wearily about, waiting only to be stroked. Outside, where hearing and breathing were once again possible, we paused to admire the stout grey geese and their squires, the ducks.

Our next stop was the first of the many church, community and Fire Department concession tents. The fairground layout, with its gently twisting roads and paths among tall exhibition halls, stables and outdoor displays, provided many a secluded corner for these tents. Some towns even provided permanent stalls where their volunteers could offer their wares. The set-up and menu was broadly the same throughout. A square green-canvas tent without sides was raised over a central post. Around the perimeter there ran a narrow plank bench at about elbow height for an adult. In one corner, large stoves were gerry-rigged, and in another corner would be a collection of fridges. Near the centre-post would be a rank of deep sinks. Tables and shelving were scattered about at random, and checked table-cloths covered most horizontal surfaces. The stoves were managed by women, men took the orders, and teenagers manned the sinks. The menu consisted of a chalkboard suspended from the central pillar. Items on offer included:

Sliced Ham Sandwich	50c
Ground Ham Sandwich	50c
Fried Ham Sandwich	50c
Hot Dog	45c
Hamburger	50c
Crab Cake	$1.00
Beef Bar-B-Q	$1.00
French Fries	40c
Bean Soup	50c
Vegetable Soup	50c
Apple Pie	50c
Peach Pie	50c
Hershey Bar	15c
Coca Cola	15c

After two Sliced Ham Sandwiches and a Coca-Cola, I was armed and dangerous.

The road curved gently now through an avenue of travelling salesmen, whose booths, placards and winning ways tempted us to improve our homes. We were shown plans for self-build sun-decks, given advice about porch-roofs, told of the strength of aluminium garden sheds, invited to test clothes washing and drying appliances, given samples of concrete, seeds and curtain fabric. We learned about the advantages of one type of swimming pool as compared to another, saw demonstrations of electric wood-splitters, tasted new and improved iced tea, and we showed appropriate wonder at the marvellous developments in the world of driveway cleaners. A thousand yards on and our pockets bulged with leaflets and our ears rang with slogans. Best of all was the gift of free equipment. C.E. had a new Farmers' & Mechanics' Bank calendar. Dutch sported a light-weight showman's cane, given to her by Grossnickel Brothers Insurance. And I had a great yardstick, gratis from Ingall's Lumber & Supply.

Now we performed a figure-8 by going perpendicular to the main road, first towards the 4-H building. The 4-H is a youth organisation, and their building was the venue for honourable best efforts. Here, on table after table, boys and girls displayed the first fruits of dedication and ingenuity. One category was for elaborate and complex table-settings, arranged to show their makers' proficiency with good manners. Agricultural displays included the difficult art of vegetable-matching – that is, growing a selection of one variety that are each exceptional as well as collectively identical. There were prepared goods like jam, pies, pastries and cakes, all of which were duly sampled by the judges. There was needlework, carpentry, masonry and model-making. Most ingeniously, each village chapter competed to form a miniature still-life dramatic vignette that embodied a particular set theme like 'hard work', 'courage' or 'pride in the home'. All were splendid, and many were to be downright cherished. Seldom have I seen so much innocent achievement so carefully arranged for public view. I need hardly tell you that, both as an incentive and as a reward, every entrant received a coloured ribbon as a prize.

From here, we doubled back through the hucksters' alley towards the other half of our figure-8, formed by the handicrafts building. This large antebellum building was one of the biggest and most crowded in the whole fairground. Inside it, every skill of the homemaker was suitably touted and proudly rewarded. Virtually anyone could and did enter virtually any thing, provided that its production demanded a display of skill. No art was excluded. One corner was devoted to amateur photography and painting, and there were cases of fine ceramics and woodwork. The bulk of the displays, however, were for the traditional mountain crafts. One entire wall, for the entire length of the building, was given over to displays of our finest prepared foods. Golden honey, spun by bees that through the long summer days fed on fruit blossom and honeysuckle, twinkled in fat jars. Sweet and sour pickles made a rainbow of colours – green with cucumbers, yellow with sweetcorn and red with hot peppers. Next, the perishables, like pies, cakes and pastries – all missing one slice – sat guarded by their glass cases. Then there were vegetables – carrots, French beans, beetroot and many others – in serried ranks, their prizes being awarded on the aesthetic of their impeccable appearance. And lastly, just to make my heart go bump, was the jam. Cherry, blackberry, raspberry, peach, all tight translucent and smug. Always straining to read the names beyond the rope barricades, we found it. A great long blue ribbon to B.Ford for a wine-dark jar of black raspberry jam, prepared in the burning afternoon of a summer's day with fruit newly gleaned from Uncle George's vines, tart with the sunshine of the mountains.

Satisfied, we inspected the quilts. How angry Dutch became if a prize was won by anyone she didn't know! She examined each one painstakingly and in minute detail, desperate to find a flawed stitch overlooked by the judges, and one with which she might vindicate her neighbours. But really, there was little need. Always, displayed to double-width at the row's end and wearing the crowning purple-blue of the Champion's Bow, would be Florry Waterman's entrant, each of its 10,000 stitches as faultless as its maker's goodwill.

Turning right through the side door, we went towards the building displaying the farm produce. The oldest, lightest and airiest of the fair buildings, it was my favourite. Inside there were countless wonders of farming prowess. One end was filled with fruits of the fields, the assessment of which must have involved the judges in mysteries of impenetrable subtlety. To me, the long columns of sweet green hay, bundled maize and glass-cased wheat, barley and oats all seemed of uniform excellence. Yet ribbons of all colours hung over them, most having none at all. The long centre of the building was filled with a double display of fruit and vegetables. Tiers of baskets piled high with apples and pears from the slopes around Catoctin, glistened like a new galaxy. Beneath them were long crowded rows of 'matched' vegetables of every description. I once got a blue ribbon of my own here for three impeccable green-striped pumpkins. At the far end of the room, the giants lived. Circling over our heads like so many stellar gods, were sunflowers two or more feet across. At ground level were the immense pumpkins, many so large that they required a forklift to move them. All of these were produced by dairy farmers who knew trick of digging a hole beside their vines and filling it with milk every night at sundown.

Outside we paused for a lemonade before heading off to the farm implements. This too was a boy's adventure. Never before did one boy's small posterior fit itself into so many upholstered seats, any number of which retailed for six digit sums. The latest innovations were on show: machines for turning over soil, filling it up, weeding it, fertilizing and spraying it, harvesting its yield, hauling it around, lifting it up, setting it down – in short, the very best of a farmer's dreams were given substance.

Somewhat jaded by my power-fantasies, Dutch led us off to see the animals. Many motives drew people towards the long low white stables. For the farmers whose beasts were on show, prize-winning meant increased profitability for their herds. For the teenagers who participated, it was a rare chance to live a gypsy life. Although no-one was obliged to do so, during fair week all the 'showers' literally lived with their animals. Walking along the endless rows of lethargic cattle, ennui-soaked pigs, and soporific sheep, I envied the older children I saw. Their bedding lay about everywhere – blankets and sleeping bags piled on straw bales. Their work seemed to fill them utterly with a prideful concentration. They exercised their animals, they practised walking in stately processions, they even rehearsed the quadrupeds' make-up. I watched spellbound as Hereford heifers had their forelocks curled, moussed and blow-dried. How bold and otherworldly, like a Druid priest, each young man of the Future Farmers of America club looked as he slowly orbited the sandy judges' ring, leading a prize Jersey bull by a halter, and bearing his family's future on his heavy shoulders.

From the animal quarters we made a sharp left towards the race track. By doing this we avoided the seamier side of fair life. To our right was the back side of a long avenue of diversions for the curious, the young, and the young-at-heart. There were noisy carnival rides with glittering garish lights. There were tents full of living oddities, human and animal, cruelly exploited. (I can still recall canvas signs for babies joined at the head, a woman who was half-gorilla, a living skeleton, a two-headed sheep, and a Clydesdale horse as big as a small bus.) At night, in a lonely corner, there was a single white van that unfolded a small stage for the riotous peep-show, known locally as the 'hootchie-kootchie' – whereon semi-clad women performed erotic dances.

My own sensual diversions at this time were directed more towards a simpler appetite. That is, in a basement corner of the largest of the two Grandstands, there was a small family-run stall that specialised in homemade fruit and spice lollipops. They were about two inches square, half-an-inch thick, and packed in their jolly paper tubes, they performed their own delicious and wildly-coloured dance in my imagination. There were at least fifty varieties, from deep black liquorice, to red-and-white-striped peppermint, from emerald-cut spearmint to purple concord grape. I pocketed at least a dozen, both as practical short-term rations, as well as supplies against future drought.

But for me, the climax of fair day came with the races. Although I had seen my grandmother in many moods and in many conditions, the spectacle of a field of horses pounding around the flat track sand animated her like nothing else. We climbed up the long wooden side stairs into the huge white-timbered Gay Nineties Grandstand. The building was a plain rectangle, open along the flat side of the great oval racecourse. There was no admission charge, there were no tickets or seat reservations, and there was no betting. The entire scene was staged for the mere pleasure of people who enjoyed watching fine animals running spiritedly. We slid along the bare benches midway up in the centre of the bleachers and made ourselves comfortable. Already Dutch's mottled green eyes twinkled with a childlike joy.

A minute later and there came the soft flatter-flatter of horses and harness making their way along the approach from the stables to the space just below the seating. Half-a-dozen horses trotted in, each one pulling the old-fashioned two-wheeled sulkie that characterises traditional American racing. Dutch smiled in spite of herself, and sat up a little straighter. As the grooms moved the contestants into place, we considered our options for favourite. There were four snorting reds, a black, and a smallish spotted grey. The grey's jockey wore striking red-and-yellow-striped silks, and Dutch and I immediately lost our hearts to his mount. In a moment, the grooms backed off and horses and jockeys tensed. There was no starting apparatus. Instead, animals and men waited nervously for the crack of a pistol shot. It came, and our hearts leapt. As they entered the first turn I stood up and Dutch leaned forward to see more clearly. Because of the distance, the distortion, and our mutually bad eyes, it was practically impossible to see who was leading. Still, as good Brethren who shunned the moral turpitude of racecourses where betting transpired, this was our sole annual opportunity to enjoy the sport, and our excitement was proportionate. As the horses rounded the last turn and started towards us once again, it was plain that the small grey was one of the leaders. Dutch's powerful brown hands began to thump involuntarily against her sides, and her round face shone with delight.

Welhay. Mohawn l'il feller, yukkan do it! Mohawn boy!

On her feet and swinging like a bell, Dutch was clapping randomly as the little grey thundered past us in second place.

Not winning made no real difference to us. For five minutes my dear grandmother was a seven-year-old child again, a thrill for beauty and sporting heroism suffused her face and she was as happy and as excited as I had ever seen her. It was the same, race after race: a group of horses assembled, we chose our favourite, and then cheered them round regardless of victory or defeat. The horses themselves alternated in different combinations, re-appearing after suitable rests. On this day, we watched our little grey win three times and lose many more.

Many races (and two lollipops) later, the afternoon wore on to its close. As a finale, the large green space in the centre of the track was transformed into a rough theatrical showplace. At night-time throughout the fair week, this space was used for musical extravagances featuring international stars with names like Buck, Roy and Conway, Loretta, Tammy and Dolly. But the afternoon crowd attracted the simpler fare of a lone anonymous acrobat. I can still recall this day with absolute vividness, because this was the first professional acrobat I had ever seen.

The stage consisted of an open square raised platform with a shiny steel surface, out of which rose an immense flag-pole. A single chair sat on the stage. There was no introduction and the crowd simply silenced itself as the blonde-haired azure-clad star climbed on to the platform and waved. He then put his arm through the back of the chair, attached a rope to his waist and hoisted himself up the pole. Once at the top, he disengaged himself from the chair, somehow attaching it to the pole. After this, he clawed his way on to the point, and started his act. On one hand, on one leg, swinging, turning, bending, the brave acrobat performed a myriad of fantastic feats fifty feet off the ground. The crowd applauded dutifully, but to me, at least, it seemed that they showed a shocking disdain for his obviously prodigious talent. Just when we thought all humanly-possible contortions had been exhibited, he brought the chair into the act and repeated the whole exhibition back to front.

Once again the crowd applauded, albeit more warmly. For my part, I was awestruck, and bewildered that no one else shared my excitement. Even Dutch's face was tightly compressed into a stolid frown. I began to feel quite bad on account of the undervalued star, especially as his work was now finished and, standing on his chair five stories up in the clear September sky, he took a few bows. For the last time it seemed the crowd clapped a tepid appreciation.

But suddenly the whole moment was transformed. As the performer's head lowered towards us, there was a terrible snap, and the flag-pole swayed to the left. The acrobat instantly spread out both arms as if he intended to fly away, but it was no use. I looked at Dutch and she had gone ivory-grey. As the pole swung downwards towards the ground, screams cut through the air all around me. We were all on our feet groaning with horror when the top of the pole reached its axis and the poor man came to the ground. But just then we were overtaken by artifice. While we watched, the top half of the pole swung neatly in an arc and, firmly attached to it, there remained a chair, clamped to which was the acrobat's foot. The loudest sigh I ever heard rushed out of the Grandstand. All at once the star rolled neatly on to the stage and began taking bows amid a hurricane of applause. I was so moved, I pounded my feet and shouted. Grinning from ear to ear and willing myself to share in the man's triumph, I looked up at my grandmother. Dear, dear Dutch smiled weakly and wiped a small tear from her eye. Another fair day ended in happiness.

CHAPTER TEN:

The Time When the Mule Walks 'Round the Press

October, fine and slow cools in the air a little above the mountaintop pines. You can hear it in the brittle tumble-bite of spinning locust leaves and the hush-and-falter from the walnut trees. It runs its wrinkled hands through the rich broadleaf maples, lifting them from apple-green to a shattering fresh butter yellow. The sycamores are dyed orange, the oaks blush crimson, and the ash and hickories are stained with blood. A quiet expectation looms in The Hollow, and every breeze loosens hundreds of unripe green nuts from the towering pecan tree. Around them, to the squirrels' delight, roll the tough green husks of walnuts.

Our best walnut trees grew in two clusters: one behind the barn, and one beside of the farm lane beside of the potato field, near the contrary springheads. The fruit of these trees, together with the large crop from the trees around The Corner and behind the Band Hall, combined to provide Dutch with an autumn income. By the bucket and by the bushel, Moose and I gathered these for her to prepare. This preparation is a long, tedious and smelly operation, not without certain risks to eyes and fingers. The American black walnut is a reluctant servitor of man's need for food. It clusters in twos or threes on the crisp and easily broken boughs of its parent where, with the aid of windfalls, it makes a superb target for little boys eager to practise their ball-throwing arm. Once on the ground it resists invasion through having wrapped itself in a deep leathery yellow-green hide. Ideally, patience in its gatherers would be sufficient to remove this covering, as it rots away after a few weeks. The difficulty with this method is that there is really no suitable place to put the harvest in the meantime. If left outside, every squirrel in the county will help himself to them at the harvester's expense.

Keeping them inside is virtually impossible because of their hideous elderflower-and-ammonia stench. The only real option is to take them one-by-one and knock their skins off with a hammer. This is also not without its drawbacks, as the acid-hot yellow juice flies in all directions, scorching the eyes and painting the hands with a semi-permanent brown. My father experimented with a few primitive alternatives. We once let the cows walk about over them, but this failed on hard ground because the nimble-footed beasts avoided them, and it failed on soft ground because the animals simply buried them with their weight. We tried laying some out on the gravel drive and reversing the truck over them, on the theory that this might knock them together like pebbles in a gemstone roller. Fortunately, we only used a few nuts for this trial, as the result was a curious green-brown mash of unpalatable splinters and vegetation.

So, we did them all by hand and delivered them to Dutch's doorstep. By the time we arrived, she had arranged a series of makeshift drying racks on the slight slope behind The Corner. These drying racks were made of old doors and planks raised on bricks, and their purpose was to hold the black woody nuts while they cured in the weakening autumn sun. In league with her cat Poodge, Dutch's early-rising habits enabled her to fend-off would-be marauders. Every day she manually turned over the nuts, selecting the driest ones for shelling, and throwing out cracked or sub-standard ones. Shelling them was one of her most praise-deserving skills. Unlike the more delicate English variety, black walnuts have an amazingly hard burr-like skull that demands real violence to crack. To do this Dutch sat astraddle a short wide elm log turned end upwards, with a bucket on either side, and a shallow tin pie dish resting on a chair in front. On her right, she had about five gallons of walnuts, while the bucket on her left was reserved for the shells. To crack them, she took each nut in her fingers and with experience-tested expertise, lined it up for a hammer blow. Little by little the shell yielded, and she drew from her pocket a small battery of cunningly shaped steel picks, like dentists' tools, to lift the kernels out. A good worker's goal was to lift out each one as nearly complete as possible without any shell clinging to it, as this could be seen as falsifying the sales-measure as well as potentially costing the customer the pain of a broken tooth. In this respect, Dutch was the best worker in the village, and she worked fast. So fast that a knuckle-bruising thumb-smashing amateur like me was no real help. Soon the pie dish was covered to the depth of about an inch with large brown-skinned cream-centred kernels. Dish followed dish until most of the flat surfaces in her already over-crowded kitchen sat full of nuts getting a final drying out period before sale. Every day she ran her fingers through the kernels, bringing each one into contact with the air so that any excess moisture, which might cause mould, was fully purged. At last, word-of-mouth brought people to her door, each one bringing an empty quart jar. Dutch weighed each jar on the old shop scales, and her satisfied customers left with a supply of nuts that would eventually adorn the fancy baking of the short winter days.

The other wood-scented crop that we brought in that year was wild honey. This came about as the result of a collaborative effort between Moose and the farmer whose land bordered our own Back Field. Midway along the far side of this field there was a hollow elm tree that sprang from our neighbour's field and overhung ours. The tree was weak, slanting and dangerous, and Moose's proposal was to cut it down himself, in exchange for half the wood. As an added boon, he was pretty certain that he had seen honeybees making to and fro journeys from a crack above the lowest limb.

The farmer agreed and we met on a fine clear morning. A pearl-bright sky hung over the brown-sweep tangles of leaves, and we walked around our three acres of standing corn, praising the cold heavy air for its (presumed) numbing effects on a honeybee's temper. I had mixed feeling about this morning's project for a couple of reasons. Not surprisingly, recent experiences had taught me to treat such enterprises with caution, and as this one involved angry bees... well, you may imagine my feelings for yourself. Besides, I was not completely persuaded of our right to deprive a colony of bees of its home and livelihood just at the outset of winter. The argument was that the tree itself was dead, and was positively detrimental to agriculture as it rained down branches and twigs, as well as threatened to fall over, smash the fence, and expose that standing corn to a herd of greedy cows. I had heard this argument before about the felling of dead trees. But I also recalled a dead elm that my father cut down at the top of The Hollow, which had once provided a home for a splendid screech-owl. As the great tree sunk to its knees with the dull grate that distinguishes dead wood, the owl popped from a hole that had once been twenty feet up. As Moose looked on, the owl, dazzled both by the sunlight and the fall, sat disconsolately composing itself among the dry broken branches. My father, afraid to approach the beautiful bird, delayed work until the owl, shaking the cobwebs from its head, let out a gripping hoot and flew up to a neighbouring tree, where it remained sadly, watching the destruction of its old home.

But, with his assistants at a suitable distance, my father used a chainsaw to put a deep wedge on the downhill left side of the tree. Surprisingly, considering the noise and obviously strong vibrations, we saw no bees. With instructions to shout for all we were worth if the defenders made a sallie, he started his cut at the side opposite the wedge. Although I watched the entrance crack until my eyes went dry, I saw nothing. Then with his usual skill, Moose laid the tree over, swinging it neatly down the hill and away from the fence. For my part, I was ready to run at the first crunching note of collapse, but I still saw no excuse to do so. Sensing with fatalistic certainty that this good luck was not going to last, I backed away just as my opposite numbers – farmer and son – moved closer to watch as Moose started to cut into the tree trunk just below the portentous crack.

Once again my father expertly made a deep cut in the underside of the fallen tree, and gravity widened this into a slight wedge. No bees. So he brought the saw down on top of the wood, and three inches into the cut the tree's weight broke it into two halves. Half-a-dozen startled warriors filed out of the six-inch hollow, and the four humans ran away like cavemen at the first glimpse of fire. When our courage returned, we gathered around the strangely deserted cavity in the log and warily peered inside. What we found was a crumbling clay-coloured tunnel, presided over by about a dozen stunned sentries, whose officers had plainly abandoned them. Their wealth consisted only of about two unbroken combs and a few fragments of wax and spilled honey. Somewhat appeased in my conscience, I did not refuse the half-comb offered to me. I had never touched beeswax, let alone whole cells full of honey. I carefully crushed each tube one at a time, and using my fingers as a spoon, ladled out the fresh honey. It was dark molasses-brown and smelt of leaf-mould and sugar. Woven from the blossoms of tulip-poplars that still filled The Hollow, it tasted of marshmallow, and ran over my tongue as cool and clean as rainwater.

Over the coming weeks I spent a great deal more time in this field. Although three acres of corn may not sound like a lot, we lacked the machinery necessary to harvest the crop, and instead, we were forced to bring in the lot by hand. Called 'horse corn' by the locals (to distinguish it from the softer 'sweet corn' eaten fresh), our plan was to store it in our new corn crib, taking it out and shelling it as required by our animals throughout the winter. To do this we had a small assembly of nineteenth-century tools.

The first job was the cutting and 'shocking' of the stalks. Cornstalks can grow to over six or seven feet tall, and at over two inches in diameter at the base, they are as tough as bamboo. To cut them, my father and I each had a special 'corn chopper', or ten-inch curved steel blade stuck perpendicularly into a two-foot long wooden handle. In preparation for cutting, we walked along every third row and at twenty-foot intervals, we tied three stalks together. These would serve as the supports for each 'shock'. When we had done this over the entire field, we started cutting. To do this, each stalk has to be held tightly at mid-height and whacked at ankle-level. One stalk is easy, but as you progress along the row you must carry your burden along with you, being careful to keep all the stalks upright. When the crook of your carrying-arm is full, you must take the lot to the nearest three-stalk support and prop them together. When each bundle has about an eight-foot circumference, take one stalk and, turning it sideways, use it to tie the bundle into a completed shock.

Altogether, I found this part of the harvest comparatively enjoyable. As we worked in the evenings after school, daylight was in an ever-shortening supply, so I could be certain of short working hours. Practically all of the work was done standing up, and even though the corn leaves were itchy, the bundles were not heavy. The ground was a funny combination of soft mud held in place by a frosty coat – somewhat like an iced sponge cake – and although rough, was not unpleasant to walk on. Besides, I liked the look of the bright orange ears, and I simply loved chopping down the tall stalks.

But the real work started about two weeks later. With the corn leaves rolling in upon themselves and fading from ginger-veined straw to blue-flecked russet, and night skies seeping upwards from the ground ever earlier, we began the task of bringing in the corn. To me, this seemed an endless process. In the slim hours of daylight between school's end and nightfall, the job went on for weeks. I sat cold and empty-hearted on a rough wooden cart as we dragged over the now lonesome hillside towards the cornfield. Inside, we lumbered diagonally towards the farthest corner of the field, every few feet of ground throwing me violently side-to-side as each of the tractor's wheels crossed a furrowed ridge. At last Moose pulled up alongside a shock, so spacing the cart as to have two or three shocks on either side. He turned the tractor off and we climbed down.

The work began by lifting the cornstalks upwards slightly and chopping through the three remaining firm stays. With these cut, the whole structure was toppled over into a horizontal pile and its tying stalk cut. Weeks of standing tightly packed in the dampish cold air had done nothing to improve the cornstalks smell, and I can still feel the charred damp-rag aroma in my nose. The work now consisted of kneeling on the damp ground amid the decaying weeds and pulling the prone stalks on to my lap one by one. Taking each stalk in my left hand, I wrenched the ears off with my right. For a small boy, this was not always an easy chore, as dried cornstalks have an absurdly illogical tensile strength. Besides, the crispy leaves can quickly slice up the hands with paper cuts. Once detached, the ripened ears need to be cleared of their leafy covering. Our predecessors recognised the challenges of doing this work on a large scale, and came to our aid with a clever invention. This consisted of a fingerless yellow leather glove, attached to which was a thin dull steel strap protruding into a hook between the thumb and forefinger. By sticking this hook under the leaves of each ear and pressing them down with the thumb, the wrappings could be cleared away with relative speed and a smaller likelihood of injury. Our supply of these utensils came from the leftovers from the Ford family store, and without them we would have been lost.

The ears themselves belied the amateurishness of their harvesters. Lovely long firm rows of hard dentine sculpture the colour of egg yolks and suffused with pink highlights, rewarded us. Once stripped of their cloaks, each was carefully broken off at the base and piled up, ready for collection. As every evening's work drew to a close Moose brought the tractor and cart near to the piles waiting by each former shock, and I threw them on to the cart. When we returned to the farm buildings we took it in turns to hurl the ears as far as possible into our proud corn crib, through the sides of which our success was plain to see. Despite the numbing cold, itchy skin, myriad cuts and days of school-time exhaustion. I was still pleased to see that we had bushels and bushels of corn to show for ourselves.

This pride operated on me at several levels. Throughout the winter I volunteered to shell the corn for the chickens and cattle. As I seldom volunteered for anything except second helpings of ice cream, my father was mystified. What I found hard to explain was my love of the strange, even bizarre combination of mathematically precise ingenuity and physical crudity that characterised the last century's farming implements, of which our two corn-shellers were examples. Both operated on the same principle, with equal drama and commensurate failure. The largest of the two we bought at a public auction. It was a lumpy iron implement weighing perhaps twenty pounds, with a crank and a rotting wooden four-legged box-container. Moose built a replacement box for this contraption, and I as always keen to use it. It was like one of those classic carnival automata gone superbly wrong. Instead of inserting a nickel, it worked like this: I got up a good head of steam on the crank and then pushed an ear of corn into a hinged orifice at the top. The cranking became a little harder, but the air was filled with a hailstorm of kernels. These were meant to have been trapped efficiently by the box, but that was (to me) a welcome impossibility. So complete was the machine's failure in this respect that we moved it to the remote corner of the workshop where the smooth wooden floor made it possible to sweep up the takings without great loss.

The machine's nearest rival was a smaller version, with a more restrained cranking action. The tool itself was on long loan from Dutch and C.E., and like our own, it relied on a wooden box to trap the newly freed kernels. It was great fun to watch. An ear was yanked downwards into the machine, where it spiralled against a studded steel wheel. As it was pulled along violently, this ear sent up kernels as fast as a roman candle throws out sparks. At the last moment, just as the operation appeared near to floundering because of a dropped workpiece, it skilfully reversed itself, and spat out a neatly-shorn cob.

I laboured in vain for months to think of something useful or decorative that could be made from corncobs. I even experimented on them, discovering that they can't be whittled, that they become waterlogged with disappointing rapidity, and smell vilely of dung when burnt. But the real natural history lesson came the following spring when I learnt all about mice. Although we had made Herculean efforts to ensure that our corncrib was a sealed web of interlocked, double-layered wire, with gaps no greater than half-an-inch, about March we discovered some alarming droppings on the then visible floor of the interior. My father decided that we had better investigate by removing the dregs of the old crop – in fact, about eight or nine bushelsful – and then cleaning up. There was a continuous light-footed scuffling as we worked, until only about two bushelsful remained. At this point some brave mousy bugler sounded the call for retreat, and the siege was raised. As we looked on, dozens of mice, of every age and calibre, emerged from the pile and threw themselves on to the wire walls, scrambling up them like ladders and looking for an outlet. In the midst of this panic there was plainly none to be found, and Moose was in a mood to give no quarter to prisoners. So he disappeared through the wire door and returned a minute later, bringing with him two of the Big Guns. Safeway and Noodle, both of whom clearly felt that Christmas Day had truly come, hit the floor running, and eventually wore themselves out with the excesses of gladiatorial slaughter. Our only explanation for the possible root cause of the whole incident was that at least two infant mice, small enough to squeeze through the wire, had gained entry. Then, growing fat on the abundant comestibles, conceived an entire race of further occupiers, until practically the whole lot vanished through the vicissitudes of Fortune.

Besides corn, our other October harvest was apples. Our crop was gleaned mostly from half-century-old trees scattered around the fringes of the fields. The variety and quality of this crop ranged widely. One large silver-barked high-arching tree, that stood giving a lonely shade to the meadow opposite the barn, produced an abundance of obscurely-named flat red fruit with soft yellow flesh. The apples here were especially large because the tree was rooted downhill from a cluster of seven strong springheads that fed our neighbour's half-acre pond, and poured a steady rill into the soft earth of the meadow. Three hundred yards down the road, the hollow tree beside the old potato patch shone with hundreds of small sharpish green-white apples, and on the hill above The Hollow, Charlie Ford's imposing copse of trees were heavily laden with dark crimson fruit, having a perfect sweet-sharp taste.

We picked them all, regardless of shape, size or colour. For the best, we dug shallow pits in the vegetable patch just behind the smokehouse, lined these with straw, deposited the fruit, covered the pile with more straw, then buried the whole in soft earth to a depth of over a foot. These lasted as cool and crisp as an autumn moon until well into February. But the rest of the crop – small, misshapen or scarred by twigs – we mixed together for making cider.

Our cider press was nothing like the majestic and professional affair managed by the Ford family of old. Still, to me at least, it was quite a piece of work. It dated from the 1890's and was constructed on a frame of four oak pillars, each about six by eight inches in thickness and over four feet tall. The rectangle formed by this frame contained a large iron crusher at one end, topped by a wooden hopper, and powered by an immense crank. At the other end there was an iron press that operated by means of a long wooden handle that slipped into an iron screw, which descended on to the wooden press base. In the open space between these two features, there were two slatted barrels, open at the top and bottom, for receiving the crushed fruit. At the very base, there was a zinc-coated wooden tray that tilted downhill to allow the cider to run off for collecting.

The first day we made cider was a sensualist's banquet. I can still feel the rough lick of the breeze turning my cheeks red, and I can hear the broken empty shouting of the crows picking over the debris of the empty vegetable patch. We set up the press on the old springhouse floor underneath the black maple tree. The ground in all directions was covered with baskets full of apples of every hue. Although it was only mid-morning when we started, the apples, warming one another by their close confinement perfumed the air with the swift head-filling aroma of pungent, lemony-blossomed fresh fruit. Our roles in this work were many. At the spout of the wide zinc tray we placed a large clean jar, topped by a funnel, in readiness to receive the floods of juice we expected. It was the cranker's responsibility to keep a close eye on this jar so that it was never in danger of overfilling with the free-flowing juice released by the crushing.

I took the first turn at cranking and Moose bounced the apples into the hopper as fast as he could pitch them in. Helped by a large iron fly-wheel, my own work met with little resistance, and the air was filled with the grinding smash of apples being torn relentlessly into small shreds called 'pummies'. As each jar filled, it was quickly replaced, until at last we had about a half-bushel-sized barrel of pummies. These were then moved over underneath the press, the heavy wooden lid placed on them, and the screw press lowered. As I watched, my father turned the great screw downwards, and the sweet slightly effervescent flood began. The apple juice was far different from the pale straw-colour of refined cider, and the anaemic watery-gold of commercial apple juice. Instead, it came forth as a deeply tanned brown liquid, with the look and texture of milk. At the end of the first pressing, with several jarsful to show for ourselves, we had our first taste. With my face lost in a misty cloud of ripe leaf-and-sugar scent, I wet my lips with the earth-cold succulent juice.

I was immediately addicted, and eagerly recommenced work in an effort to increase our stores of this ambrosia. Through lunchtime and into the afternoon we took turns at the crank. While one of us was pressing, the other filled the hopper and kept on crushing fruit, so as to improve our speed. Our yield, after necessary deductions for further partakings, was about one gallon of juice for each bushel of apples. Heaven only knows how much fresh juice I drank that day. Overjoyed with my discovery of the deliciousness of this new substance, I could hardly stop myself. My father, with the foresight to know that the juice's future fermented status would be denied me, did nothing to discourage my imbibing. Although in retrospect I can say that the secondary effect of my indulgence was a disconcertingly loose bowel, I don't regret swallowing a single drop.

With less to do in the fields at this time of year, Moose reckoned that it was a good time to service the machinery. He was also conscious of the fact that as we had to work on the equipment outside, it would be better to complete our repairs and refinements before the onset of the sometimes savage winter cold. So in spare moments we replaced broken bolts ('sheared pins' as they're called), filed blades to sharpness, welded joints, changed tyres. More daunting was the prospect of finding out what internal mishap was the cause of our new tractor's reluctance to start.

You see, we now had two tractors. Our second one was a leaf-green John Deere 'A', of about 1920 vintage. I shall leave it to you to infer its relative power based on the appellation 'A'. Now John Deere tractors have always held a mysterious attraction for my father, probably because of their extreme quirkiness. Named after the inventor of the first all-steel plough, they are the only green model in a world of red, orange, yellow and grey peers. They also possess the only examples of large petrol engines that fire on only two pistons – a fact which gives them a distinctive 'putt-putt' sound, recognisable for miles.

Just why any of this makes them appealing I could never tell. But somehow I was not surprised that Moose should be drawn to them. We bought our own on a chill autumn morning from a second-hand tractor dealer in a neighbouring county. I thought it was a bad sign when the dealer, unable to make the machine start, disappeared into his office, and re-emerged with an aerosol tin. Spraying this into the air above one side of the tractor, he turned the engine over with the other hand and, as if by magic, it started on its putt-putting way. 'Ethyl-alcohol,' he explained. I had never seen any mechanical device that required smelling salts in order to function, but I felt instinctively that this item would not prove to be a wise investment.

But my objections went unheard, and the tractor was delivered the following week. For a while, depending more on the barometer than on any improvement in its nature, the tractor worked well and gave the lie to my reservations. But as the weather grew colder, its former crankiness re-emerged. With his customary insistence on doing things for himself in spite of all obstacles, Moose carried on trying to find ways to bring the beast to heel. Saturday mornings found us working in tandem to get the John Deere mobile by dragging it into the open and launching it like a fledgling robin. That is, Moose reversed the Farmall up to the John Deere, and I joined them together with a log-chain. I then climbed into the John Deere's seat, put in the hand-powered clutch, and steered the silent tractor while my father towed us to the top of the hill near the apple trees. When we reached the crest and just began to drift, he stopped and I leapt up, pressing down on the steel brake-pads with all my weight. Like tanks, tractors have separate brakes for each wheel, and I had to stand on the pedals to bring mine to a stop. Locking the brakes in place with a side lever, I jumped down and disconnected the chain. Moose and I then traded places, and I drove the Farmall off out of the way to the right, being careful not to turn too sharply on the steep hill, as doing so could cause the tractor to upset. After this, with me watching anxiously, Moose aimed the tractor downhill, towards the swamp at the foot of The Hollow, and let go the brakes. The silent morning air rebounded with the rattling stutter of a fifty-year-old starter, as my poor father raced Time, Fate and Gravity to make the machine start before it reached the level ground at the bottom. If it worked, the tractor would run for the rest of the day. If it failed, we repeated the whole process, until overcome with ennui, the tractor was persuaded to co-operate.

This comparatively cheerful episode in my relationship with our John Deere was followed by more dramatic incidents. Besides its somewhat labour-intensive starting procedures, this tractor also suffered from a slipping power-take-off. That is, the two inch fluted steel rod that projected from its rear end just above ground level, and which converted engine revs to turning power for implements like mowers, was sometimes unpredictable, causing disturbances in other machinery. I awoke one morning to the somewhat alarming news that Moose proposed to fix this himself.

I was not – on this occasion at least – bothered about this proposition from selfish motives. After all, my part in the operation would consist solely in passing tools, shining torchlight, or gathering up bits and pieces. I was mostly fearful of the serious damage that could be wrought accidentally to one of our more sizeable investments. The spot chosen for the work was the level area just beyond the young orchard. This was as near as we could bring the tractor to the workshop, and the light here was unusually good.

With tools laid out on the grass, Moose considered his options. The logical place to begin the surgery was in the area surrounding the injured limb itself. This area was a rectangular iron plate about eighteen inches by twenty-four, and covered with boltheads of all shapes and sizes. Of course (of course!) we had no instruction manual, and despite his wide experience in mechanical matters, my father had never done anything quite like this. So, he began by identifying a number of identically-sized bolts which circled the perimeter of the plate. On the theory that these held the structure together, he removed them all. Nothing happened. He then began to remove each and every bolt, separately convinced that each was the key to the mystery. Finally, although there were no more bolts to remove, the whole thing remained intact. Puzzled, he took a long sturdy screwdriver (one that he had made himself) and slipped it into the thin joint between the plate and the tractor's central framework. There followed a sudden sucking noise, like a huge animal choking, and then the plate fell off. With it there also came gallons of a gluey beige petroleum product, that tumbled hopelessly on to the ground. We both looked on in astonishment, too immediately shocked to be instantly angry. Without ever realising he had done so, Moose had removed one entire side of the tractor's gearbox, thereby releasing the complete store of very expensive gear oil. This weighty Dijon-mustard-coloured fluid, vital to the tractor's movement, plopped in heavy globules on to the grass. Besides rendering the tractor utterly useless in the short-term, we had also created our own private oil-slick where, despite our clean-up operations, the soil refuses to support vegetation even to this day.

Eventually, however, we righted the problem, and the power-take-off was restored to its full potential. But from the standpoint of my free time, this was a disaster. Not because we were able to use the tractor more often, but rather because it emboldened my father to try his hand at even more serious mechanical exploits...

This time, the problem lay in the fact that under the strain of a heavy load, the tractor's reliable bass putt-putt was joined by a tenor staccato of ticks, accompanying a lessening of its power. Having armed himself now with an instruction manual (!), Moose learned that unlike more modern engines, the pistons of a pre-war John Deere tractor were made purposefully smaller than their cylinders. Most newer engines, in which the piston slides smoothly against its cylinder, wear out when these two surfaces no longer match perfectly. John Deere's designers anticipated this problem, and instead of a smooth fit, they made the piston a fraction smaller, making up the join through the insertion of a steel ring that fitted into a groove in the piston itself. The intended result was that as the crucial joint gradually wore down, causing a loss of power, it could be replaced without having to rebore the engine block.

It was an ingenious idea, and no doubt those intrepid designers expected that the task of replacing these rings would fall into the capable hands of trained experts, suitably equipped. But our case was different. Work started on a Monday evening after school. The days were very short now, and Moose brought the tractor round to the waggonshed where we made use of the electrical outlet to power a hand-held light. The initial stages of the process went smoothly. In other words, we didn't break or lose anything. After a few evenings' work we had succeeded in stripping the engine block of most of its protrubences, and we were ready to draw the pistons our of their cylinders. How easy that sounded. What actually happened was that my father wore himself down with constant tugging at the pistons which, as if to insult his efforts, simply swished back and forth rhythmically, exchanging places with one another. At last, with both his feet propped against the iron frame, he pulled until the veins on his temples stood out. There followed a hollow swoosh and the heavy piston sunk down into my hands. The worrying thing was that the tightly sprung metal ring fired off with a ping against the plank wall.

My heart froze. Night after night for a week I had devoted my evenings to ripping apart a nearly useless hunk of old iron and steel. When I went to school I suffered the embarrassment of oil-grey hands, and I could scarcely afford to neglect my homework any longer. Now, there hovered before me the dim spectre of more nights' work, toiling to get a replacement steel ring, equally springy, back into a cylinder the tolerances of which could only be measured with a micrometer. The situation was made worse by the working conditions: only one hand-held torch for light, damp chill evenings to embitter the heart and stiffen the hands, and, for me, no ripe incentive other than anxiousness to be released from my duties.

But still, we persevered. I shall never forget the surge of energy that filled me when miraculously on the 181st try, we succeeded in sliding the second piston back in, through dint of muscle and the fortunate compression of the awful ring by a god-directed screwdriver. In no time, the rest of the tractor was re-assembled and putt-ing away as well as ever. Overall, I'm sure it worked no better, but at least I was spared future involvement with its health and hygiene.

Two events marked the end of October, and one of them was Halloween. Our celebrations were little different from other rural communities. One of our own orange pumpkins, suitably carved and lit by a candle, guarded our porch steps. I banded together with friends and went door-to-door in the darkness, knocking loudly, but speaking shyly, 'trick-or-treat.' Later, I returned home with a pillowcase full of fruit and sweets. Older children, more interested in tricks than treats, spent the night colouring in stray car windows with soap. The highlight came on the Saturday night nearest Halloween, when the Band Hall sparkled under the starlit sky and the Harmony Community Club hosted a Halloween party. All of the village children put in an appearance, if only to claim a share of the cold apple juice and warm gingerbread. Most of us took part in a costume parade, trying to win the prize of a whole ginger cake. I, myself, dressed in a pair of C.E.'s trousers, with one of my father's worn out shirts puffed out with a pillow, and my face suitably dirtied, was entered as a hobo. I had never seen a hobo, but I trusted my elders, and felt supremely good about myself, even though I didn't win.

The other great October happening was the arrival of a real travelling circus. Never before in my short life had one come so close, and I was in ecstasies when my parents said we could all go. The scene of this momentous event was a large, now-emptied hayfield on the outskirts of a small market town about six miles away. The night of the performance was a golden one: a crisp-as-celery autumn night when the air gathers in frosty clouds around you, and the stars are near enough to brush your sleeve.

We parked the truck alongside a great many other trucks in a far corner of the field, and walked towards the green canvas sphere that loomed in the moonlight like a dropped cone of ice-cream. A triangle of light opened up, and my mother bought three tickets and a program. Although I felt a momentary twinge of disappointment that the great round tent held only one ring and not three, I was so excited that I lost all ill-feelings immediately. We sat down on folding red chairs, midway up on the right-hand side of the entrance, and we had no sooner sat down than I experienced an overwhelming craving for popcorn. With the telepathic ability characteristic of all entrepreneurs, a young man suddenly appeared with just this commodity. So now, suitably provisioned, I waited.

As the church bells struck in the still night air, the tent suddenly fell into a murmuring darkness. A drum roll began from a low corner of the tent, ending in the crash of a kettledrum, and the flash of a spotlight on to the centre of the ring. There stood a tall man in the traditional red-and-black suit of the Ringmaster. His roaring voice called out, Ladies and gentlemen, boys and girls, children of all ages…Sit back in your seats, for the show is about to begin!

In the maze of spotlights that suddenly swung round the high wires overhead, and the skidding tinkle of band music, I gave myself up, transported by the thrills of the show. There were tightrope walkers and trapeze artists, there were half-a-dozen trained poodles, there were clowns who piled out of tiny cars, juggled hats, doused themselves with water and the crowd with confetti. There were men on stilts, jugglers and acrobats. I was lost in a whirlwind of colour, sequins, gaudy music and death-defying extravagance.

Apart from the trained dogs and five beautiful Appaloosas (whose riders sat, stood and somersaulted over their backs) there was only one other non-human species in the show, and that was the elephant family. I knew they were a family because there were three of them – papa, mama and baby. The people I knew who lived nearby the site of the circus told how the largest of the two adults helped the roustabouts to set up the big top tent. For Appalachian farmers, the spectacle of an elephant dragging huge tent poles, pulling ropes and carrying canvas, was truly otherworldly. Indeed, for the old folks, who referred to all non-American dominions as 'them places', and whose geography was somewhat sketchy, the sight of the packaderms conjured up images of Noah, Joseph and Nebacaneezeer.

I too thought they were marvellous. Although they had a rather melancholy look in their eyes, and I thought their tricks and stunts an embarrassment to their profound dignity, I was sure they loved one another, and in that spirit, I enjoyed watching them.

I shall never forget their entry. Papa, mama and baby strode in as if on parade. They wore jaunty headresses with feathers, and had matching blue-and-gold waistcoats. They also held hands in their own way, trunk-to-tail, and poor baby with his short strides often got left behind and had to run to catch up. They were definitely the biggest animals I had ever seen – papa was as big as five cows stacked up – and their exoticism was enthralling. When they passed by the air swarmed with the green-brown fermented smell of the jungle. Papa elephant even fulfilled my dearest wish just before exiting by evacuating his bowel in a grand manner, and ejecting a lump of faeces as big as a football.

But for me, the star of the show was a great unknown. I noticed him first as the 'straight-man' among the hordes of clowns, and I was surprised when he later appeared as a juggler. He was tall, robust and handsome, with a brightly flushed fair face, and a head of tight ginger curls. He was spectacular. Once I had identified him, I followed him with my eyes throughout the rest of the evening. When he walked the tightrope with his beautiful assistant, he wore a sky-blue one-piece outfit, open to the waist and picked out in rhinestones, and when he led the elephants his suit changed to a matching cut in yellow. He wore green when he bounced on the trampoline, and ivory when he tumbled with the acrobats.

But then late in the evening I lost him for a while. Well that is, three or four acts went by without him. I began to despair of ever seeing my hero again, when a late-comer to the show sat down in the empty chair to my right. The stranger wore a long brown overcoat and a felt hat, and I took no note of his face, as I was lost in the beginning of the magician's act. But while I watched the top-hatted man in the centre of the ring display his skill at cutting off bits of a young woman in a box, I noticed that the stranger began to fidget. My attention was drawn back to the ring by the applause that followed the girl's triumphant re-assembly. Then the stranger began to cough and rock about a bit. He took a strangely-shaped bottle from his pocket, and quickly knocked back a good swig, wiping his mouth on his sleeve. The older folks exchanged looks and muttered about what a shame it was that such a nice family show should be marred by drunkenness. Meanwhile, the principal player and his assistant had cleared away the centre of the ring and set up a round pedestal, over the top of which hung down a circular steel ring with a curtain. The magician mimed for his assistant to stand on the pedestal, but she refused, gesturing plaintively that she was still in too much pain from having recently been cut up. The audience was tickled, but the magician was so woebegone that I could have wept for him. The Ringmaster appeared and called for volunteers, and dozens of little hands shot up, mine included. As if on cue, the drunk stood up and bellowed something inarticulate, reeling and staggering down the wooden steps towards the bright circle of light. When he was close enough, the Ringmaster seized him by the collar and gave him a shake, and it was then, as his hat rattled forward, that I noticed that the drunk had ginger hair.

My pulse speeded up. It was him, and I was sure of it. The Ringmaster plonked the man down violently on the pedestal and took his bottle away from him, smelt it, and threw it down in disgust. He then called the magician over, and with much struggling, they hid the man behind the curtain. There was a drum roll and the crowd clapped in time. The magician circled round the curtain once, waving his arms, and from inside the curtain the drunk's hat flew out. The magician circled again, and the overcoat flew out. After the third revolution the band struck up a loud 'ta-da,' the curtain dropped, and we all discovered that the drunk had vanished. Amid the applause, the Ringmaster rolled away the pedestal so that we could all see that it was empty. Then he replaced it in the centre, and the curtain was drawn up again.

Another drum roll, and the crowd chanted a wordless drawl. The magician made three more revolutions, and the band struck another 'ta-da'. The curtain dropped and there, in a crimson suit, spangled with sequins, my hero appeared in his full shining glory. Stomping our feet, all of us who recognised him (and by now there were hundreds of us) cheered ourselves hoarse. Alongside us, the little tin-pan band struck up a glorious salute to the performers who now marched in proud symmetry round the ring. And as for me, thoroughly drunk on excitement, I felt my evening well-rounded-off by magic.

CHAPTER ELEVEN

Over the River and Through the Woods

The November of my memory rolls as slowly as an echo through the frost-grey mists of the forest. Skies, sombre and yellow-blue, weigh dumbly on the backs of the trees, and twist in gauzy fronds with the silent breeze. Chased by a cold sun, that breeze mounts ten thousand dove-blue horses, whose feet clatter briskly in the stiffened branches. No bird sings, and only the quick hop of rabbit feet in dry leaves startles the sunrise-drowsiness of the autumn-bared mountain. Walking fondly with a head still full of wastrel dreams, I raise my eyes to the sun-dyed and sterling-tinged branches, ice-drawn against the morning light. I see the patterned hollows knocked into the limbless dead trees by the woodpeckers. Deer tracks lay fresh in the hardened streamside mud, and beside them cluster the tiny paw-marks of racoons, who washed their food here in a midnight feast. A clip-hip overhead and the rittle-tack of a falling shell betrays the work of a hungry squirrel. I walk over the low-lying stone-scattered level by the stream where, in a month now gone, I counted the yellow veined peter-in-the-pulpits, and gathered the daffodils watered by the marsh. Now at my feet nothing stirs but the ever-turning wave of red-wire brambles. Away to my right, South Mountain is lost in fog, pink-washed by the dawn. I snap the ice fringes that cling paper-like to the edges of the water, and puff out my cheeks to blow a ghost-like halo around my hands. On the slopes before me, on the banks of Little Catoctin Creek, a few black-mottled cows cough out the cold, and the village lamps go down as Harmony dresses itself for work.

An early Saturday morning, with not much work of my own to do, made a good time for a walk. For me, walking was the music of country life – an accompaniment to Time when, lit by a watery sun, I found it easy to unroll my heart in the quiet of a leafless wood. So sitting on a woodpile in the laurel brakes, I used to look for clues about myself. I looked for reasons in the poems I wrote, poems that revealed so much yet gained so little of the affection they sought. I was a boy who read Shakespeare and Plato, and who used popsickle sticks to build replicas of Fort Donelson. I floated downstream with Shelley, I drew complex diagrams of factories, and I burnt away summer days with fantasies of great riches earned on board ships that sailed an ocean I had never seen. I taught myself to sketch portraits, and I combined faces to make an Artemis as fine as Ovid's and worthy of the girl whose fancy I hoped to inspire. My loneliness was the seed of occupation. Like all of my family, I gave my time to 'improvements'. I looked for that family as I looked for myself, and I sought them in places that they had left long ago. From out of them I hoped to create a Self worthy of the passions that drew out my weak eyes in books. And like all children, through them I hoped to grow strong.

The strangeness of those days makes me laugh, but their heroism makes me cry. Three fields above the meadow, where the summer before I had watered the cows, there was a hayfield that belonged to Obidiah Taylor. Near the top of this field there is a narrow and deeply rutted lane, beside of which is a small cluster of gravestones. These stones mark the final resting place of Obidiah's grandparents. There is no writing on the stones, but careful tending keeps the ground around them free of weeds and briars. Standing beside the graves it is possible to see for about two miles up the valley towards the Wistman Lane Falls, and about three miles south over the whole of Obidiah's farm and the entire village. It is a lovely spot and it is not surprising that Obidiah's people should have wanted their remains to be laid there. For much of the nineteenth century farming families all around Harmony preferred to be buried on their own land – land that they had cleared of trees and stones, laboured over and grown to love, land that fed them, warmed them, calloused their hands, and the beauty of which calmed their spirits.

Such places fascinated me as a boy, and I spent many hours exploring fields and woods looking for the monuments of people whose lives were just out-of-reach. I wanted to walk in their footsteps and by so doing, see my world through other eyes. In one of the fields where my father and I had worked beside of Hoover Kenwood in the broad steamy light of a July afternoon, I found a rectangular stone enclosure, cramped between a cypress tree and a crippled root-stunted tulip poplar. The walls were just taller than my head and there was no gateway or entrance of any kind. Climbing up the poplar tree, I dropped inside the walls among the company of about ten graves. Hoover's kin – men described as 'farmers' and women as 'consorts' – lay all about me. Beside almost all the women's graves were the small unlettered stones of their children, lost in infancy. Overhead, the trees rocked and at my feet the dried-out stalks of daisies grated, humming the same hymn season after season.

I found Dutch's people on a hillside near her own birthplace on the southern slopes of the mountain. Here, in a stone-strewn triangle of locust and hickory trees, there is a scattering of about twenty graves, many from the eighteenth century and most written in German. The stones themselves are narrow blue columns of slate, about eight inches wide and two inches thick. The writing was deeply cut to ensure its longevity in the face of the extremes of our weather. Though ornate, the writing was clearly executed free-hand directly into the stone, as there are letters of irregular sizes wedged together with many abbreviations. I could read none of the words, but I contented myself with sitting on a pile of greenstone boulders to consider the scene. I saw a small family of Bavarian immigrants – stumpy round-faced women and blue-eyed men – all in the heavy black of old-fashioned mourning. The sun sat wanly astraddle the distant peak of Sugar Loaf Mountain, and a frost-heavy wind climbed hand-over-hand up the slopes of Catoctin. A narrow grave had been pounded out of the icy stone-rich ground, and the children stared open-mouthed at the sweet-smelling pine coffin that lay beside it. Who among those shapes shares my blood? Which one of you would be glad of my tears? I hear the hymns sung, and see the coffin lowered. In a mossy shroud of clouds the sun grows warmer and the family, my family, return to their cabin where a small fire still burns.

I am not alone in the strength of my feeling for these sites. A mile down the road, in the rich glossy brown soil of the valley, is the largest collection of family graves in the vicinity. Nestled in a brushing grove of maple trees at the edge of the old Hawbottom Road, this plot was looked after lovingly by one of the last survivors of the Martin family. Already an elderly man in the 1940's, 'Old Man' Martin kept his family's graves free of weeds and softly decorated with daffodils and grape hyacinths. But at last this centuries-old peace was threatened in the years immediately after the Second World War when the federal government proposed to lay out the path of U.S. Route 40 directly over his forebears' heads. Earnest and with homespun eloquence, Old Man Martin refused the government's offer of re-interment elsewhere, stating his objection as one of feeling and not one of practicality. Against all odds, the old man's arguments proved to be persuasive. Today, the thousands of interstate drivers who pass unknowingly by the deserted gates of the Martin family's homestead do so around a wide bend, skirting the now-untended graves.

By mid-November I could begin to look forward to snow. Although it brought many strange terrors to adults, I found the whole experience to be one long invitation to shameless self-indulgence. Every evening that held the promise of school the next day, I watched the television weather reports anxiously. What I wanted was a great big low pressure system to roll across the Mississippi River, slow down over the Deep South, then bounce its way up the Atlantic coast before being sucked inland along our own Chesapeake Bay. Whenever this happened, the likelihood of our getting a deep snow was pretty good. Sometimes things went wrong – that is, the storm might not drink up enough water to give us a good one, or it might get confused and miss the Bay, crashing into New York City instead. But, perhaps most disappointingly, were the near-misses, when counties on either side of us took the brunt of the inclement weather.

So on nights like this I went to bed early as a sacrifice to the snow gods who, favouring me, would grant me my wish. In the morning, as soon as I knew I was awake, I opened my eyes very slowly, eager for the rush of stunning white light that signals a good snowfall. In any case, I rolled over and looked out over the porch roof for confirmation. If I was neither gratified nor disappointed outright, I could expect hours of intense frustration. If it was actually snowing at the time, I threw myself down the cold wooden stairs with the patience of a bear with a burr under his tail, swooping into the kitchen for a radio update. What I wanted was to hear either A) School was called off; or B) School was one (or two) hour(s) late, but stay tuned. If it was only late, then the ridiculous logic of willpower led to arguments.

Mother – It's letting up…

Son – No, it's not!

Dressed for school, in other words wrapped up to the eyes in coat, gloves, hat and scarf, I scuffed off through whatever snow there was, silently cursing the plain foolishness of adults who simply couldn't see things from the right perspective, and whose evident lack of faith no doubt acted detrimentally upon the snow gods.

Waiting for the school bus had its own frustrations. Practically all of our school's big crude yellow buses were privately owned by farmers and driven either by themselves or their wives. As such, the care and maintenance, not to mention safety matters, were somewhat at the discretion of individuals whose agendas did not coincide exactly with that of the school authorities. Consequently, the eight or so half-frozen children who stood about waiting in the snow began to pray that A) the driver was too timid to risk the journey B) the driver was too mean to risk wrecking the bus C) the snow-chains were broken and the trip was impossible D) the bus was harmlessly in a ditch somewhere.

Thinking back, none of these options ever actually happened. Even if one had done so, I've no idea how we would ever have found out, as there was no means of getting the information to us. So while we waited, we amused ourselves by sliding on the frozen road, and cracking the ice on the flooded part of the nearby meadow. On more than one occasion we convinced ourselves that some lucky misfortune had befallen our transport, and propping up each other's honour, marched off towards home. Whenever we did this, always with a frequent glance over our shoulders, the tormenting snow gods would cause the yellow apparition to creep along the horizon. As we scampered back to our places, the driver would push on the brakes and the lumpy misshapen hulk would skid to an eventual stop.

The other great thing about deep snow was the inevitable power cuts. On long winter evenings in a silent valley, blurred into translucence by a million million snowflakes, nothing is sweeter in the early-grown darkness than the sound of supper hissing on the woodstove, and the greasy-cedar smell of kerosene lamps. How I loved to see these fine glass dragons brought out. Jane dusted them down, and Moose carefully wound out their wide cotton tongues, that rooted downwards into the fumey broth. I wanted these nights never to end, and I wanted the snow never to stop falling. Two feet, three feet, until the snow drifts covered the fence-posts and blocked the roads in all directions. If the telephone was working we called Dutch and C.E. to see if they were well. My mother cooked hearty warming meals of pancakes and red-eye gravy, and we rationed milk. When it was safe, I ran outside and built a huge dirty snowman, and amassed an arsenal of snowballs. Sometimes I cut the snow into great blocks and built forts, tunnels and jagged igloos. Always there was a maze of paths to be dug – to the barn, to the smokehouse, to the workshop. When the streams froze over we went out with axes to chop holes for the cattle, deer and other animals to drink. When the roads were safe, we walked down to see to it that Charlie Ford's whiskey supply had not been too far depleted.

But the short month of November haunts me still because of its many chores of blood. That is because November is the month for slaughtering pigs. The scarcity of food, together with the cold, often harsh conditions, made this the time for replenishing the larder and smokehouse in preparation for winter.

It was the same throughout the village. Slaughtering pigs, or just 'butchering' as it was called, was an enormous operation and required a large team of workers and a wide stock of specialist tools and know-how. Moose had been preparing all of these things for months. Ours was a family of three 'at home', plus a married daughter and one set of grandparents. For this number of people, four large pigs were reckoned to provide an adequate supply of pork for one winter. Accordingly, my father had chosen the best of our piglets and raised them with care – two boars and two sows. The boars, in keeping with local custom, were castrated early on, by hand with a specially curved razor. The loose testicles, known as 'mountain oysters', were given as payment to the neighbour/surgeon who performed the operation. For six weeks prior to butchering day, the pigs were fed exclusively on our own homegrown corn.

The day chosen for the butchering was the third Thursday in November: Thanksgiving Day. Jane and Dutch planned to supervise the traditional feast for all the workers. Other preparations took weeks to complete. A special supply of dry hardwood, neatly split into long strips, was piled up in reserve. Specialist wooden tools that could not be bought secondhand, were built from scratch. Some steel tools were welded up out of spare parts. Supplies of salt, pepper, saltpetre, sage, brown sugar, cornmeal and flour were bought in. Containers like loaf tins, crocks, bowls and cast-iron kettles were scoured clean. In short, this one-off time-sensitive process - dependent on weather, manpower and equipment, and made worse by the fact that pork is easily spoilt –

meant that there would be no second chance to achieve the perfection that the whole performance demanded.

Then, Fate played its awful card. It was 3.30 a.m. and my father rose to light the first fires for the planned 5.00 a.m. start. When he walked downstairs, he saw that the electric clock on the kitchen shelf had stopped at 12:02. He looked outside at the thermometer. It was four degrees Fahrenheit (minus sixteen centigrade), and the landscape was buried under a foot of newly fallen snow. For Jane, the terrible news was that the electricity had been off for hours, and she was still expected to prepare a Thanksgiving Day feast for upwards of fifteen men, five women and one boy, all of whom could be expected to be ravenous after a morning's gruelling work. In any other circumstances, the wisest thing to have done would have been to have postponed the butchering to a better time. But the very nature of the work precluded this option. In the coming weeks, most of these men would themselves be butchering, and there would not be time enough again to have assembled the whole crew.

So with no other choice, Moose went out to light the fires. When they were burning well, he came back in, wet with damp, hoarse with cold air and smelling like a cinder, to drag me from bed. I would keep the fires going while he brought all other things to their final state of readiness. By 5:00 a.m., ten of the men had appeared and were drinking coffee brewed on the woodstove. Inside, Dutch, Jane, their cousins and assistants began the work of preparing the day's meal. Meanwhile outside, the men divided themselves into working parties. Each party needed men of different skills and strengths, because much of the ensuing work was highly technical, financially precarious, not to mention potentially dangerous. The honour of the first kill was given to Dick Taylor, Moose's old baseball crony, who was reckoned to be the best shot present. With three men to help him, Dick led the way into the barn. Two of the men were armed with meathooks, one carried an extremely sharp long thin-bladed knife, and Dick himself carried a .22 calibre rifle. No one else was allowed inside.

The order of events was like this. One of the two hook-carrying assistants would lead a single pig out of the box-stall where it had lived with its three companions, and into a kind of holding area in the centre of the barn. Once here, both the hook-carriers backed away, and Dick took aim. A good mark was to draw an imaginary cross between the animal's eyes and at a level with its ears. Properly carried out, and one such shot was lethal. And indeed, this time it was. There was a single, surprisingly quiet snap, and a soft hush as the pig dropped to the straw. Instantly the knife-wielding man – in this case, Obidiah Taylor – leapt over the wooden partition and drove the long blade into the animal's jugular, while the still-beating heart quickly emptied the carcass of blood. When no more blood came out freely, the two hook-carrying men locked their tools into the flesh just behind the tendons of the pig's hind legs, and began to drag the animal away, while their helpers steered and lifted with the other two legs.

From now on, the timing was crucial. The new carcass, still intact, was dragged to the level area on the downhill side of the waggonshed, where a special apparatus had been constructed. This apparatus consisted of a 150-gallon flat-sided steel oil drum with one of its sides removed. The drum was half-filled with water and it lay on its side over a long narrow ditch, in which a steady fire burned. At one side of the drum a wooden platform was laid out for the men to work on, and on the other side, room was left for two men to operate the log chains that were used inside the water. All eyes watched as a thermometer in the water told when the correct temperature was reached. The water had to be as hot as possible without actually boiling. That is, hot enough to relax the animal's skin, without damaging the meat or cooking it. No time could be lost, as the work was easiest while the muscles remained supple, and the bitter air could stiffen the carcass quickly.

At last the signal was given and the pig, wrapped in the two log chains was lowered into the water. Working very cautiously and in close time, the men rocked the pig back and forth, trying to ensure that all sides were evenly scalded. The precise moment of fitness is judged when an expert touch can lift off a handful of pig's hair easily and without pulling. When this stage was reached the chains were passed across the tank to the men on the other side. A shout went up, and all hands dropped whatever else they were doing to help hoist the pig out of the steaming cauldron.

Working with speed and intensity each man grabs a 'scraper' and sets to work. These scrapers consist of a round galvanised steel saucer about the size and shape of a man's palm. They are not sharp, but using the wooden handles that stick perpendicularly from their backs, the men remove practically all of the animal's short bristly hair without scratching the skin. This needs to be done quickly, because if the carcass cools and the flesh contracts, the hair cannot be loosened a second time. When the hair is completely removed, four or more men lift the pig on to their shoulders and carry it to the 'poles'.

A set of 'poles' is a homemade wooden tripod, about eight feet tall, with hooks on two of its supports at a level of about six feet. The clean carcass, once again suspended by the hind legs, is hung here to enable it to be reduced to manageably-sized parts. With the pig safely hung up, the second working party returns to the barn, and most of the crew takes a breather in preparation for the next session of scraping.

While this is going on, one man, usually the most experienced, together with an assistant, starts to work on the cleaned pig. On this occasion that man was Dutch's cousin George, and (with my fires burning happily), I was his assistant.

As I look on, George begins by making a single steady cut completely around the animal's neck at the place where the soft fleshy jowls rub the firm muscles of the shoulder. Any blood not freed by the 'sticking' drops out now in heavy clots. When this gorey patter is finished, I slide a flat ten-gallon two-handled galvanised tub under the head and take hold of the animal's ears. Using a sharp hatchet, George takes three blows to cut through the spine, and I drop the severed head down, face up into the tub. I then carry this away to the floor of the waggonshed and return with another tub. While I am doing this, George begins to disembowel the animal. He does this by making a careful incision around the pig's anus, which he then draws out, tying a knot in the large intestine. Then with real delicacy and surprising speed, he makes a gradually-deepening cut into the thin plate of muscles on the animal's underside. As he does so, a wide unbloodied V begins to open up and the multi-coloured entrails begin to sag forwards. George is careful not to open the cut too suddenly so that the pig's insides are torn by their own weight, and he is especially careful not to cut into any of the organs. In either case, the result could be a spilling of bile, faeces or fluids that are both foul-smelling and unhygienic. When the incision is complete, George lays aside the knife and pries open the chest cavity. Gallons of gluey-white-membraned guts pour into the tub, and I drag these too away, eventually carrying them off to a corner near the front porch where George's youngest daughter would come out to clean them and prepare them for use. With the carcass now open, George once again picks up his hatchet and expertly hacks his way downward through the animal's spine, until all at once the carcass falls open into two workable halves.

By the time all of this is done, another pig is ready to be raised on a second tripod. This time old Hank takes over with the knife and hatchet, and I continue as before. When the fourth pig is raised in the same way, and my fires are all burning nicely, I am sent off to the kitchen to fetch coffee.

The atmosphere inside is one of noise, laughter and steam. All the kitchen sides are covered with carrot and potato peelings, and bowls of these vegetables, along with sweetcorn and french beans, sit in water, ready for cooking. Standing over the woodstove, our neighbour Ebbie is stirring a pot of stock, and my mother is working behind, dicing the sweet potatoes. Dutch has disappeared, taking the turkey off with her to The Corner where it will be roasted in the coal-fired range in Charlie Ford's kitchen. Guessing why I have come in, Jane takes the constantly boiling kettle off the heat and pours it into our huge coffee pot. While I am waiting for the coffee, the mist of outdoor cold turns to sweat on my forehead, as the room is very hot. George's second-oldest daughter Kathy grins a 'hello' above the washing up, and I look over our dining room which has been stripped to the bare essentials to make room for the men, who will come in to eat in two shifts.

At last the coffee is ready and I go back outside with a teetering tray. It is just before 7:00 a.m. and the grey-black sky has faded to bluish-yellow streaked with pink. The horizon over South Mountain is empty except for the hot morning star, and it promises to be fair and cold for the rest of the day. When I return, the men are arranged along two long trestle tables set up in the waggonshed. Each of these tables has a top made of a single poplar plank two-and-a-half foot wide, eight foot long, and three inches thick, sawn from the same tree brought down in The Hollow. On each table the men are gathered round a half-pig, and the room echoes to the sound of bone-saws, cleavers, and knives sharpened against round 'steels'. I am instructed to mind my fires in the following way: let the fire under the scalding tank go down, and salvage any fuel that can still be used; fill up the 'kettle' with clean water and stoke the fire to boiling. I am also given a pan of fat diced into one-inch cubes and told to divide it between the two medium-sized 'kettles', stoking up the fires under each.

These 'kettles' (there were four in all) were a source of pride amongst the villagers. Everyone, even people who never butchered, had one or two about, out of admiration for their design and noble execution. Made of cast iron, each one was a cauldron about three feet wide across the top, and two-foot deep in the centre. They were about an inch thick in the thinnest places, had a round arching handle, three stubby legs, and weighed about 100 pounds. The very best ones – the two medium-sized ones and the very largest one not yet fully fired – were beautifully smooth inside, kept that way to prevent food from sticking to them. The fourth kettle, slightly smaller and not quite as smooth inside, was used to supply hot water for the day's hygiene measures. All four kettles were perched on 'furnaces' made of fifty-gallon steel oil drums cut in two and with a small hole inserted, through which I could tend the fires.

As I got on with my work, the men got on with theirs. One by one, each trotter was cut off and the ham and shoulder removed. The trotters were reserved in a bucket to one side for Dutch, as she was the only person who knew how to prepare them, using them eventually to flavour rich warming winter bean soups. The hams and shoulders, as the most treasured individual pieces, were manicured to a fine finish and carried off singly to rest on specially prepared shelves in the smokehouse. Likewise, the great square slabs of bacon, two from each pig, were carried away separately to remain out of harm's way until evening. Other cuts of meat followed: chops, roasts, tenderloin. But making these was skilled work in which I did not participate. My own special contribution to the cutting-up process was in reducing scraps of meat and fat into small chunks. The purpose of this was twofold. The fat, in silky pearl-white lumps, would go into one of the two medium-sized kettles to be rendered into lard – an essential ingredient in Appalachian cooking. Each pig would yield approximately five gallons of smooth, feathery soft lard. The meat scraps, misshapen but surprisingly lean, were piled up in readiness to be turned into sausages.

From now until midday there was a swirl of activity. When enough trimmed fat was ready, it went into the kettle, filling it to a depth of about three-fourths full. Using a metal-pointed wooden stir that looked like a hoe with a long narrow blade, the men took turns keeping the seething mass from sticking or burning. When the fat could be rendered no further, a conical galvanised strainer at the end of a three-foot handle was used to lift out the shrunken bits, dropping them into a waiting tub. The lard, ladled out a quart at a time, was poured into five-gallon stainless steel cans and put away to cool. Meanwhile the strained fat was dropped little by little into the cast iron sausage stuffer. This machine – ours was a century old – had a two gallon capacity. It looked like an iron bucket with a heavy crank-powered screw-press at the top. Inside there was a close-fitting cylindrical colander through which the lard drained, pouring out a small channel at the bottom and into a waiting can. After each pressing, the colander was lifted out and a roaring hot cake of compressed fat was tipped on to the table. Shyly, singly, men came by to pick over the 'cakes', looking for lean bits, deep-fried like a fondue.

When all of the top cuts of meat had been taken away to the house for wrapping, and hams, shoulders and bacon were safely stowed, work started on the prepared dishes. The piles of loose meat chunks was scattered thinly over the table and sprinkled heavily with salt, pepper and sage. Slowly, and with great relish, old hands rub the spices into the meat, before it is passed through a zinc-plated 'grinder', turning it into a coarse puree. Then, with the lard-pressing over and the machine is cool, clean and dry, a bucket of prepared 'casings' is brought out from the kitchen. These casings are in fact four complete sets of small intestines, emptied, scraped and washed, turned wrong-side out and packed into water ready for use. Long sections of casing are then threaded on to a projecting zinc tube at the bottom of the machine and, with its colander removed, the machine is filled with minced spiced pork. As evenly and steadily as possible, the crank is turned, forcing the machine's iron plate downwards and extruding the meat into the casings. The finished sausages, about two inches thick and three or four feet long, are not linked, but rest in coils in a galvanised tub. Later they will be taken to the smokehouse and hung from the rafters to 'rest' overnight.

Hank and Obidiah, as 'headmen' were given the heads to clean. Each man began by pouring hot water into the tubs containing the heads, and then using old-fashioned straight-razors, they carefully shaved their respective customers. When each head was smooth, it was lifted out and placed on the table. The meat on this particular article, although as soft as tenderloin, is very difficult to extract. But gradually a pile of choice bits was built up and put to one side. Making well-aimed blows with their hatchets, both men then extracted the blue-grey globes of the brains. As this is not an article that my family relishes, they were gratefully given to the men who procured them.

At the other end of the table there was a pile of organs that had been cleaned and washed indoors and returned for use. Four livers, four hearts and eight kidneys were diced up and mixed with the meat reserved from the four heads. When the sausage-making was finished, this meat, coarsely pureed, was mixed with a bit of lard and dropped into the second of my two medium-sized kettles. The fire was then lowered and one of the men was given full-time responsibility to stir the mixture. In time, the meat was reduced to a thick aromatic mash that was ladled into clean crocks to cool. When cold, this 'pudding' as it was called, resembled a coarse pate, and stored under an unbroken layer of fat, it could last out a winter without further preservation measures. Spooned out and warmed to spreadbility, it was generally served as a wintertime breakfast topping to small round cornmeal pancakes.

The fourth and best kettle was reserved for making 'pon hoss' (or 'scrapple'). This was regarded as a delicacy, as it has to be eaten fresh. To make it, I began by lowering the fire to a steady even warm. A ladleful of lard is poured into the kettle, together with about ten gallons of boiled water. A few handfuls of fresh sausagemeat are also dropped in for extra flavour. As the water simmers, several quarts of flour and cornmeal mixed with salt and pepper are swished in through the fingers, being careful to avoid lumps. Once again the men take it in shifts to stir the mixture rapidly, breaking up lumps and preventing it from sticking. Because of the low heat and the actual volume of food being cooked, pon hoss takes a long time to make, and the stirring wearies the men, all of whom by now are looking a bit tired.

As midday approaches, C.E. and Dutch drive up in the Machine. Normally the road, having been snow-ploughed only once by this time, would not be worth risking, but Dutch is eager to see that the turkey is ready and on the table in time for lunch. A brightening rush of anticipation passes over the haggard faces of the workers as the turkey, wrapped up like a child, is carried past. C.E., seldom an early riser at the best of times and always averse to anything like farm work, gets a good hiding from the others for his tardiness. Still, he is welcomed at once when, seeing me working at a fire, he asks,

Hey, Bub, yever hear 'bout my days asa farman?
Someone shouts,

You warnt never no farman, nothin uh the kyind.

T'ell wi you, ya no account, lop-eared drag-ass!

Smiles spread over every face, and C.E. tells us how in the 1930's he worked briefly as 'fireman' on board the old Baltimore & Ohio line. His job was to shovel coal as fast as possible into the hell-mouth of the great 4-8-8-4 'Big Boy' locomotives (the biggest in America) as they dragged their mile long freight trains north into Pennsylvania. One of the lads irreverently starts to sing 'The Ballad of Casey Jones':

He was goin' doun na grade makin niney miles an ower whan 'is whissle bruck intoo a scream,

He was foun' in na wreck with 'is hand on na throttle, scalded ta death by the steam.

Roars of laughter. Someone pipes up that at the end of the day's work the coal dust must have left C.E. looking a little like John Henry – the legendary African-American steel-driver. In grinning fury, C.E. turns his colourful invective on his accuser,

What'nee 'ell you know 'bout it, ya shit-fer-brains skwinty-eyed son-of-a-dog-catcher?

Whistles of merriment.

Hey, Clarns, I heyeer yuh fly planes too!

C.E. tells the story of his once-in-a-lifetime flight, made as a young naval recruit. Having survived the bouncing tumbling landing of the cargo plane that transported him to a field near Norfolk, Virginia, C.E. crawled out to commiserate with his nearest mate, a black Virginian.

C.E. – How ya feel 'bout flyin' now, Henry?

Henry – Well, suh, I doan like it too much.

C.E. – Nossir, me neether.

Henry – Way I sees it, ifya ina caa, an na caa breakdown, ya puss ow ya foot, an dauh you is. Buh if you inna plane, anna plane breakdown, ya puss ow ya foot, din whauh is ya?

Hoots of approval are interrupted by a stern look from the back porch. It is Dutch announcing Thanksgiving lunch.

Hey! Iffin any you foul-mouth fellers walln any dinner, yeh bes git on in yere.

The men divide into two groups and half go in to eat. The half that stays behind keep on stirring and sharing stories with C.E., who waits (decently) for the second shift.

I, of course, go in with the first group. What I find is a kitchen transformed. There is no washing up and no waste. Instead, the kitchen sides are covered with the pies and cakes brought out from the larder. Bowls of vegetables sit warming around the sides and back of the stove, and steaming plates of food lie semi-covered everywhere. In the dining room the large round pine table is covered with a white cloth, and places are set at comparatively wide intervals to allow the men, heavily-dressed even without their coats, a bit of elbow room. The men themselves, having washed up in the kitchen sink, look stiff and awkward in this altered context, and shuffle about, filling up their seats. The women, like old-fashioned butlers, stand behind the chairs, passing food to and fro and filling dishes and plates.

The food on offer spans a wide variety, is cooked simply, and offered in prodigious quantities. As there is no room to carve, the centre of the table is dominated by a large 'blue willow' pattern charger, piled to the eaves with sliced turkey. Beside it, there is nearly a third of a ham, roasted under a sauce of mustard and brown sugar. Fanning out around the table are steaming bowls of mashed potatoes, sweetcorn, peas, French beans, beetroot and candied sweet potato. There is homemade cranberry sauce, gravy and a huge flat dish of bread stuffing, redolent with sage and thyme. After the whole party works its way through Olympian-scale platesful, and the speed and clatter of cutlery slows noticeably, the women clear the entire spread, and return with dessert. This course consists mostly of a range of pies: apple, peach, blackberry, huckleberry and pumpkin. Like the vegetables, all of this fruit is home-produced.

Scarcely able to move, I felt my eyes glaze over with satiety. How steady, how evenly the calm of exhaustion hovered just above our heads. But rousing themselves with laughter and compliments to their hosts, the men rolled on to their feet and, heads down, went back into the cold air. By the time the two dining shifts changed, the women had once again re-stocked the dishes, washed and restocked the cutlery, and resumed their places behind the chairs. It was only after the second crew finished that the women themselves took their well-earned places at table.

When I got back outside, the pon hoss was nearly done. The long plank tables, earlier used for cutting up the meat, were now scrubbed clean, and covered with crocks and pots of pudding. Each man brought with him a pot or two of his own, to be filled with the day's produce which he could take home and enjoy as a 'payment' for his day's work. These 'payments' all dutifully made were grouped together at one end. Each one would later be recompensed as neighbours went to one another's houses in turn, giving a day's labour to all who asked it. Likewise, the pon hoss. When all agreed that it was of a satisfactory consistency, it was slowly ladled into oblong loaf tins, that were then lined up to cool alongside the pudding.

When the second round of lunch was finished, the clean-up operations began. All of the kettles were put to use heating water, and all hands joined in scrubbing the wood, iron and steel tools. Gallons of now cold water, used in the morning to scald the carcasses, was poured down the embankment by the waggonshed, and a sackful of pigshair was raked together to be burnt as soon as it was dried out. All of the mechanical tools, like the sausage-stuffer, were polished to brightness and greased with lard. Cleaned and emptied tubs were piled high with bones, and divided among the workers who wanted them. By mid-afternoon, the ground was cleared of debris, the fires put out, and the kettles cleaned and greased. Each worker, worn-out, but well-fed and happy, went home with at least one dish of pon hoss and one of pudding as a reward. Some few took sausages and bones and offal as well.

As sunset comes early in November, Moose and I hurried to finish the last of the day's work. Moving methodically, painstakingly, and with a caution that belied his weariness, my father stood in the semi-darkness of the smokehouse beginning the task of curing the reserved hams, shoulders and bacon. The curing mixture was made up of salt, pepper, brown sugar and saltpetre, and Moose worked with a craftsman's concentration to rub this mixture into each slab of meat. Over and over he passed his hands through the mixture of ingredients and massaged the dampish surface until there was no trace of exposed flesh. When at last he was satisfied, each piece was slipped on to a double hook and suspended from the ceiling. The whole curing process was repeated nightly for weeks. When finished, the meat was shrunken, rosy pink, and impervious to decay for nearly two years.

My day ended with a late walk. Waiting my turn for a bath, I strolled out behind the naked walnut trees and forlorn lilac bush to the barn. Winter had truly come, and little caps of snow sat on every fence post. Drips from the pigpen eaves, melted by the midday sun, formed crinkly icicles in the cooling night air. No birds sang, and there was no sound but for the swishing of cows' tails as they milled about after their supper of hay. A trampled, and by now icy trail, led downwards from the barn to the waggonshed, and I followed this back to the stable-door leading into the pens. Under the weight of silence, the cobwebs bowed to the breeze my passing raised. As I looked down at the floor in the centre of the room, I saw four round patches of blood-soaked straw, each one about three feet across. Tired as I was, this sight gave me an aching hollowness. I knew the value of what we had done today, and no one would enjoy the results more than I. We had done our work well and expertly, giving as little pain as possible. And yet... how sad that room felt. With blood on my hands, and blood under my nails, never again could I consider my life, or any life, in quite the same way. But with a grain more knowledge of its infinite responsibilities and confusions, I wondered at its brevity and its mystery.

CHAPTER TWELVE

Go Tell it on the Mountain

December hangs like ice, unmoved and reflecting. Every tree is a fountain, frozen motionless in Time. Every stream is a pathway of glass. The forest floor is a shallow carpet of snow, rippled and broken by the pattern of leaves, and furnished with the tangled yarn of bare honeysuckle. Spots of olive-hued laurel and deep-water-green cedar give colour to the brown and blue-grey skeletons of undergrowth and the tracks of animals, newly-minted in the dawn.

My favourite discovery on a December day was the daisy-chain prints of the deer. The coming of the bitter weather means a shortage of food that drives these beautiful creatures downwards from their usual home at the top of the mountain. For centuries, this change spelt good fortune for the inhabitants of Catoctin Mountain. The Tuscarora, moving with the herds, kept a winter camp in the water-rich pasture-land beside Schultz's meadow. Once in a while, in the late autumn, the farmer ploughed this field to re-seed the grass, boosting the summer grazing. In the interval between the ploughing and the seeding, C.E. always found time to give the field a close-eyed once-over. What he found was a wide variety of stone-chipped arrowheads. Practically all of them were of two types: there was a narrow featureless sort, about three inches long and chipped from a kind of grey shale; and there was a short stubby fluted variety, fashioned out of deeply-scored quartz. To me, both were precious, first because of their magically indeterminate age – the handiwork of a lost people who had walked the mountain I knew, and who, like me, knelt to drink from the clear streams. And I treasured them because I knew the effort they had cost C.E. to find. With eyes little better than my own, he walked over a newly-ploughed field, and from the seeming infinity of jagged stones, found those that human hands had worked.

Other stone tools were found all around us. A triangular hole-prick-

patterned hide-scraper turned up in a gravelly patch a hundred yards from The Corner. When Charlie Ford still lived in the farmhouse, he picked up a really grand tomahawk in the vegetable garden. All of these things marked this history of a life that, although altered, continued unbroken. The annual running of the deer still stirred men to action, and hunters flocked to the deep woods throughout the short hunting season. Some built rough huts high in the trees as places to await the passing of small herds. In time, I grew used to the shy company of deer. Whole families of them, startled from their haunts, hungry, or wrecked by the skill of rifle-fire, wandered all about us in the early daylight hours. The refugees had two favourite paths. One was to come down the mountain along our own small stream, crossing the field beyond our vegetable patch, and along the farm lane to the lower stream, then over the hilly fields that lead to South Mountain. Most, however, followed the edge of the forest by the field opposite our barn, before joining up with the paths followed by the others. On this route, with the old Indian hunting camp just out of sight to their right, the animals always paused. I can still see them – eight, ten, even sixteen of them – standing about in the quiet snow-bright air. Their soft intelligent faces with stunning eyes, alert to the least sound, movement or scent, they waited for a few minutes to catch the breath that circled in misty clouds around their heads. With each herd, there was generally one awesomely proud stag. These bold creatures, swinging about with their great racks of antlers, were bundles of raw nerve. Leaders, and among themselves fighters, they made an inspiring sight in an otherwise bleak landscape. Sadly, I thought, they were the most prized by hunters, their graceful, fine-lined heads exhibited as trophies mounted on walls, the very closeness of which was antithetical to all they stood for. To me it remained a telling fact that all experienced hunters spoke of a condition known as 'buck fever'. This came about as a reaction to the splendour of these noble animals as seen across the sights of a powerful rifle. Symptoms included a weakness in the knees, a churning stomach, trembling muscles, and a feeling that the blood had drained from the heart. The result was that the precious quarry, defenceless against its invisible assailant, simply walked away unharmed. In my own childish way, I believed that the deer, one family at a time, halted their journey across our fields to mourn their losses by the winter home of a brave people now vanished, with whom they had lived on even terms for thousands of years – a people whose eternity made room even for the animals.

For younger sportsmen, ice and snow meant sledding. Because few cars attempted to climb Coxey Brown Road after a snowfall, local children could be assured of many hours of open racing. The bravest sledders started at the kiss-your-arse corner beside of Clarence Farley's cabin. From here the road bumps its way downwards without serious curves for nearly a mile to the junction with the Harmony Road. On a perfect run, a good sledder, lying face-down on his wooden iron-runnered sled, could expect to reach speeds upwards of thirty miles per hour. Mishaps were frequent, but serious injuries were few. The worst risks arose when the packed ice and snow wore through, exposing gravelly patches. If struck at an angle, these could snag or slow one runner, and thereby pitch the sledder off on to the frozen ground or into the rocky roadside ditches. I shall never forget the sight of a small, closely-wrapped human being hurtling down our road amid a shower of blue and orange sparks.

Although I longed to join in this deviltry, once again my poor eyesight hindered me. The bumpiness of the road meant that realistically the only way to stay on board a sled was to lie face-down, steering with the hands, six inches from the snowy ground. My problems were two. Whenever I tried this my steaming breath fogged over my glasses so that I could barely see where I was going, or the spray raised from the projecting runners meant that I couldn't see at all. Also, I knew that if I was thrown off and lost my glasses in the white fracas of the crash, I would have virtually no hope of finding them again. As the cost of my many replacement pairs was already the stuff of legend, I thought it best to avoid further issue. Besides, with Christmas so near at hand, I didn't want to think that my parents' resources might be wasted on pragmatic utensils like new specs.

I think I looked forward to Christmas shopping almost as much as I looked forward to Christmas Day. For obvious reasons, I couldn't go shopping with my parents, so I always went with C.E. and Dutch. Well, Dutch really, because C.E. disappeared minutes after we arrived. Our route took us over Catoctin Mountain, through the rolling farms to Frederick. Frederick is the county-town, and in those days it had a population of about 30,000. I thought it was an urban metropolis. The shopping district that Dutch gravitated towards was the very heart of the city, where most of the buildings dated from 1750-1850. C.E. always followed the same route down a steep hill beside a pair of green fields called Baker Park. I always felt desperately sorry for people who lived in houses that touched one another and for whom these two green patches, no bigger than a good-sized hayfield, represented the outdoors.

From here, we went through a leafy suburb, and parked The Machine in a little backwater called Court Square. This was one of my favourite places in town, because I was moved by its quiet Federalist-style elegance. The square was dominated by a slightly lumpy 'classical' brick building that had once been the home of the County Court. After the court was relocated to another street, the building was used as the public library. I can still recall vividly my first venture inside the building. While my mother waited impatiently, I wandered about open-mouthed, lost in a wonderland of more ideas than I had ever dreamed possible. Without the least guidance of how to find anything, I have the honour to report that my first loan was a history of the Plantagenets.

Anyway, looking left from the courthouse, there were two splendid adjacent brick houses, identical except that one was burgundy and one was white. They were built by a father and son. Opposite them was a tall narrow building called The Spite House. This was built by a man who, learning of a planned road improvement next to his own abode, quickly filled in the gap with a new dwelling.

But my favourite feature of Court Square was the fountain. As a small boy in the Appalachian mountains, (where brick houses were a surprise) this was the only fountain I had ever seen, and I treasured it. Deep grass-green bronze, in springtime its frothy pool reflected the cherry-blossom, in summer, its shaking crystals cooled the hot breezes. I mourned its winter leaf-choked silence, and wrote many elegiac poems to its beauty.

From here we walked two blocks to Patrick Street, past the church where Stonewall Jackson fell asleep listening to an anti-Confederate sermon. Our goal was a shop called Quinn's. This was one of those old-fashioned hardware stores – the sort where loose items were sold out of bins, and weighed-out by the pound by knowledgeable old men whose fathers had followed the same trade. Indeed, Quinn's had been in business since the mid-eighteenth century, its bare wooden floors showing the scrapes the vicissitudes of Time. Our purpose in coming here was for me to buy a present for my father. As our whole lifestyle was bound up with matters of wood – its procurement, refinement and uses – I came to know its practices well. Time after time I watched as Moose laboured to split the short twisty lumps of hardwood we burnt as fuel. His tools consisted of a sledge-hammer and three steel wedges, the soft heads of which mushroomed out from long use, and sometimes broke off, flying about dangerously. So with this in mind, I determined to buy him a new wedge. I remember it exactly: long, heavy, shiny black, and costing $3.00 – that is, six weeks' pocket money.

Carrying the heavy wedge, we crossed the street to Schroeder's. This was a gentlemen's tailor shop, and our mission here was for Dutch to buy C.E. a pair of carpet slippers. Dutch and C.E. had a tacit agreement that every year, regardless of other presents they gave one another, each bought the other new slippers. No doubt that while we were inside, C.E. was somewhere else making a similar purchase. While the business was being transacted, I had a moment to look around. My attention was almost evenly divided between speculating on the shoe size of the gigantic old man who always sat on a chair in the front corner of the room dangling his enormous (although beautifully-shod) feet into the aisle, and the unbelievable softness of a taupe camel-hair jacket adorning a mannequin. I noticed that the price-tag on the jacket read $400 – 800 weeks pocket money – and I marvelled at the luxuries available to adults.

Once outside, we turned the corner on to Market Street and walked to Fanny's. This was a traditional family-owned five-and-dime store, a kind of forerunner to the more common Woolworth's variety. Dutch, never able to reconcile herself to the term 'five-and-dime', persisted in calling it 'the ten-cent store'. This time it was my turn to buy a present for my mother. Feeling virtuous, I passed by the glass spheres of the gum-ball machines and the contraption for minting your own ID discs, and headed for the glassware 'department'. What I chose was a small violet glass vase that I thought would 'go' nicely in the glass-fronted corner cupboard that Charlie Ford had built my parents as a wedding present. It cost $3.00 and the assistant wrapped it in tissue paper and packed it tightly in a box.

After all of this intensive shopping, our thoughts (or at least, my thoughts) turned to food. Taking the hint, Dutch directed our steps to the corner of Fourth Street, to a small grocery that she called 'Capello's'. Mr Capello had run the grocery shop here in Dutch's youth, and although the shop had changed hands shortly after the war, she continued to refer to it by its old name. Mr Capello was best-known for his in-house bakery, which the 'new' owners wisely decided to maintain. This bakery – one of only two I had ever seen – produced many fine things, but my own favourite was a special variety of cookies. These cookies were round wavy-star topped, semi-sweet shortbread, yellowish in colour and topped with a sprinkle of parti-coloured sugar beads. I was certain that in the wave of strong aromas borne outward on the rush of warm air as we opened the door, that I could distinguish their particular flavour. At fifty cents a dozen, they were a rare hedonistic indulgence.

But I was not allowed to eat them immediately. Instead, Dutch put the little white bag among her other shopping, and we headed off to the White Star. A visit to the White Star is a trip in a time machine. For this little restaurant, founded around the turn-of-the-century, progress seems to have halted in the early 1950s. The premises consisted of a long narrow room painted mint green. For almost the entire length of the room's right-hand side, there was a tall formica bar with rotating steel bar-stools, and at the far end of the room there was a cluster of small formica tables with steel chairs. On the rear wall hung a copy of the famous unfinished portrait of George Washington, and to the right there was a low old-fashioned sliding-top Coca-Cola cooler with an outside bottle-opener. Behind the serving counter there was a long worktop storing crockery, cutlery and glassware, and most of the cooking was done in the light of the large shop window facing Market Street. The cooking itself was, shall we say, limited in scope, as 99% of the food sold consisted of one type: hot-dogs. I can truly say that without the merest hint of exaggeration, they were the finest hot-dogs in the galaxy. The founder of the company – a Greek so they say – discovered a peculiar type of hot dog somewhere in Texas, and had them delivered especially for his new business. Unlike the usual sort, these hot-dogs were short, fat, tough-skinned and linked like sausages. They were prepared by being split lengthways and fried on a huge grill in the shop window. I can still see them, lying out in long rows, as I pressed my nose on the cold glass, masticating them with my eyes. When cooked, they were dressed with a lightly-chilled beef sauce, mustard, and a vast quantity of finely-minced onions marinated in lemon juice. They were a boy's dream food, and I recalled enviously the story of how C.E. once ate nine of them at a sitting.

Too shy to sit at the public bar, Dutch found us seats at one of the small tables. The waitress/cook/cleaner came round in a moment, less to ask us what we wanted, than to ask how many. Alongside of them, Dutch ordered one Coca-Cola for us to share. The waitress divided this by first setting out two aluminium objects that looked like a pair of cones stuck together at the points. Into each of these she dropped a conical paper cup, which she then filled with the soft drink. She then laid two paper-wrapped paper straws on the table, and went back to chatting with the regulars at the bar.

Later, with our own meal finished, Dutch ordered two more hot-dogs 'to go', and the waitress/etc. wrapped these up tightly in grease-proof paper. These were for C.E., who would eat them on the drive home. The whole meal, including C.E.'s share and the tip, came to $2.30.

After a bit more shopping, we returned to The Machine where C.E. was waiting for us. On the way home, I thought about Christmas. I was sure we would cut our tree from the same hillside where we always cut one, and that, as always, my mother would half-bury us in pine and holly. Christmas was a particularly busy time for Jane as, despite the usual routine of holiday cooking, she also made a frenetic effort to re-fit us with new ornamentation. Her typical chore of replacing seasonally-relevant decorations – fresh flowers, dried flowers and so on – accelerated into a drive to replace practically everything used as decorations the year before. She busily made little ceramic Nativity scenes, sewed new table-napkins, crocheted fresh doilies, painted yellowing woodwork. Anything that could be made to look new fell under her sway. There was, of course, food in abundance, including special items like walnut cookies and eggnog, and the whole family came to our house to eat.

Meanwhile, for the entire school holiday I spent my time re-living the summer. I did this with the help of my extensive model farm set. My father had built me a large scale-model replica of our barn, and for years my presents and pocket money tended to be spent in the direction of small animals, implements and accoutrements. With my usual thoroughness, I set up a good 'permanent' base of operations (farmyard), in the unused square between the sofa, the grandfather clock and the bookshelf. To my mother's perpetual horror, I forbade her ever to clean this area of floor, as her depredations upset my carefully planned layout. For the rest of the house, I prepared detailed maps of fields, allowing each to be treated as part of my personal 'crop rotation'. To do this I had to make allowances for a number of pragmatic and topographical features. For instance, with Jane running about in high gear, it was useless to try and play in any of the major walkways, so I designated these as pastures. Scatter rugs were treated as individual fields, my favourites being two large ovals with alternate green and brown stripes. These I treated like the famous 'contour fields' of our neighbours' farms. (A 'contour field' consists of a beautifully arranged pattern of narrow strips, all of which follow the rise and fall of a hillside, each strip being planted with a different crop.)

My only onerous chore this time of year was to bring in wood for the stove. All summer long the limbs of trees that we had cut for timber lay in neat four-foot-long piles, scattered about the corners of the farm. The larger chunks, stumps or pieces too crooked for other uses, were hauled to the level place by the waggonshed and split by hand. But as time permitted, and necessity demanded, the other piles were gradually cut into shorter lengths and hauled to a sheltered spot near the garden cave. This made a kind of ready-reserve pile, from which my first chore was to carry in bits to the large stockpile on the back porch. From here, a small helping was kept inside to replenish the stove. On warm dry days, moving the wood about was relatively simple. But in the cold early-darkening evenings, I found the whole thing much harder. Despite its tarpaulin covering, the wood, dampened by snow and ice, froze together in great clots. Prying it apart, I often scratched myself up the elbows and caked a strange powdery dirt under the nails of my numb fingers. Besides this, there was always an indeterminate rustling of small bodies somewhere down inside the pile, whose defence of their winter homestead I felt could easily have become menacing.

I knew how they felt. The December solitude turned my thoughts inwards upon my home as well. After a year of intense labour and fantastic journeys into uncharted territories of space and spirit, I too was proud and ready to defend my security. I thought of our new home's resources. We had defiantly reclaimed the broken shell of a building that had once housed the dreams of my forebears, restoring it to beauty and functionality. The crumbling buildings upon which their livelihood (and our own) depended, were repaired and brought back from the brink of real collapse. I thought of the fields, the site of so many hours of sweaty toil for men and women like Charlie and Sadie Ford, once overrun with the swift tide of rubbishy briars, ungoverned trees and the rubble of broken walls and fences, that were now cleared for crops, grazing and fruit trees. In the spaces around the house itself I saw the trees and flowers, so lovingly planted half a century before my birth, uncovered and released from their wild disfigurements and once again the givers of solace. I thought of the many animals whose lives and whose deaths I had learned from – animals that only one year before were to me as abstract and remote as the stars in the night sky.

I thought also of the whole family's struggle to lay down food – good, wholesome, safe food – to last a whole winter. Outside, the smokehouse held eight new hams, eight shoulders and eight sides of bacon. Our new cave was crammed with potatoes, and bushels of apples lay buried in the vegetable patch waiting to be dug out. The top shelves of the larder held jars of dry walnuts, and underneath there rested cans of lard and crocks of pork pudding. In the darkest corner beside of these were large jugs of cider, blackberry-, cherry-, and Concord grape wine. There were two enormous chest freezers filled to capacity with three-fourths of a home-reared and home-slaughtered beef, choice cuts of pork, and dozens of chickens. Besides this they also held strawberries, cherries, dewberries, black raspberries and huckleberries, as well as carrots, sweet corn, lima beans and cabbage. On the cold cellar floor there sat a huge crock of sauerkraut, and clustered around it were pumpkins of all colours, while overhead hung plaits of onions. On the wooden shelves to the right there sat rows of pint jars full of sweet and sour cucumber pickles, apple butter, loin of pork, and jam made from plums, black raspberries, cherries and strawberries. Beside of this there were racks full of quart jars holding French beans, peppers, beetroot, turnips, peaches, pears and tomatoes (whole, juiced and pureed). Our hens laid more eggs daily than we could eat in a week, and Jane sold the extra for pin money. Despite the elusive marauding mice, our corncrib was packed to the rafters and the barn fairly bulged with hay. All together, the fruits of a long season left us provisioned far in excess of our needs.

So mostly, as I sat in the backseat of The Machine listening to Dutch and C.E. grizziling amiably with one another as we drove back along the long road to Harmony, I thought of the people I had come to know. Sometimes gentle, sometimes brutal, I felt myself becoming one of them. I knew then that a 'country life' is hard. It is often dirty, it is sometimes dangerous, and its rewards can lie hidden throughout the hours when you need them most. I felt myself standing in the footsteps of people whose heartbreaks were no longer strange to me, and whose promises – as impossible now as on the day they first made them – I too would work to fulfil. I held their tools in my hand and their stories in my head, and if I could never touch them, I could at least remember what is so easily forgotten: the life of a community, as precious to the human heart as April sunshine on a robin's wing. I knew then that I could never be still when so much all about me lay unsung. So from the gingery-flecked buds of the tulip-poplars to the dark noisy eddies of the streams, I dressed myself in the richness of those fortunate days, and wrapped up my boyhood like the priceless gift of Harmony.

Maryland, My Maryland

When I was twenty-five years old, I left Harmony. The combination of good grades when I was in school, a lot of hard saving and a small legacy, enabled me to become the first member of my family in its two-and-a-half centuries on Catoctin Mountain to leave home for university. Apart from some long holidays, I have never really returned.

Since that time a new world has settled itself down there like dust, rapidly and irrevocably hiding the old world I knew as a boy. The narrow gravel roads, that once had time to turn a little to the left or right out of consideration for a fine old mountain ash, are widened now and paved, and the great iron bridges have all gone except for one – kept as a curiosity on a farmer's lane. The farms, the beautiful farms, the vision of whose grandeur brought tears to the eyes of soldiers who marched over them to the maelstrom of battle, are vanishing. In their place there is an ever-strengthening net of streets, beside which live burgeoning communities of newcomers, eager to root themselves in a land whose ways they do not know, whose seasons they do not share. Even the rich forest, where the patchwork of shadows trembling with spines of light once harboured deer and racoons, has been invaded and become a home for strangers.

Few of the old-timers remain now to tell their stories. Floyd, Obidiah, Hank, Florry, Guy, Ebbie, Lancelot, a whole generation has passed away, and none rises to take its place. From my own family, Charlie Ford and Sadie Mae, C.E., Viola and others have gone, resting peacefully on the breast of the mountain that had for so long given them life. But like Dutch, the few who remain – all in their ninth or tenth decades – still hold a low fire in their hearts for the days that have passed. A word, a look, the touch of a sympathetic hand can stir the embers, raising a still-strong light to the eyes, a light that shines with the dignity and merriment of time well-spent, and time happily shared.

Some of my own friends too have gone. Tom Fox, the brave silent boy who defended third base on a hot summer's day, ended his own life – blowing out his brains for the love of a heartless girl. My dear friend David, who with his father and brothers staged private recitals for his mother, was killed a few years ago. With characteristic courage, he risked his life to save a complete stranger trapped in a terrible blizzard.

Yet Harmony's life goes on in its own slow way. On Sundays, the Brethren and Lutheran children still wait impatiently for the chance to play together, throwing stones into the stream by The Mary House. A few of The Loafers still gather, and old jokes re-echo with laughter.

Old Man – Hey, li'l feller, knoa whut at air is?

Boy – Yessir, at's chicken shit.

Old Man – Yeppun, ya see at whyat stuff in na middle… knoa whut at is?

Boy – Nossir.

Old Man – 'At's chicken shit too!

Maryland, my Maryland, you are not as you were, and I mourn the loss of you. I have stood by your side in the frost-white autumn fields, and I have listened to your footfall in the clapping rush of March-filled streams. Together we have counted the stars of a December night and tasted the clover-sweet days of summer. I know now that we shall never leave one another, and I would give you as a gift to all those whom I love. I believe in your future as surely as I hold your past inside me. And I will make it my prayer that your sons and daughters may grow to be like you, with the courage to claim a mountain, and the wisdom to live among their dreams.